D1564751

DAVID DINKINS AND NEW YORK CITY POLITICS

DAVID DINKINS AND NEW YORK CITY POLITICS

RACE, IMAGES, AND THE MEDIA

WILBUR C. RICH

STATE UNIVERSITY OF NEW YORK PRESS

Published by
State University of New York Press, Albany

For information, address State University of New York Press,
194 Washington Avenue, Suite 305, Albany NY 12210-2384

Production by Marilyn P. Semerad
Marketing by Fran Keneston

Library of Congress Cataloging-in-Publication Data
Rich, Wilbur C.
David Dinkins and New York City politics: race, images, and the media / Wilbur
C. Rich.
    p.   cm.
Includes bibliographical references and index.
ISBN-13: 978-0-7914-6949-1 (hardcover: alk. paper)
ISBN-10: 0-7914-6949-2 (hardcover: alk. paper) 1. Dinkins, David N. 2. New
York (N.Y.)—Politics and government—1951–   3. Press and politics—New York
(State)—New York. I. Title.
F128.54.D56R53   2007
974.7'044092—dc2   2006003063

10 9 8 7 6 5 4 3 2 1

CONTENTS

ILLUSTRATIONS

Photographs

Tables

Figure

PREFACE

Journalist Robert Turner once asserted, "Mayors are chronicled by novelists but ignored by political scientists."[1] I am a political scientist who has spent most of his career watching and writing about mayors. Yet I do agree that mayors are "character actors of politics."[2] They are certainly not the lead actors or stars of the American political theater. Occasionally, a city mayor appears on the political stage, attracts a large following, and is able to speak to the American people at large. Richard J. Daley of Chicago, Coleman Young of Detroit, Sam Yorty of Los Angeles, and Rudolph Giuliani of New York are examples of mayors who achieved national visibility.

This book is about the political image of David Dinkins, the first African American mayor of New York City. It does not attempt to explore all aspects of New York City politics. Politics is just part of what is happening between a political leader and constituencies. Obviously the most attentive constituency is the media. This project began as an attempt to understand the media's interpretation of what can now be called the "Dinkins interregnum" between white mayors of the city.

This research project began as an attempt to deconstruct journalists' understandings of the politics of New York City. As I delved further into the writing process, I realized that I needed to include more contextual information about the political career of David Dinkins and the media's reaction to him. For this I gained much insight from psychology, sociology, advertising, and social construction theory scholars. So the story that is developed in this book is one of media meanings and perceptions. I have always wondered how media stories are constructed and why certain events are highlighted and others are ignored. I confess to being envious of journalists' access to mayors. They enjoy a proximity advantage over political scientists that allows them to see mayors at their best and their worst. Reporters behave similar to emergency medical services (EMS) personnel during political events. They rush to the scene, interview people, and sometimes make suggestions to actors as the event unfolds. Because they are close to the action, they collect telling quotes from politicians. Accordingly, their written reports, notes, and broadcast selections matter because they are the basis for public discourse about city life. It has been said that journalists write the first draft of history. This is true, and there is much to be learned from this draft.

In my interviews with reporters, I found most of them knowledgeable and modest. Many were particularly conscious of their influence on the discourse on race. Although race is an attractive subject for editors and reporters, it does not rank with sex and financial scandals as a crowd puller for newspaper readers, television watchers, and radio listeners. Nevertheless, race stories do sell newspapers and attract viewers and listeners. When a black person is elected mayor of a major city, editors and reporters are given a cornucopia of possible story lines. There are a variety of angles to explore and new frontiers to examine. Having studied several black mayors, I began to appreciate the role that print media plays in the construction of images of these mayors. I wondered if it played the same role with white mayors. It does but not with same lead lines or angles. During my research former mayor David Dinkins offered two admonishments for my study. First, he said, "You historians. You have to rely on news clips and interviews and what not, and it gets to be a function of whom did you talk to [and] what did you read. . . . If you are not part of it, you were not here. How would you know? You take what you are told."[3]

I agree with the mayor. I was not there. However, history can only approximate political events and suggest possible interpretations. Retelling rarely provides unchallengeable explanations for an event. Historians cannot talk to all the participants, and even if they could there is always the possibility they would get different interpretations of the same event. We who write history try to collect as much data and as many impressions as possible and then place the work in the academic marketplace. Accordingly, this book is just one interpretation of the Dinkins years, and as an outsider I may never know what I have missed.

This book examines the leadership of David Dinkins as mayor of New York City as seen by the media. For this study, leadership is understood to be transactional, situational, and relational, and through it, I aim to capture how Mayor Dinkins related to the various constituencies of the city. A mayor's relationship with constituencies involves feedback and adjustments. As a study of political communication, we scrutinize the rhetoric, policies, and symbols used during Dinkins' tenure. Journalists have different roles as they write as events take place and often shape the discourse about events.

Readers who are familiar with my earlier work are aware that I have always been a proponent of the transformative capacities of the mayoralty. Mayors matter. Their personalities matter as do social and economic conditions. Thus a city hall leader can convince others to join him or her and to literally change the image of a city, promote economic growth, and lure new residents and businesses to relocate to their city. Alternatively, the wrong person in the office can undo much of the city's positive image or reinforce the negative image.

This book is ultimately about how David Dinkins became the mayor of New York City, the staffing of his administration, his reactions to political events, his relations with other political actors, and his legacy. More specifically, it examines the intersection of the New York City media with the first African American mayor, his job performance, and racial discourse. This brings me to Dinkins' second admonishment: "It is very difficult to compare me with the mayor of another city, even if it is a white mayor or a black mayor of another city. There is an essential difference. You have to compare apples to apples. You have to compare me with other New York mayors. One has to factor in the times."[4]

It is difficult indeed to compare the mayor of New York City with mayors in other cities. No single book could hope to cover every aspect of the tenure of Dinkins, so my selections are designed to highlight the media role in the shaping of the public's perception of him. I endeavored to be sensitive to the role "the times" (economic conditions) played in his image.

ACKNOWLEDGMENTS

I would particularly like to thank Mayor David Dinkins and his former staff members. They were gracious in our interviews and in allowing me to construct my own analysis of them as individual and elected officials.

I am deeply indebted to a great team of manuscript chapter readers, including Jeff Henig, Marion Orr, John Mollenkopf, Marion Just, James Jennings, Jim Sleeper, Clarence Stone, Bryan Jones, Daniel Schulgasser, and James Bowers. J. Phillip Thompson allowed me to read his unpublished manuscript on the Dinkins administration and New York politics. It was extremely useful in helping me understand the internal dynamics of the administration. I am also indebted to my colleagues who patiently listened as I tried to explain what I was doing. Jim Sleeper, a serious and thoughtful journalist, listened patiently to my groping for a way to understand what the troubled Dinkins administration was about. I also owe much to the listening skills of Professors Andrew Hacker, Martin Kilson, and Charles V. Hamilton, who were generous with their insight and their time. Writer Stanley Crouch provided me with one of the most comprehensive overviews of black politics in New York City that I have ever heard. I also appreciate the time given me by reporters such as Paul Delaney (former *New York Times* reporter), Leland Jones, Albert Scardino (Mayor Dinkins's former press secretary), Sam Roberts (of the *New York Times*), and Joyce Purnick (of the *New York Times*).

One of most memorable hours with reporters was my visit to the *New York Times*. I thank Sam Roberts for inviting me. I would also like to thank all the reporters who spoke to me by phone:

Todd Purdum, Joe Klein, William Murphy, and others. I deeply appreciate the time and assistance allotted me by Norman Steisel, former deputy mayor of New York City; Ruth Messinger, former Manhattan borough president; and many others who wish to remain anonymous.

I would also like to thank the Russell Sage Foundation for allowing me to spend a year in New York as a visiting scholar. The foundation research staff, especially Mariam Manichaikul, aided my search for information. With the foundation fellowship I got the chance once again to experience the aura and spirit of New York City politics and to spend time talking to John Mollenkopf, a fellow visiting scholar and expert on New York City politics. I am also grateful to Wellesley College for providing a faculty research award for this book. Special thanks to Dr. Michael Rinella and Marilyn Semerad of SUNY Press for their suggestions and support of this book.

I am grateful to my family, who always supports me whenever I start down a tunnel that leads to a book, especially my daughters Rachel A. Rich (Reynolds) for her editing and Alexandra Rich for her Spanish translations. Finally, thanks to Fred W. McDarrah for giving permission to use the photographs included in this book and on the cover.

I dedicate this book to the newest member of my family, Kailani Alexandra Reynolds, my granddaughter.

CHAPTER ONE

INTRODUCTION

Increasingly, city politics revolves around mayor-centered coalitions. Within these coalitions, it is the mayor who commands the media attention, serves as the principal communication intermediary with a whole host of groups and individuals, and acts as a lighting rod for public dissatisfaction. As a high-profile spokesperson, New York City's mayor's responsibilities make possible opportunities for pubic success and failure. This book examines how David Dinkins, the first African American mayor of New York City (1990–1994), used this opportunity in hopes of problem solving, maintaining his electoral coalition of blacks, Latinos, and liberal whites; and satisfying the media's appetite for news. Each member of Dinkins' electoral coalition had different expectations of him. Not only would maintaining the loyalty of his supporters require nimble political skills, but also Dinkins had to ingratiate himself to the permanent governing elite who ran the city. The latter required being able to project a stylish image of the city. Considered a clubhouse politician, David Dinkins posed an image challenge for the business leaders who cherished New York's reputation as the center of urbane America. Concerned that Dinkins' highly localized political biography—as state legislator, city clerk, and Manhattan borough president—could hurt the city's image as a magnet for the transnational elite, media sought to inflate the attractive aspects of his personality. In order to make Dinkins look suave, reporters were assigned to write attention-getting stories about the new mayor. It is axiomatic that no mayor-centered coalition can function effectively and efficiently with a mayor with a less-than-attractive image. Mayors with negative images can distract from the overall image of the city. As the most visible member of the governing coalition, a mayor's reputation is essential to the success of the city's governing process. Accordingly, the entire governing coalition, particularly the business sector, endeavors to support a positive image for an incoming mayor.

At first glance, David Dinkins seemed to be a perfect case study for media analysis. Carefully trained and nurtured as consummate insider before he assumed office, Dinkins was cast as a deracialized leader and a transracial politician. A Harlem politician who was well liked among his peers and among reporters, he moved easily along the corridors of the city politics. Furthermore, he had done favors for several important politicians and activists. In effect, local politicians owed him. The mantra of New York City politicians is, if an officeholder helps them, they will reciprocate.

A closer examination of city politics revealed that several local politicians felt a reciprocal obligation to Dinkins. Many reporters, however, did not share this feeling of obligation. Since most of the reporters and readers were white, there was a strong tendency to treat a black mayor in a race-declarative manner. Often this race recognition relied on stereotypes that disparaged David Dinkins and flattered the reporter's white audience. This holds for most black politicians as they are rarely on an even playing field with reporters. Reporters have the advantage of being merchants of meaning and can adjust the product to suit the customer—the public. Every time Dinkins spoke publicly, to use a baseball analogy, he either hit a home run or struck out. There was little middle ground. Once the words were out of his mouth, the media was free to add their own meaning.

Political Life in a Media Age

We are told that we live in a media age. Blumler and Kavanaugh claim that we are now living in the third era of political communication.[1] The first was the pretelevision age when political parties and interest groups delivered the political messages. The second era was triggered by the rise of the mass media along with press strategists, pollsters, and performance coaches. The latter were increasingly employed by politicians and others with political messages to be delivered. Although not household names, political consultants such as David Garth and John Martilla became important players in local municipal elections. The third era is marked by the rise of market research and the advent of new opinion-assessment technologies (such as focus groups and audience feedback). The selling of candidates and policies borrows much from the commercial world. This era, characterized by a proliferation of electronic channels, is hungry for new content. Not only is the media ubiquitous and avaricious, but it is also able to create the illusion that we are participating in the great events of our times. What is more important, it introduces us to people, events, and places we would not have ordinarily known.

New York City has fifty-one newspapers, fifty magazines, forty-six radio stations, and forty-three television stations. This is a community of professionals that reads and listens to each other. Members of this community live in a fluid environment in which changing employers and venues of presentation is not uncommon. Newspaper reporters appear on television and radio. Broadcasters write editorials in local dailies. They interact and affect each others' work and attitudes.

The *New York Times*, a powerful newspaper that is read nationally, is the standard for local coverage. This means that it has to compete with a variety of New York City tabloids, weeklies, and special niche papers. Although the *New York Times* has a national audience, its metro section is well written, and some of its best reporters are assigned to cover local news. It follows the mayor and city politics with regularity. What the *Times* reports or editorializes, matters. The *Times'* political clout comes from the fact that most opinion leaders read the paper, and reporters often use their comments to reinforce a theme within an article. The *New York Daily News* and *New York Post* are tabloids but are also widely read by the so-called working public. Their specialties are eye-catching headlines and photos. These three papers are clearly the attention getters in the reporting of city politics. Most other newspapers are weeklies, ethnic journals, alternative tabloids, or borough-centric. The one exception, the *Village Voice*, also a weekly, is less a player than it once was in politics. *New York Magazine* covers city hall with great enthusiasm. The *Irish Voice, El Diario, Amsterdam News,* and the *Jewish*

Press, considered ethnic papers, are read by city intellectuals, political pundits, and politicians, but they have a limited mass readership. This is not to say the ethnic-oriented or specialty-oriented newspapers and magazines are ignored; they simply do not have the impact of the major dailies. Indeed, mayoral candidates often grant interviews to such specialized outlets in the hopes of reaching their readers.

The broadcast or electronic media also covers politics. Television stations, in particular, are very competitive. Most network-affiliated stations have reporters and trucks on the street daily who cover most political events. The 6:00 news is a major part of a station's identity. Winning the top-rated newscast is highly prized among stations' owners. They use their anchors to advertise their stations. With the exception of so-called all-news stations, most radio restricts the news to the hour break. Yet broadcast media gets the advantage over its print competition when it covers breaking news with images and sound.

Interestingly, it is the print media that provides the news framework for the coverage of broadcast media. As the old saying goes, go into any radio or TV newsroom, and you will find anchor people reading newspapers. This is not to gainsay the role of TV reporters and talk show hosts. These interview shows and call-in programs can affect a mayor's image, but it is the print media coverage and its interpretation of a mayor's actions that reifies the image. Television reporters and talk show hosts glean most of their topics, quotes, and information from newspapers. As one television reporter explained when I asked him why he did not just look up the information he asked me for in the library, "You got us confused with newspapers. This station doesn't have a library."[2] Yet television, with its moving pictures, appears to be on top of a story. Although it can often air breaking stories as they happen, there is generally little, if any, follow through in local politics.

In our media age, we are deluged with a variety of messages. Sorting out these messages requires an inquiring and discerning mind. However, the media is not always rational or objective, nor are its viewers, listeners, or readers. The media world is made up of both fantasy (for example, Horatio Alger themes, good trumps evil endings, and the omnipresence of glamor) and reality. Separating the two becomes more difficult when the media's version of life mimics real life. This is particularly true in politics. Politicians, and their celebrity auxiliaries, dominate media life, crowding out others in what Ferdinand Mount calls the "theater of politics."3

Most of us will never experience a media life since few of us will become politicians or celebrities. Accordingly, the media can safely ignore us. Although many of us are content to lead lives of relative anonymity, there are some who may experience *coverage deprivation.* This group may either envy the attention and visibility politicians receive or decide to seek it for themselves by making episodic forays into politics. Soon they discover that political visibility and media coverage are not without their perils. Sometimes the coverage is flattering, and at times it is not. In effect, nonpoliticians and noncelebrities function as aliens in the media world. Unlike ordinary citizens, politicians are expected to be denizens of the media world and demonstrate an expertise when "handling" the press. However, even for veteran public performers, the media can be either a tool or a pair of manacles.

"Managing the press" should be a part of the job description for an elected official. This is particularly true for big city mayors. Since intense coverage is inevitable, and the appetite for news is unrelenting, the challenge of a mayor is to maximize positive self-representation and offset negative ones. To do this, mayors must carefully construct images that they wish to project and campaign hard to sell that image to their constituency. It is not uncommon for campaign rhetoric to include undercurrents of altruism, self-confident promises, and crusading slogans. Subsequently, when the media covers city hall, it endeavors to create what it believes is an "ecological image" of the mayor and his or her administration. In other words, the media attempts to analyze incumbents as they react to the uncertain environment of city politics. For the media, politics is a game of rules and violations, winners and losers, bad calls and luck. This may or may not be commensurate with a mayor-projected image. When it is at variance, the potential for conflict exists. In their struggle to frame events and assign political meaning, the mayor and the media can find themselves at loggerheads. This conflict constitutes the essence of urban politics in a postmodern and media age.

Media and Mayors

Journalist Phyllis Kaniss claims that mayors employ six media styles—paranoid media avoiders, naïve professionals, ribbon cutters, dancing marionettes, colorful quotables, and liars.[4] Obviously these styles are not mutually exclusive, yet the media may be inclined to incorporate one of these styles into the overall image of the mayor. Doris Graber asserts, "The images that the media create suggest which views and behaviors are acceptable and even praiseworthy in a given society and which are unacceptable or outside the mainstream."[5] Edward Rubin asserts, "The politicians are created in the reportorial image today. The reporters are created in the entertainment mold. Coverage increasingly relates to the politicians' present success or political prospects as contestants in elections."[6] This is particularly true of high-profile city mayors, because their actions are closely linked with the city's image. Therefore, the images of a mayor can be either an asset or a liability in the marketing of a city. Outside investors look to the mayor for project pitches, political support, and reassurances; members of the city council look to the mayor for the setting of city priorities; members of the governing coalition look to the mayor for articulating a motif; and the public looks to the mayor to exert influence and provide services. The media role is to monitor those expectations and alert the public as to whether the mayor is meeting them. The mayor's image and media style are essential to telling this story. The media coverage of a mayor is crucial to a city's image, to the work of a city, and to the public's satisfaction with their city.[7]

Since urban residents have become media dependent, they glean from news coverage a construction of local political reality. They are routinely told that the local media strives for an independent and unbiased coverage of mayors and political events. Even when there is evidence to the contrary, the public wants to believe that the media is unbiased.[8] Phyllis Kaniss observed that "while there is much in the news and editorial columns that is critical of local officials, this criticism is limited when compared with the amount of information that is taken directly and almost unquestioningly, from official bureaucratic sources."[9] To insure objectivity, the public expects mayors and reporters to create a degree of personal and political distance. Yet maintaining a free and impartial relationship is difficult, because the media is forced to work closely with mayors. John Soloski asserts, "News sources, then, are drawn from the existing power structure; therefore news tends to support the status quo. Although journalists do not set out to consciously report the news so that the current politico-economic system is maintained. The selection of news events and news sources flows 'naturally' from news professionalism."[10]

If the public presumes news professionalism, then it will have to accept the view, as Solski does, that professional norms serve to create ethical guidelines for journalists. Nonetheless, there are hazards in a symbiotic relationship that as its primary goal attempts to facilitate the flow of information. There are three functions that differentiate the roles of the mayor, media, and public. A mayor's role is to provide leadership and govern, the media's role is to provide political information, and the public's role is to act in response to political stimuli. Unless it is well informed the public cannot perform its electoral and policy feedback roles. Since the media is closer to the "governing process," it can find itself deemphasizing certain issues that could seed public discontent, thereby leaving the public with less than the whole story. Conversely, overemphasizing some issues at the expense of more pressing but less attractive ones can be equally misinforming.

The relationship between reporters and mayors raises a series of questions. Are current journalistic norms and practices sufficient to protect the public from insufficient information? Are news stories simply a matter of negotiation? If so, what will happen if the mayor does not understand or disagree with the negotiation process? More important, can media coverage interfere with the normal business of governing and social accounting, that is, a mayor's ability to explain his or her behavior?

Despite academic writings that celebrate the professional autonomy of print journalists, reporters are not free agents. Rather they serve as extensions of their editors and publishers. One reporter put it bluntly: "The editors decide what gets published, therefore what is seen or heard. They are like directors. Reporters get the facts. Editor decided where to play the piece."[11] Paul Delaney, a former *New York Times* reporter agrees.

There is usually an informal story conference in which the editor lays out his ideas for the story. A reporter is free to debate or express his ideas. In most cases a reporter will win an argument, but you know what the editor is looking for. Editors are quite open about what they want as a story. They will say, "here is the story." Here is what to look for. You are being programmed. You know what will impress the editor.[12]

Reporters also understand that editors are the corporation representatives. Although some reporters did not like to think of themselves as working for a profit-oriented business, editors cannot afford this self-delusion. Editors have to walk the line between journalistic impulses and the bottom line. If sensationalizing the news sells papers, attracts viewers and listeners, or allows them to be the most popular, then editors will urge reporters to accept that challenge.

Editors provide the parameters for the media discourse, but reporters get bylines. Accordingly, mayors direct their attention to beat reporters. These are the people they see and know. The mayor and his aides try to negotiate with reporters to little or no avail because reporters can either seek refuge in journalistic professionalism or in protection from editors. An editor can remain relatively blame free and quasi-anonymous.

A reporter's job is to create readable and acceptable copy within a short time. Readability is pitching a story so it is available to target readers. Acceptable copy is that which is catchy, factual, and free of legal trip wires. Saltzman found that "after working on a newspaper or magazine for a while, every reporter soon came to understand what stories would get into print and which would not, or what stories would finally be printed under protest but buried inside and below the fold."[13] Journalists are trained to work within acceptable boundaries.[14] A journalist who strays from these parameters must make a cogent case for his or her wayward behavior. These boundaries also permit journalists to construct images.

The Political Construction of Mayoral Images

Political images are social constructions made necessary by Blumler and Kavanaugh's second era of political communication. Although seldom called "image consultants," these individuals

play a critical role in mayoral politics. Although these constructions are not fixed and often undergo quick and unanticipated
changes, politics is delicately choreographed. Because unanticipated political events have the potential of altering images,
many politicians feel obligated to expeditiously frame situations. City politicians continuously struggle with the local
media over the construction of an accurate and appropriate
image. The old axiom of Watzlawick and colleagues that "one
cannot not communicate,"[15] is certainly true for mayors. Every
public statement, gesture, no comment, appearance, and pre-
meditated silence sends a political message. Indeed images can
send a message even though a mayor may not be personally involved in a policy.

During the mayoral campaigns, would-be mayors and their
staff propose an image that will resonate with the public and one
that will aid the election process. If their candidate is elected,
staff will try to refine or reinforce the officeholder's persona in
the course of governing. The image offered by a successful candidate, and now an officeholder, may be called a "preferred self-
image." This is the officeholder's ideal self. Much of what passes
for political discourse is the media's attempt at challenging a
mayor's political and personal image. The media will take the
preferred self-image and revise and modify elements of it to
make it fit into ongoing political discourse. This modified image
may or may not be consistent with the mayor's image of himself
or herself. In order to govern effectively, mayors have to decide
whether to embrace, refute, or ignore media-constructed images. Mayors often try to offset negative images by instituting direct and personal interaction with as many constituency groups
as possible. This can be a time-consuming enterprise.

Over time a modified public image emerges that is the combination of a mayor's *preferred self-image* and media revisions. This
is usually the first image the public understands. Again, events
serve to intersect, contradict, or overwhelm the public image. In
that event, a public image is altered, and the officeholder is left
with a *prevailing image*. Prevailing images are extremely difficult
to change. If a mayor's prevailing image is positive, then the
public will be searching for evidence to reinforce that prevailing
image. Conversely, if the prevailing image is negative, any mistakes or misjudgments serve to strengthen the image.

What is more important, a mayor's prevailing image plays a role in defining the public's understanding of political events. Standing alone events may have multiple meanings, but language defines which of these merits public consideration. Murray Edelman has related the understanding of political events to the construction of political language. "It is language about political events, not the event in any other sense, that people experience; even developments that are close by take their meaning from the language that depicts them. So political language *is* political reality; there is no other so far as the meaning of events to actors and spectators is concerned."[16]

Images are a part of the political language. The prevailing images of the mayor become a prism through which events are understood. Unfortunately, for some mayors, their prevailing images are beyond their control. They are not simply a matter of skill and personality, although both are important and affect responses to events. A mishandled crisis can seriously damage a mayor's prevailing image. This point will become clear when we discuss the impact of the Red Apple and Crown Heights crises on the prevailing images of Mayor Dinkins.

The challenge for the media is to create an alternative or more realistic media image to the one offered by the mayor and his consultants. Many journalists just look for a new tag line and stay with it, while others search for that critical and public political decision or statement as the defining moment for the administration. A few focus on stereotypes, some of which involve race.

Race, Ethnicity, and the Media

The relationship between race and the media resembles a series of dance steps. What is this metaphoric dance between white-owned media and black mayors? One must be careful not to miss required steps or to step on others, but as long as one is not obviously out of step, then one escapes notice. Making a racist remark or trafficking in racial stereotypes is, without question, a misstep. The question then is, are the steps different from those of the media and white mayors? Was the *Los Angeles Times* more critical of Tom Bradley than it was of Sam Yorty? Was the *Detroit News* less forgiving of Coleman Young than it had been of Jerome Cavanaugh? Could an opinionated local television anchor such as Bill Bonds gain a reputation for toughness if Coleman Young had been white? Was the *Washington Post* pickier about Marion Barry's behavior than it is about that of Anthony Williams? Does a talk show host provide airtime for callers who repeat racial stereotypes in order to hype his rating and gain attention, or is it all a matter of perception?

There are no simple answers to these questions. Race images may be activated only if attention is called to them and if the audience has a history to bring to the characterization. Minorities might be more attentive to press criticisms when the mayor is a minority, and minority mayors might be more interesting than an average white mayor. What we see and hear is, in part, a function of our socialization. Reporters are not exempt from this socialization. Whether they admit it or not, much of a person's self-image is bound up in race and ethnic distinctions. Since the social construction of race and ethnicity has undergone years of clever evolution and subtle change, the meaning of actions and beliefs is not self-evident. Meaning is often created in social interaction, and sorting it out in terms of preconceptions and objective conditions can become more difficult. Nevertheless, race becomes a part of the silent ideology that characterizes how we define events. Peer and Ettema assert,

> We look at urban politics as a terrain on which race is socially constructed. At a time when "all politics is local politics," the urban landscape is a battleground for different racially and ethnically-defined groups fighting to advance their interest. . . .
>
> The construction of racial reality, or of race as a political reality, is an important example of news as ideology. As ideology, the news invoked a framework for understanding urban politics and provides a narrative which features race as the key to politics.[17]

The media reflects on the ideology of race to frame the discourse in its coverage of the election of a series of black mayors. In the history of racial constructions, a black mayor is a rather recent case: before the 1960s, the concept of a black mayor was unknown. In majority black cities such as Mound Bayou, Mississippi, black men were elected mayor for years, but without the racial construct. After Carl Stokes was elected mayor of the majority white Cleveland, Ohio, he became the first "black mayor." The racial construction took on serious political meaning. Two ways of construing mayors of African descent emerged. The first involved the election of a black mayor as a sign of race progress and racial maturity. The second construed the election of a black mayor as a symbol of white abandonment of cities (that is, a racial takeover). In either case it is a construction that takes on a different meaning for whites and blacks.

We learn to be comfortable with these constructions and resist rethinking them even in the light of new information. Entman and Rojecki call the tendency toward mental inertia a "joint product of cognitive economy and of cultural influence." Accordingly, we use schemes and frames as mental shortcuts. They define schemes as "a set of related concepts that allow people to make inferences about new information based on already organized prior knowledge."[18] For example, many white Americans believe blacks are less able, intelligent, and responsible than whites. News items about wrongdoings and mistakes by a black officeholder might trigger a series of stereotypes or schema stored in the minds of the audience. Given our racial history, it is unlikely that most Americans can be truly race neutral. Entman and Rojecki assert,

> This is where culture comes in. We define the mainstream culture as *the set of schemes most widely stored in the public's minds and the core thematic frames that pervade media messages.* Lacking much opportunity for repeated close contact with a wide variety of Blacks, Whites depend heavily on cultural material, especially media images, for cataloging Blacks. The mediated communications help explain the tenacious survival of racial stereotypes despite a social norm that dampens public admission of prejudice. And they help explain pervasive White ambivalence that shrinks from open prejudice but harbors reactive fear, resentment, and denial that the prejudice itself widely exists.[19]

The social construction of race and managerial competence evolved in this way. Given over thirty years of electing black mayors in America, journalists now have enough stories to make this fallacious proposition: black mayors cannot manage cities as well as their white counterparts, and they are less likely to protect white interests. Whites are more likely to believe this proposition than are blacks. It becomes a part of the constructed reality.

Neuman and others argued that journalists are a part of the process of constructing reality. The first construction takes place at the source of the story—politicians, spokespersons, public affairs people, and so on. These key people interpret the news for reporters in hope of having their views, characterizations, and frames included in the reporter's story. The reporter, in turn, continues the process of interpreting the news. Neuman and others conclude, "Journalists reconstruct reality for an audience, taking in account their organizational and modality constraints, professional judgments and certain expectations about the audience. Finally, the individual reader or viewer constructs a version of reality built from personal experience, interaction with peers and interpreted selection from the mass media."[20]

One of Jeffrey Pressman's preconditions for an effective mayoral leadership is a supportive press.[21] A hostile or second-guessing media can make leading constituents more difficult. As purveyors of these mayoral stories, reporters can be classified as theme setters and theme followers. Theme-setting reporters try to preempt or override the discourse about a mayor or his actions by framing events in their terms. If a reporter has a flare for colorful and memorable characterizations, he or she can set the tone for the political discourse. These reporters help focus the lens of history with words and images. They seem to know how to ask the right questions and how to churn the right story. Theme followers, however, are not as creative. They are content to anchor their work on existing social themes.

Race and politics are ongoing topics in all news outlets. Depending upon the nature of an event, news directors and editors of these outlets can cover any personality anywhere within hours of an event. The promise of technology is that no story will be left uncovered by the media. Furthermore, competition among media outlets insures that even minor events will get some coverage, which is particularly true with respect to racial incidents. Many black politicians believe that they are under the strict scrutiny of a racially biased national and local media. A common complaint among black officeholders is that the media concentrates on their racial backgrounds and ignores other dimensions of their personalities and performances. Some of these officeholders claim that the media rarely asks them about issues such as citywide economic and cultural development. What are the problems inherent in attributing this one-dimensionality for black politicians? What effect does this practice have on the public's assessment about their competency? Why are black politicians so closely linked to the racial progress of their black constituency? To what extent does "racial progress ideology" influence the coverage of black mayors?

African American politicians are relatively new players in the highly competitive news market. Most are aware that as "targets" of both the national and local press, their policy decisions, as well as their lifestyles, will be heavily scrutinized. This may explain why some politicians are reluctant to talk to reporters and academic researchers.

Moreover, there are few black reporters and columnists.[22] Minority-led cities do not have counterparts in the news business. For example, there are no black-owned dailies.[23] There are some black-owned weeklies (such as the *Amsterdam News*) with small readerships. They cannot match the opinion-making ability of the *New York Times*. Minority-owned television and radio stations tend toward small stations that concentrate on entertainment and cultural events. As a result, white-owned media may not treat minority politicians as legitimate city leaders, but rather as interlopers.

African American politicians claim that they receive a disproportionate amount of negative publicity and are portrayed as ineffective policy makers. Anju Chaudhary's study of nineteen newspapers showed that "the length of stories on black elected officials in newspapers is greater than those of white elected officials."[24] She also found that such stories were placed in less desirable positions and were more negative than those written about white-elected officials. Several black mayors have felt that the media was biased against them.[25] Recently former Cleveland mayor Michael White barred the largest city newspaper, the *Plain Dealer*, from his retirement news conference.[26] Ironically, the national media has featured him as the prototype of the new black politician.[27] These "new black politicians" are supposed to be race neutral and more mainstream in their approach to governing. Does this mean they are more competent than their predecessors? Have they overcome the "antipower bias" that precludes them from exercising effective control of government operations?[28] Do they provide more leadership than their predecessors? What role does the structure of city government play? Is the role fragmented or centralized?

The issue of agency versus structure and the issue of accountability to followers are the heart of mayoral leadership. Bryan Jones is correct when he suggests that "creativity versus constraints"[29] is the key to understanding political leadership. The discourse about African American mayors has been biased toward issues of agency. Can they act independently? Will they be creative enough to overcome the structures of the office? The subtext of this discourse is whether the mayor is competent in a creative sense.

The Subtext of Competence

Was Mayor Dinkins competent? Spitzberg, who defines competence as ability, asserts, "It represents those capacities a person more or less possesses or acquires that enable the repeated enacting of goal-directed behavioral routines. The assumption is that possession of competence permits the optimizing of positive reinforcements while minimizing negative ones relative to effort and expenditure, and alternatives."[30] A competent mayor would consistently perform tasks necessary to govern. Such individuals would improve their performance as they mastered the routines of governing. The competence question takes on racial overtones when directed toward a black mayor. The nation seems to be still debating the mental ability of black people, therefore, it remains both an implicit and an explicit part of this nation's racial discourse. This may explain why editors allowed their reporters to use so much precious space accusing Dinkins of not paying enough attention to office obligations and routines. At the same time, he was charged with not providing enough visible leadership on the big issues. By raising the question of competence, reporters were trying to explain why nothing seemed to be happening.

Part of the race story is that blacks may be equal before the law, but it seems to be permissible for the public to hold reservations about their intelligence and their work ethic. Powerful equalitarian norms preclude explicit messages touting the inferiority of blacks, but there is a lot of what Tali Mendelberg calls "implicit racial appeals."[31] On the role of politicians and parties, Mendelberg observed,

Politicians convey racial messages implicitly when two contradictory conditions hold: (1) they wish to avoid violating the norm of racial equality, and (2) they face incentives to mobilize racially resentful white voters. White voters respond to implicitly racial messages when two contradictory conditions hold: (1) they wish to adhere to the norm of racial equality, and (2) they resent blacks' claims for public resources and hold negative racial stereotypes regarding work, violence and sexuality.[32]

The same characterization could be made for some journalists. Not only are these messages implicit, but also the messenger is sometimes unaware that he or she is a part of a larger racial discourse, that he or she is a message deliverer. Journalists convey racial messages implicitly when they construct stories that reinforce white readers' socialized beliefs of racial superiority and entitlement. Research suggests that some whites have been socialized to believe negative racial stereotypes regarding the intelligence and work ethics of blacks.[33] Some whites perceive a black demand for equal opportunity as a demand for preferential treatment.

The journalistic challenge is to cover a David Dinkins without the filter of racism. Many still regard an elected black officeholder's insistence on deference as problematic. This is why covering a black politician is so disappointing and predictable. Presenting black politicians in term of their race usually goes unchallenged. Labeling can lock a journalist into a tunnel, which may preclude presenting the black officeholder in more three-dimensional terms.

This book analyzes subtle stereotypical messages, second guessing, and racial signaling contained in stories about politicians. Black politicians bring with them a whole set of prepackaged images that white politicians do not. These prepackaged images include negative stereotypes that blacks are less competent and less intelligent. Black politicians are also supposedly more attracted to the perks of the office than to the substance of the job. These images are triggered either after something goes wrong or after black politicians complain. That means that if things get tough, as they did for Dinkins, the first reaction among the public was "Well, what do you expect? He is black." The white public tends to allow extra slack for white mayors. Because they have more slack, it takes longer for misjudgments and mistakes to affect the prevailing image of white mayors. It is not uncommon for black and white politicians to receive different evaluations from the public for making the same decision.

Because of the white public's stereotypes, if a black politician is called "incompetent" the label has a better chance of sticking than it does with a white politician. When an officeholder is labeled "incompetent" this characterization has to be documented and sustained by stories of mistakes, misjudgments, and mismanagement. Usually reporters solicit quotes from academics, businesspersons, or politicians that either imply or reinforce this label. These stories need to be referential to appeal to the public. In the case of mayoral competency, the public has a propensity to believe stories that resonate with their preconceived notions of the incumbent and their own personal value systems. In many ways, the labeling of mayors sends a variety of messages. In some cases it is simply a matter of using the right adjective. Political scientists Anne Schnieder and Helen Ingram list some of these positive or negative adjectives. For them, "Positive constructions include images such as 'deserving,' 'intelligent,' 'honest,' 'public-spirited' and so forth. Negative constructions include images such as 'undeserving,' 'stupid,' 'dishonest,' and 'selfish.'"[34]

For mayors, we might add positive words such as *savvy, evenhanded, fair,* and *open-minded*. Negative words include *strong partisan, vindictive, thin-skinned,* and *combative*. These words or characterizations take on an entirely different meaning when applied to minority and women office holders. Being called a "vindictive mayor" is considered harsher when applied to a woman than to a man. Stating that a black mayor made a stupid decision may be interpreted differently than the same characterization applied to a white mayor. Because many readers carry stereotypes about the intelligence of black people, any message that reinforces these stereotypes will provoke a reaction. Because it plays into racial stereotypes, an "inarticulate" black mayor is somehow more negative than an "inarticulate" white mayor.[35] Such characterizations reinforce stereotypes.[36] When I interviewed reporters, most seemed quite aware of their readers' beliefs and used such references to develop their stories.

Framing Events to Fit the Overall Story

The media, particularly the print media, is often faced with a story that does not fit the overall narrative being nurtured. The story can be reshaped (consciously and unconsciously) to fit by stimulating or otherwise activating dormant social beliefs by framing political issues in constructed group terms. Journalists can do this by framing issues in zero-sum, racial, class, gender, or spatial terms. For example, if group X gets Y, then group Z is made to feel it got nothing. If blacks get more jobs, then whites will get fewer jobs. The advance of women can only come at the expense of men. When neighborhood A gets more municipal services, its property values will appreciate, and neighborhood B, receiving fewer services, depreciates. These characterizations create the impression that some groups are being left out, double-crossed, or even ignored. Conversely, some groups are made to believe they are at an advantage or privileged. Gamson and colleagues observe,

> We walk around with media-generated images of the world, using them to construct meaning about political and social issues. The lens through which we receive these images is not neutral but evinces the power and point of view of the political and economic elite who operates and focuses it. And the special genius of this system is to make the whole process seem so normal and natural that the very art of social construction is invisible.[37]

This elite supportive view has been criticized by a variety of media commentators.[38] It is not uncommon for the media to run photographs of business leaders with celebrities, especially on occasions when they are being philanthropic. However, leaders are rarely questioned about their role in decisions regarding the city's economy. Although most reporters work for large corporations, it is very important to them that they have credibility and are seen as independent of their corporate employers. Publishers and editors understand this need and allow some negative stories about leaders to reach the public. Therefore, some stories are critical of politicians and powerful business leaders. Reporters often will invent nicknames for politicians and criticize them in cartoons, which helps the reporters cultivate a skeptical image. Yet the images reporters create are not very helpful in organizing a meaningful public discourse, nor do they contain enough information to mount a response to elitist decisions.[39]

Professional journalism espouses objectivity in reporting, but in practice, most journalists support the views of the existing politicoeconomic system. Political scientist Benjamin Page claims that newspapers use a series of techniques to slant the news, such as how a story is presented, selective reporting of facts, use of evaluative words, and framing.[40] This slanting permeates the entire paper, not just the editorial pages. As noted earlier, Soloski disagrees with this view. He believes that objectivity in journalism is not the same as in social science and resides in the behavior of the journalist. Reporters are not impartial observers of events, but rather "they seek out the facts and report them as fairly and in as balanced a way as possible."[41] Soloski makes an argument that professional norms serve to control the behavior of journalists. He cites a quote by E. B. Philips: "By definition, then, journalists are turned into copying machines who simply record the world rather than evaluate it."[42]

In other words, the crusading reporter is a myth. Reporters are primed to hear and see events in a particular way. Hence, their views support the status quo. Reporters make political judgments based on what Meryl Louis calls a "cognitive script."[43] These scripts allow them to make sense out of various political situations. The scripts allow them to identify triumphs, mistakes, and inconsistencies, override official accounts and interpretations, and anticipate a reader's interest. Jim Sleeper makes a similar observation.

> We in the media do carry "scripts" in our heads, storytelling devices that help us make sense of conflicts into which we are thrown, on deadline, with only fragmentary evidence to guide us.

The more seasoned we become through diverse encounters with the people we write about, the more refined are our scripts. But they can also remain tainted by the private guilt, anger, cynicism, or hope we carry with us. Above all, we know that the greater the horror, the "better" the story; journalists, too, operate within a "pack" psychology.[44]

One could argue that the more diverse the city, the more a journalist must tailor his or her stories to engage the audience. Equally important is the ability to incorporate one's own personal script with the overall story of one host city.

The City as a Story

Cities attract people for a variety of reasons. High-profile cities such as New York now compete globally for resources, companies, residents, and tourists. Each city has formulated a central story that identifies why it should be the place to live and work. A city's central story often takes years to formulate, revise, and refine. The story is more than civic jingoism or boosterism. Stories provide points of emotive references that explain why we invest in some cities and divest in others. New York is the grand American city because its political and economic stories are among the most compelling ones in the nation. The city draws upon history to make the case for uniqueness. The grand story locates people, inveigling them to buy into a common purpose of living and working there: "We are all New Yorkers." This is not a shibboleth, as it is essential for mobilizing and governing in an increasingly disparate urban community. In a society that divides people into occupations, classes, races, ethnicity, and neighborhoods, a common element can hold everyone together. The telling of these stories is done through media outlets, but politicians act out the drama.

New York residents believe they live in an extraordinary city, in part, because the media flatters them. They are made to feel lucky because they live in New York. According to these positive messages, New Yorkers are a steady group blessed with resiliency and boundless coping mechanisms. They can arrive anyplace in the city by subway. Sure their apartments may be small, but they live in the "City." There are stories about the high cost of living in Manhattan, Fifth Avenue matrons, Broadway, Wall Street, and expensive restaurants. There are also stories about people (mainly movie stars, international financiers, and rich Europeans) who could afford to live anywhere but prefer living in New York. Paul Delaney observes, "The Bible of the *Times* is the idea that the city is sacred. The *Times* propagates the New York culture passionately. They live by it. The first thing they ask new reporters. How do you like New York? The paper is a true New Yorker."[45]

Overview of This Book

The introduction of this book provides an opportunity to examine the political communication literature as it relates to race and mayoral images. Indeed, I am trying to expose the media's role in image construction and raise questions about its process and the role images play in politics. I am suggesting that David Dinkins represents different meanings to different audiences independent of the political events of his tenure. This is not to say that events shaped the construction of his mayoralty but rather to say that race complicated his image and politics. This analysis borrows much from the research of social psychologists, journalism theorists, sociologists, and literary theorists.[46]

I interviewed former mayor David Dinkins, his principal staff members, and the reporters who covered him. In my interviews, I attempted to engage interviewees with respect to interpretations and conclusions drawn from media discourse. I also used the newspaper accounts of Dinkins' tenure. The cases selected for review included mayoral appointments, race relations, public unions, employees' unions, and school politics. Each of these provided a challenge to the mayor's image.[47]

Chapter 2 is an analysis of the social and political background of David Dinkins. Some New York City politicians are considered *greenhouse politicians*, because they are trained to be only local politicians. Greenhouse plants are grown under controlled conditions—the proper lighting, temperature, water, and fertilizer. Such plants are never exposed to the environmental vicissitudes of the outdoors, but once out of this controlled environment, they cannot survive. 'Greenhouse politicians' refers to black politicians who were nurtured in the idiosyncratic white, liberal politics of New York City and became true believers in positive government. However, such politicians are provincial, and when in office they behave with a New Deal bent. They have a limited vision about what cities can do or be. Furthermore, New York City politicians do not believe that they can learn from other cities or non–New York politicians. Such politicians could not function outside the city. Could the greenhouse politician characterization be applied to mayor David Dinkins? Was he a victim of the backlash toward black males who assume agency?

Chapter 3 examines the proposition that Dinkins' election represents a regime change. It discusses the economic, social, and structural conditions that greeted him as he entered Gracie Mansion and city hall. The Dinkins era corresponds to the advent of a new city charter and a nationwide economic recession.

Chapter 4 examines the staff appointments of Mayor Dinkins. The first sets of high-profile appointments are critical to a mayor's public image. Dinkins' appointments reflected his notion of inclusion and ethnic representation. Potentially, the mayor's team can either facilitate or impede his or her goals. The internal dynamics of city hall reveal a great deal about Dinkins and how he assigned responsibilities.

Chapter 5 describes how Dinkins dealt with the racial crises in Queens and Crown Heights. The Crown Heights incident (a conflict between Jews and blacks in a Brooklyn neighborhood) was a critical marker for his administration. Although he had racial problems during the Korean store boycott (the boycott of a fruit store in Queens) and a series of interracial murders, Crown Heights stands out as the watershed of Dinkins' tenure.

Chapter 6 reviews the relationship between Dinkins and the employee unions. For a variety of reasons, public employee unions have emerged as some of the strongest interest groups in the city. They are the second most attentive public the mayor has, and their leaders play a major role in electoral politics. Politics in many ways has become a cycle of collective bargaining. Mayors are often judged by how they manage the demands of the unions. Mayors who alienate union leaders do so at their peril. The press is particularly attentive to the opinion of union leaders because work stoppage and job action can disturb city activities.

Street crime remains the top public issue in most industrial cities. This is especially the case in times of economic downturn. In the current crime-phobic society, mayoral candidates are forced to outline what type of *safety compact* they plan to impose if elected into office. The discourse about crime is that everyone is a potential victim. A commentary in the *New Yorker* expanded on this point by saying, "Crime is at the center of the issue of public safety, which also encompasses a range of other affections that give an air of menace to life in many parts of many cities, New York included: aggressive panhandlers, graffiti, and violence in and around public schools."[48]

Mayors run on anticrime platforms and take every opportunity to be constructed as effective crime fighters. This image making includes soliciting the police union's support in campaigns and in appointing commissioners with crime-fighting reputations. A crime incident in the city can change the image of a mayor. Chapter 7 reviews street crimes and Dinkins' reactions to the demand for more safety in the streets.

Chapter 8 examines New York City school politics. Most mayors have to deal with public school politics. Although they can appoint members to the central board, mayors generally have very little control over school board policy. In an earlier work, I suggested that policy was controlled by a coalition of central board staff and union leaders, the public school cartel (PSC). Chapter 8 examines how Dinkins fared with this cartel. The last chapter brings together the findings from the case studies and outlines some implications for media and mayoral politics.

CHAPTER TWO

THE MAKING OF A NEW YORK
BLACK POLITICIAN:
DAVID DINKINS

American cities have been electing mayors of African descent since the 1960s.[1] The election of a black mayor is no longer greeted with the excitement or apprehension of the sixties and seventies. The eighties and nineties were times when certain cities anticipated electing the first mayor of African American descent. Most black mayors have proven themselves to be relatively good stewards of their cities.[2] White voters have increasingly supported black mayors' bids for reelection.[3] Therefore many pundits were surprised that New York lagged behind in producing a serious black candidate for the city's top executive job. Even Newark, a city often the butt of jokes for Manhattanites, could boast of electing a black mayor long before New York City.

Historically, New York City has always been ahead of other cities in electing blacks to municipal offices. In 1919, James C. Thomas was elected to the city council (then the board of aldermen). During the Great Depression, Harlem became the center of black politics. The concentration of black Manhattanites in Harlem helped to form a natural political base. Many famous black politicians started their careers in Harlem. In 1944, Rev. Adam Clayton Powell Jr. was elected to Congress. Then in 1953 Hulan Jack became the first black president of the borough of Manhattan. Granted, the latter is not a powerful executive office but is a seat of the Board of Estimate, which has jurisdiction over the budget, zoning, and franchises.

In 1964, J. Raymond Jones became the first black chairman of the New York City County Democratic Party, inheriting what was left of the once powerful Tammany Hall political machine. Tammany Hall had lost its clout as a political machine and its appeal to voters. Yet being elected chairman of the Democratic Party had symbolic value. The task for the nascent black political class was to translate party prominence into citywide elective office. In the sixties, the evolution of black politics in other boroughs lagged behind that in Manhattan. Citywide offices such as mayor, city council president, and comptroller were beyond their reach.

In addition to an underdeveloped citywide view of politics or supportive political organization in the outer boroughs, black politicians were unprepared for the shifts in the economic base of the city. As the manufacturing base gave way to the financial and service industry, Latinos began to outpace the new immigrants to the city. By the 1980s the city had changed demographically, and the dream of a black mayor suddenly became more realistic. The question was could the black community mount a serious campaign for the mayoralty?

In the introduction I described New York African American politicians as "greenhouse politicians," that is, as politically socialized under ideal conditions. Trained in political clubs and befriended by white liberals, they lack constituency networks that could develop mentors outside the city. This type of politician cannot survive outside his or her borough. Some never leave the life in the black political clubs. Leaders may know of their counterparts in other borough clubs, but they rarely meet. Someone once said, "You couldn't get these guys to meet as a group unless some famous white politician called them together. They don't really need each other."[4] Unlike other cities with large minority populations, New York does not have rampant white flight. In addition, the separation of blacks into five different boroughs divides black leaders and inhibits cross-borough coalitions.

The political context of New York City politics is heavily biased toward liberal views and coalition politics. Indeed white liberal activists have sponsored the careers of black politicians with fund-raisers and publicity. At the beginning of Dinkins' term, Rev. Calvin Butts, pastor of the Abyssinian Baptist Church in Harlem candidly stated, "As an African-American person, I see David Dinkins as a symbol of our progress. Whether he will be an actual tool for progress remains to be seen. Dinkins is as much a machine, clubhouse politician as he is African-American."[5]

New York black politicians rarely face challenges from insurgent civil rights and labor activist leaders. They are not required to build grassroots constituencies beyond their clubhouse. Few of these politicians achieve visibility outside New York City. The city is so large and impersonal that name recognition becomes a factor in citywide elections. Politicians of both races need attention from the media. There is no political party to promote them as potential mayoral candidates.[6] Ironically, before the nineties, the man who would become the first black mayor of New York—David Dinkins—was not mentioned consistently in the newspaper or broadcast media. The powerlessness and invisibility of black politicians were pondered in a 1987 *New York Times* series on race relations in New York City. An article by Michael Oreskes reported a telephone poll that asked, "[W]ho do you think are the two or three most important white/black leaders in New York City?" Of the 62 percent of the 1063 respondents who couldn't name any black leaders, 65 percent were whites and 54 percent were blacks. Benjamin Ward, the police commissioner, received the higher percentage of nominations with 17 percent of whites and 16 percent of blacks. In the survey, 14 percent of whites and 13 percent of blacks named David Dinkins.[7] The future mayor of New York had two years to define himself and gain citywide name recognition.

Dinkins, The Man

David Norman Dinkins was born to William Harvey Dinkins Jr. and Sally Dinkins on July 10, 1927, in Trenton, New Jersey. Trenton, the capital city of a highly industrial state, was known for its pottery porcelain. William Dinkins was employed by a cable factory and was also a barber. He was active in the Masons and the NAACP. Later William Dinkins became a real estate and insurance broker. According to black family standards, the Dinkins family fell within the middle class. However, David Dinkins' early childhood was in the midst of the Great Depression.

David Dinkins moved to Harlem, New York, at the age of six when his father and mother separated, but later returned to

Trenton at age fourteen to live with his father. In 1942, the nation was involved in World War II. During the war, Dinkins served eighteen months in the Marine Corps at Camp Lejune in North Carolina. At that time the corps was one of the most segregated branches of the American military. After the war, Dinkins entered Howard University, considered the elite of historically black colleges and universities, where he majored in mathematics and graduated in 1950.

Dinkins returned to New York in 1950, and in 1953 he met and married Joyce Burrows, the daughter of a former Harlem politician. During the nascent civil rights movement in the South, Dinkins attended Brooklyn Law School. He graduated in 1956 and then began practicing law in Harlem with Fritz W. Alexander. Dinkins' political career also began in the fifties as he became active in the George Washington Carver Club, headed by J. Raymond "the Fox" Jones, a city councilman and erstwhile mentor for Adam Clayton Powell and Percy Sutton.

The Fox was known as both a politician and a tutor. Charles V. Hamilton, Columbia University professor and longtime analyst of black politics in Harlem, concluded, "[W]hatever else J. Raymond Jones was, he was a crafty politician. He understood votes and counting, and he had no illusions about the necessity to bargain and compromise. Likewise, he was not apologetic about the use of patronage as a means not only of gaining party loyalty but as a means, an important one, for laying a 'base' for further economic development."[8]

In a later article *New York Times* reporter Todd Purdum claimed that Jones was the quintessential go-along-to-get-along politician, who drilled into Dinkins and his generation the idea that dogged loyalty and quiet perseverance were keys to success.[9] Dinkins asserted that Jones was not his role model. "I didn't want to be like him."[10] At the urging of Jones, Dinkins ran and was elected to the New York State Assembly in 1965 and as Harlem Democrat district leader in 1967. He served one term in the state assembly. In 1972 Dinkins was elected the first black President of the Board of Elections.

In Harlem, members of the Carver Club rarely debated the genesis of the first black mayor; they assumed he or she would come from Harlem. They accepted Manhattan hegemony in city politics. Harlem political club development was further ahead of its Brooklyn and Queens counterparts in building a political base and nurturing politicians that had visibility beyond the borough.[11] Harlem politicians contended that a black mayor of New York was inevitable and that an acceptable personality was needed to appeal to white liberal politicians in Manhattan. The assumption was that white, liberal reform clubs and Democratic regular organizations would be able to deliver the white voters, if black politicians could agree on an acceptable candidate—or when the time was right. Were these assumptions consistent with the potential for mobilizing the black voters?

Black Voters/Black Politicians

The connection between black voters and politicians is a weak one in cities such as New York with its ineffectual party organization. Charles V. Hamilton suggested that the inchoate development of black politics could be traced to lack of incentives for political participation. White, liberal candidate victories, civil service reform, and the U.S. Supreme Court holdings against the use of patronage had defanged the Tammany Tiger. The New York City political machine was dead. Consequently, "voting early and often" did not offer the same incentives for blacks as it did for the early white ethnic immigrant groups. According to Hamilton, white immigrant groups had a patron-client relationship with political parties.[12] They realized direct benefits by supporting party A over B or candidate A over B. Clients were given jobs, assistance with the police and tax collectors, food, and personal attention. These benefits continued even after civil service reform and up until World War ll. After the war parties began to lose control over welfare services, and white ethnics began to move to the suburbs. By the time black immigrants such as David Dinkins gained some influence in the Democratic Party it was a relatively empty vessel. The political clubs could help black politicians to get elected to local office, but they had little patronage to distribute to keep the electorate close to the organization. Poor blacks developed a patron-recipient relationship with the welfare department. They were not the exclusive clients of the Democratic Party, because they voted for Democratic candidates, not the party itself. David Dinkins would have to make it to Gracie Mansion on his own volition and not as a Tammany man. In order to get citywide visibility, Dinkins needed a citywide office. This opportunity came when Mayor Abraham Beame, the city's first Jewish mayor,[13] attempted to appoint Dinkins deputy mayor of planning and development. The appointment fell apart when the media discovered that Dinkins had not paid his income taxes. Dinkins had not filed a federal tax return or New York state or city income tax returns, between 1969 and 1972. Dinkins withdrew his name from consideration for the deputy mayor post and paid a total of fifteen thousand dollars worth of fines as well as interest and penalties. He contended that he thought he had paid everything. Dinkins' image went from that of a young, aspiring politician to an alleged tax cheat. For many black aspirants, this disclosure would have ended their upward mobility within city politics.

Two years later, however, Mayor Beame appointed Dinkins city clerk, another patronage job. The clerk's office sells marriage licenses, receives reports, and registers lobbyists. In the same year Dinkins, along with several black political notables, joined the Black Americans in Support of Israel Committee (BASIC). Founded by Bayard Rustin, the civil rights activist, BASIC was a platform for blacks to express their support for American Middle East policies. Ambitious black politicians knew this association would serve them well in a citywide race. (One cannot succeed in New York politics unless one has the right views on Israeli politics.) The Jewish voting bloc played a critical role in city elections. Moreover, many black leaders had long-term friendships with Jewish liberal activists and were adherents of coalition politics.

Lessons from Sutton's Race

Traditionally, citywide minority mayoral candidates were washed away in the Democratic primary because white liberals would run and split the minority vote. There was also the problem of multiple minority candidates. Black and Puerto Rican leaders would field competing candidates, offsetting each other. The result was a classic example of a divide and conquest strategy, which was encouraged by white politicians.

In 1977 white liberals Mario Cuomo, Ed Koch, and Bella Abzug ran in the primary. Abzug was a former congresswoman and feminist heroine who had earned a reputation as a gadfly in Congress. Edward Koch, a congressman from the east side of New York, was known mostly for his wit. Mario Cuomo had been active in neighborhood politics in Queens and was thus considered a "comer" in city politics. Herman Badillo, a Puerto Rican congressman, was the other minority candidate.

Black political pundits thought that if the Jews split their votes among Beame, Koch, and Abzug, a black candidate could win the primary. All they needed was an ideal black mayoral candidate. (They reasoned that Cuomo was from Queens and thus represented no threat. New Yorkers have traditionally elected Manhattanites to the top job at city hall.) A successful black candidate had to be articulate, urbane, and well liked among whites. All he or she would have to do is consolidate the minority and garner some help from his or her liberal friends. This scenario was enhanced by the rumor that Percy Sutton (Manhattan borough president), the most visible and highest ranking elected, black official, had made a deal with then mayor Abraham Beame for future endorsement of him as a mayoral candidate. The problem with these political calculations was that New York was in the throes of one of the worst fiscal crises in its history. To make things even more complicated, Mayor Beame decided to run for reelection.

Nevertheless, Percy Sutton entered the race for mayor. Sutton served as president of the NAACP and had an exemplary resume. In his early career, he had had little or no support from other Harlem politicians. Indeed, Sutton described himself as an outsider in Harlem politics. By all accounts, he was part of the new generation of black activists of the sixties. He had been arrested during the civil rights movement and had acted as lawyer for several controversial political activists, including Henry Winston, a Communist leader, and Malcolm X. Sutton had served in the state assembly before being elected to the borough presidency. Malcolm X campaigned for him when he ran successfully for an assembly seat. Along with Basil Patterson and Charles Rangel, Sutton changed the name of the old Central Democratic Club to the Martin Luther King Democratic Club. Dinkins' name was added to the leadership of this group, and the members became touted as the "gang of four."

The major issue in the 1976 mayoral campaign was the fallout from the 1975 fiscal crisis. Who could put the right fiscal face on the city and keep the city's promises to the municipal bonds community, Emergency Financial Control Board, and Municipal Assistance Corporation? The media never constructed Sutton as a possible rescuer in the fiscal crisis. All of the city saviors were white males. For many white political leaders, this was the wrong time to debate the efficacy of electing a black mayor of New York. The fiscal problem trumped the racial problem.

Sutton said some important things in the campaign but could not establish a reason that he should be elected. Subsequently, he received only 14 percent of the vote (approximately the percentage of blacks in the primary electorate) in a crowded primary race. The media decided that Mario Cuomo was the new star. With the Queens community activist background, Italian ancestry, and good speaking voice, Cuomo was the man to watch. The media virtually ignored the Sutton candidacy.

Only about a third of the black voters voted in the primary. The low turnout was related to some of the points made by Professor Hamilton and to Sutton's weak organization and mobilization skills. Sutton was surprised that the press ignored his campaign. He recalled being praised by the media.

> I had been rated the best Borough president in the history of New York. I had been called highly intelligent. They said that I mixed well in public. But they also said that I didn't have a large constituency.
>
> I got no coverage. The only coverage was my radio station. I held a news conference on the top of the Empire State Building. I had the president of Diners Club, major bankers, and convention people. I said New York should be exploited for trade and commerce. New York is the capital of the world. New York is the tourist capital of the world. The *Daily News* came, but nothing came out."[14]

This quote suggests that Percy Sutton was not off message but out of the construction. The decision to ignore a press conference of the city's first serious black mayoral candidate had to have been made by editors and reporters who concluded that there was no story there. The media decision not to engage Sutton on the fiscal issues also signals whites that his was not a serious candidacy.[15] "I couldn't get my message across."[16] Other candidates were simply more interesting. Governor Hugh Carey, one of the heroes of the 1975 fiscal crisis, supported Mario Cuomo. Ed Koch and Bella Abzug were colorful characters in their own right. Sutton admitted that all candidates were liberals, and they split the vote. During our interview, he would not confirm the rumors that he had made a 1973 deal to support Abraham Beame, the first Jewish mayor, and that Beame would support him in 1977. In fact, Beame stayed in the race and tried unsuccessfully to defend his record.

Percy Sutton received 14.4 percent of the vote, and Herman Badillo received 11 percent. Combining their votes would not have put either man in the runoff.[17] The surprise winner in the primary, Ed Koch, had been successful in framing the primary race as a vote on the competence of Mayor Beame. In a race among three prominent Jewish politicians, Koch disassociated himself with liberal politics, embraced highly nuanced conservative themes, and won. Mario Cuomo survived the primary and was defeated by Koch in the runoff. Sutton and many black voters supported Koch in the general election.

A closer analysis illustrated that neither minority candidate, Sutton or Badillo, received 90 percent of the vote in heavily black or Puerto Rican precincts. Why? Because of the campaign organizations and strategies of the two minority candidates. Both men were extremely articulate and urbane individuals but failed to connect with nominally minority constituencies. Black voters who thought Sutton should be borough president were not enthusiastic about the mayoral race. Badillo, who considered himself a role model for many young Puerto Rican politicians, was not an ethnic mobilizer. Although he had served in Congress, he was not known as a Puerto Rican grassroots advocate. He carefully nurtured a reputation of being an independent politician and did not have the networks of grassroots activists.

More important, Sutton's poor showing surprised some black leaders and presumably Dinkins. Many black leaders believed the "your time will come" rhetoric of their white, liberal allies. Either white liberals were hypocrites, or they were not ready for a black man in the highest city office. Sutton seemed to have had everything—elegance, wealth, political connections, and a forceful personality. This candidacy provided another example of the "greenhouse mentality" of black politicians. Granted Sutton had a weak and underfinanced campaign structure (he claims he spent four hundred thousand dollars of his own money on the campaign) and started late. "I couldn't raise money."[18] Sutton had few political connections in the big population centers such as Queens and Brooklyn. He had black supporters in the other boroughs but very little white support. Yet many blacks felt that he should have made it to the runoffs despite the crowded field.

Martin Kilson, a political scientist, reviewed the failed Sutton campaign and deemed that it was an example of weak political incorporation. Kilson concluded that Sutton represented client political incorporation. According to Kilson:

> [Sutton] [s]o shaped his politics around political brokers—especially Tammany head Frank Rossetti—that his own ethnic organization flagged. . . . The politics of client-incorporation enable politically skillful leaders to carve out a power niche for *themselves* but not their constituency. This power niche produces sizable personal clout for black leaders, as well as some wealth and business opportunities. But it seldom facilitates effective political incorporation for blacks in general.[19]

Charles Green and Basil Wilson were less kind. They concluded:

> Sutton chose to run for mayor when the white backlash movement was at its zenith and initially chose not to base his campaign in the black community. Although there was an increased number of black elected officials, there did not exist any concerted black effort in support of Sutton's candidacy. . . . Sutton's campaign was too conventional and unimaginative and did not have much of a historical impact. It left Sutton in a shattered state. He has indicated that the campaign was the most disheartening, deprecating, disabling experience he has ever encountered and that he was not prepared for the isolation of his candidacy based on the color of his skin.[20]

Dinkins served as city clerk from 1975 to 1985 and got a chance to watch his associate Percy Sutton make a quixotic attempt at city hall. Phillip Thompson, a political scientist, observed,

> When Sutton ran for Mayor, black City Clerk David Dinkins ran to fill his seat as Manhattan Borough President. Dinkins reasoned

that should Sutton lose, it was important for a black person to
maintain a seat on BOE. But Sutton and Dinkins both were tap-
ping the same limited sources of financial support. . . . Dinkins
and Sutton worked at cross purposes, [and] both campaigns were
strapped for money. . . . As it turned out, they both lost.[21]

Although they both lost, there were lessons to be learned for the
Sutton campaign. Not only did blacks lose a seat on the Board of
Estimate (BOE), but it also marked a time when there was not a
high-ranking, elected, black official in municipal office.

Reporter Jim Sleeper makes the connection between the Sutton campaign for mayor and the subsequent rise of David Dinkins. According to Sleeper, Sutton's decision not to resign from
his office to allow Dinkins to be appointed to the borough presidency forced Dinkins to become an "honorary black insurgent."[22] Reformers put up two candidates, Robert Wagner Jr.
and Ronnie Eldridge, a woman, splitting the vote and allowing
Andrew Stein, scion of a wealthy Jewish family, to be elected
borough president. Dinkins spent the next four years building
his image among reform groups in New York City politics. He
tried again for the borough president in 1981 but lost again to
Stein even with what Sleeper described as "lavished support"
from white reformers, although he came close with 47 percent
of the vote. When Stein decided to run for City Council President in 1985, Dinkins took advantage of the opening and was
elected Borough President.

Chris McNickle claims that Dinkins' election to borough president elevated him to a new status. Unlike Hulan Jack who had
won the presidency as a junior partner in an ethnic coalition,
Dinkins "won his as the senior partner in a racial one."[23] The coalition of blacks, Latinos, and white liberals had enough voters
to elect a Manhattan borough president. Sleeper concluded:

> Dinkins finally became Manhattan borough president the old-
> fashioned way: he earned it, not just by inheriting the local black
> band of Jackson's Rainbow but by befriending the new, white re-
> form establishment, which suppressed its lingering misgiving and
> embraced him at last. Dinkins had also proven himself to the more
> conservative "permanent government" of realtors, developers, and
> contractors who'd always been close to his mentors in Harlem.[24]

David Dinkins (left) and Percy Sutton (right), February 15, 1990.
© Copyright Fred W. McDarrah.

Dinkins Elected Borough President

Created by the 1901 charter the borough president is the borough representative, not a county executive. Each borough president had a seat on the Board of Estimate. This legislative body made decisions on zoning, land use policy (such as the Uniform Land Use Review Procedure), and contractors, tax abatements, leases, and franchises. The BOE acted as a second legislature dealing with the capital budgets, franchises, and planning. Among the most important tasks of the borough president is appointing members of the community boards, the board of education, and the city planning commission. Borough presidents also appoint five members to the New York Public Development Corporation, the agency responsible for overseeing economic development. Borough presidents are expected to advocate for their borough (counties) before city hall.

In 1953 Hulan Jack was elected as the first black Manhattan borough president. For twenty-four years, until 1977, a black had been elected Manhattan Borough President. In 1977 Dinkins ran for the job against the well-financed Andrew Stein and the son of a former mayor, Robert Wagner Jr. He ran a poor third. In 1981 he ran again and received 47 percent of the vote against Stein. When Stein decided to run for city council president, Dinkins was victorious against a relatively unknown state assemblyman, Jerrold Nadler. Dinkins was the first black to serve on the BOE in the twelve years of "the Stein interregnum."

Dinkins had been city clerk for ten years. The borough presidency gave him more visibility, and he began to speak to a wider range of community groups. Politicians and the media began to notice him. As Dinkins was the highest ranking elected, black official in New York City, his views on racial matters were solicited. Also, his views about the infamous Tawana Brawley drew a lot of attention.

In 1988, Dinkins got involved with the Tawana Brawley controversy. Brawley, a young black woman, claimed that she was abducted and raped by a group of white men. Many people questioned whether she was telling the truth. The case became a crime icon of black/white relations in both New York City and the state. The circumstances and the resulting trial are beyond the scope of this book, but suffice to say that the trial created more questions than it answered.

Dinkins criticized Brawley's advisors, Rev. Al Sharpton, a civil rights activist, and lawyers Alton Maddox Jr. and C. Vernon Mason, for engaging in name calling and for making wild accusations about white officials. During a television interview, Dinkins asserted, "I don't think they help their cause or ours by calling the Governor and Robert Abrams and others names." Dinkins also declared, "[T]he wild charges are unsubstantiated and, I am confident, untrue."[25]

The *Times* editorial reaction to Dinkins was interesting. It asked, "What took so long?"[26] The piece pointed out that other prominent blacks had already expressed disapproval. It scolded what it characterized as the "highest ranking black elected official" for not getting involved in the controversy. The article created the impression that Dinkins was siding with those who did not believe Brawley's story. A different reading of the Dinkins statement would suggest that he was against calling the two highest ranking Democratic politicians, Governor Cuomo and

Attorney General Robert Abrams, names. Dinkins responded with a letter to the editor. He wrote,

> Besides my concern about the assumption that black officials must always "speak out" on any issue involving blacks, while white officials are allowed to stay above the fray, it is also distressing that it is so easy to get column inches and air time in New York City when criticizing Tawana Brawley's advisors or when, like them, one plays to the news media's hunger for sensationalism; whereas it is nearly impossible to get coverage for criticisms of or recommendations to improve the criminal justice system. . . . You accuse me of not speaking out soon enough. In this case, as in all my works as a public official, I must work on my own timetable, not one dictated by news deadlines and headlines.[27]

The Brawley incident and his reactions to it were important for Dinkins' image. Although he claimed his first comments were taken out of context, the letter to the editor may have been designed to deflect charges that he was kowtowing to the white media. This must have been reassuring to his black constituency, many of whom had not yet made up their minds about the Brawley case.

The eighties were coming to an end, and the prospect for black unity looked bleak for a black candidate aspiring to be mayor. Although there was no shortage of willing white candidates, finding a black one would be difficult. Before the 1989 mayoral primary, black leaders held several major meetings trying to agree on common goals and a single mayoral candidate. Recovering from the lackluster 1985 mayoral bid of black Assemblyman Herman "Denny" Farrell, a new optimism among black politicians emerged. This was due partly to the political enthusiasm of the Jesse Jackson 1988 presidential candidacy.[28] Jackson had stimulated black and brown voter registration and had energized New York City black voters.

The Symbolic Significance of Jesse Jackson

The two presidential candidacies of Jesse Jackson (1984 and 1988) served to mobilize many new black voters nationwide.

Dinkins was one of the only visible black, elected officials to support Rev. Jesse Jackson's 1984 campaign. Most black leaders supported Walter Mondale. The 1988 campaign was extremely significant for New York City. Many blacks registered in order to help the Jackson campaign. Others wanted to test the theory that an incumbent mayor could be defeated if enough minority voters went to the polls. Jackson repaid Dinkins by campaigning for him in his bid for the mayoralty. Ironically, the 1988 Jackson campaign had a negative effect on black-Jewish relations. The Jewish community leaders were active in the liberal reform movement that black leaders counted on for support. Jackson's infamous "Hymietown" remark forced several black politicians, including Dinkins, to disassociate themselves from him.

Many black politicians including Dinkins had supported the Jewish community's stand on Israel and had strong political ties with Jewish politicians. Dinkins had repeatedly stated his support for Israel. In New York, local candidates for mayor are expected to be pro-Israel on the Middle East issues. Black leaders wanted to capitalize on the growing anti-Koch sentiment among white liberals.

By the 1989 New York election, Professor Kilson had cited Dinkins as an example of a transracial politician who could win the mayoralty. Kilson's characterization was meant as a compliment to Dinkins. It did not suggest that Dinkins was above race, but rather had a personality that could generate respect across racial lines. Dinkins had managed to keep the race issue at a distance. There was no indication that Dinkins was making a bid for the title of the leading black personality in the city. By all indications he was content to be borough president. Ruth Messinger, his successor, stated, "David loved the job, and the job loved him."[29] In an interview she stated she had begun to raise money in 1988 to run for an "unknown" citywide office. She asked Dinkins if he was running for mayor, but he kept saying "no way that he was going to run for mayor."[30]

Someone had to take on Koch. There was a core of progressive Democrats who wanted to defeat him. Messinger believed that Dinkins was a reluctant candidate. "He was reluctant to give up a job that he loved." In 1988 Dinkins said, "I have never had the ambition particularly to be the city's first black mayor," but by 1989 he was warming up to the idea of running. It is not clear why he changed his mind. Koch was losing his image as an enlightened neoliberal, yet few people envisioned Dinkins as an ideal candidate. Would the race be a recap of the Sutton and Farrell race? Was Dinkins up to the job? Joe Klein, then of *New York* magazine, wrote a column that addressed this.

> Toughness seems a euphemism—for acuity, I suspect. There is a complacent quality to Dinkins; he lacks rigor. His unwillingness to confront the mayor—or anyone, for that matter—may seem statesmanlike but might just as easily be construed as an allergy to serious thought. He has commissioned several worthy studies as borough president and colleagues admire his staff, but little of their effort seems to have percolated upward. When asked a substantive question—about anything—Dinkins will flee to the nearest platitude.[31]

Once he entered the race, Dinkins became a serious and committed candidate. He carefully disassociated himself from Jesse Jackson's remarks but not from Jackson himself. He received the endorsement of several liberal whites and public service unions, yet few politicians actually expected Dinkins to win the race.

Dinkins versus Koch

At first glance, an Ed Koch versus Dinkins bout seemed an unlikely and uneven match. Dinkins claimed that he entered the race because "Koch was the way he was."[32] Koch, hero of the neoliberals and self-described law and order man, was pitted against a black politician who was not well known outside of Manhattan. Dinkins' tenure as president of the Board of Elections, city clerk, and Borough President were not perceived as good stepping stones to the mayoralty. Black voters accepted Dinkins, in part, because the chances of electing a fiery Jesse Jackson type candidate were nil.[33] In 1989, the Hart polling organization conducted a survey that predicted Dinkins beating Koch in the primary.

Upon entering the race, Dinkins would face city comptroller Harrison J. Goldin, MTA chairman Richard Ravitch, and incumbent mayor Ed Koch, all Jewish candidates. At first, Dinkins was

Ed Koch and David Dinkins. © Copyright Fred W. McDarrah.

hesitant to run. Despite all of Mayor Koch's political problems, he was a proven vote getter. Koch still had supporters who had been with him throughout his long political career. The coalition Dinkins was trying to put together was untested. Running for mayor also meant that Dinkins would have to give up the borough presidency, then the highest ranking position held by a black in city government. There was also considerable uncertainty about whether Dinkins' candidacy would appeal to white voters in Queens, Staten Island, and Brooklyn.

The main issue in the Democratic primary campaign turned out to be whether Koch's rhetoric had inflamed racial tensions. There had been several infamous racial incidents during his tenure (for example, Bensonhurst, an incident in which a black man who was searching for a used car was attacked and killed by whites), and the city voters wanted someone less confrontational. Dinkins' campaign burden turned out to be his tax-paying habits and his relationship to Jesse Jackson. He also fielded an allegation that one of his staff members was anti-Semitic and that the campaign had paid $9,500 to the Committee to Honor Black Heroes, a black nationalist group headed by Sonny Carson.

Koch Undoing Himself

New York is a city of political symbols. The 1977 Koch victory was the epitome of white, liberal reform club insurgency and clever appropriation of the conservative law and order rhetoric. However, Koch governed with a neoliberal philosophy. "He was always arguing with someone, even if only playfully. . . . He kept a steady banter with reporters, communing with them exhaustively. . . . His joyful, brusque chutzpah seemed right for New York, especially as it returned from its staggering bout with bankruptcy in the 1970s."[34] By his own account, he told Jews off as well as blacks. White ethnics appreciated his frankness about the declining social conditions of the city, and in cultivating an image as a fiscal and social conservative, Koch became a very popular politician. However, by 1989, Koch's standup act had worn thin, and racial incidents such as Bensonhurst, coming twenty days before the primary, raised questions in the minds of his liberal and ethnic supporters about his approach.[35]

In the 1989 primary, Koch was challenged by a variety of liberals—David Dinkins, Richard Ravitch, former chair of the Metro-Transit Authority; and Harrison Goldin, city comptroller. However, it was the Dinkins campaign that provided the most contrast. Joe Klein of the *New York* magazine characterized Dinkins's campaign

> His campaign for mayor is wearing well. He's been a class act so far in a race rutted in trivia, vituperation, and anomie. He may, in fact, be embarked on that most hallowed, if infrequently observed, political rite of passage; the man of apparently modest talents who finds himself in the right place at the right time and seems to grow in stature and ability as he pursues high office.[36]

Blacks continued to see Koch as an opportunist using the race issue to get himself reelected. To many of them, his cynical behavior showed his insensitivity to their struggle to survive in the city. Columnists also turned against Koch. Pete Hamill of the *New York Post*, Jimmy Breslin of *Newsday*, and Jack Newfield of the *Daily News* wrote anti-Koch articles that questioned his ability to lead the city in those racially tense times.[37] Yet many liberals supported Koch because of his record of appointments and spending priorities. They knew and liked him. So what if he occasionally put his foot in his mouth as long as he was able to do the job? Yet black politicians who disliked Koch's antics were powerless to remove him.

Ed Koch was a man to whom few people could remain neutral. One either loved him or hated him. His autobiography portrays a man who is fighting for acceptance while centering himself at the core of the city's political life.[38] He was a self-proclaimed Jewish nationalist, political showman, and shameless narcissist. New York enjoyed watching and reading about him. The city had not had such a flamboyant mayor since Mayor Fiorello La Guardia.

Koch may have been able to survive the racial incidents, but a series of kickback scandals involving close Koch allies Donald Manes (Queens borough president) and Stanley Friedman (Bronx borough president) compromised his prevailing image of an abrasive but competent leader. Even Bess Meyerson, another close friend of the mayor, was caught up in a separate scandal involving influence peddling.[39] These incidents raised new questions about how well Koch was informed about activities within his administration and what he knew about these cases.

Rival black leaders and their erstwhile white allies came together to criticize the mayor. Koch was put on the defensive, and he never recovered. Browne, Collins, and Goodwin introduced their biography of the colorful mayor with this lament:

> When he came in office in 1978, he said he hoped to be the best Mayor the city ever had. Now he says only that he wants to be mayor forever.
>
> In that sense his own book tells a tragic story. As time has passed Ed Koch has frittered away a potentially brilliant career in pursuit of fame, fortune and clippings. What a pity.[40]

Dinkins won the primary receiving 537,313 votes (51 percent) over Koch's 445,816 (42 percent). The other votes were divided

New York Democrats with David Dinkins. (Left to right) Daniel P. Moynihan, Ray Flynn (Boston), Steven Solarz, Floyd Flake, Elliot Engel, George Mitchell, Charles Rangel, Thomas Manton, Eudolphus Towns. © Copyright Fred W. McDarrah.

between Richard Ravitch and Harrison Goldin. Dinkins got 29 percent of the white vote in the primary, and Dinkins won an estimated 94 percent of the black vote. Running against Jewish opponents, he won 26 percent of the Jewish vote. Hilary Mackenzie of *MacLean Magazine* summarized the Canadian view of the race.

> The road to Dinkins's victory was pitted with disbelief that a mild-mannered black, who ran a cautious and uninspired campaign, could unseat the controversial Koch, a Jew who seemed to personify the liberal spirit of many New Yorkers. Throughout the campaign, Dinkins was battered by accusations that his campaign was directionless, that his speeches lacked spontaneity and that he delivered them in a boring monotone.[41]

For many black and brown New Yorkers, September 12, 1989, was a triumphant day. They finally got rid of Ed Koch. But more important, they had nominated the first mayor of African

American descent as the Democratic candidate. Black politicians celebrated the end of the years of trying to coalesce around a single candidate for mayor. In Dinkins' primary victory the audience booed when Koch's name was mentioned. Dinkins responded, "[N]o, oh no, we're all together now. All together now. Remember me? I'm the guy that brings people together."[42]

How did they do it? McNickle claims that Dinkins' minority coalition was "ironic" but was insufficient to win citywide. He needed white votes to win a citywide election. He asserts, "Dinkins won those votes because of his personal commitment to ethnic politics—a willingness to accommodate the interests of different groups."[43] McNickle acknowledges that expanding Dinkins' electoral coalition would be difficult despite his personal style. Would this electoral coalition hold together? Could the electoral coalition be converted into a governing coalition? Were blacks finally politically incorporated into New York politics? Did Mr. Dinkins win a hollow prize? In order to answer these questions, one must understand the history of black politics and the ancillary role blacks played in the elaboration of New York City liberalism. More important, could this politician from Harlem manage the city's $27 billion budget and over two hundred thousand employees?

The defeat of Ed Koch marked a turning point within black politics in New York. Black politicians had perceived themselves as quasi-insiders since the days of J. Raymond Jones, but now they had one of theirs literally inside Gracie Mansion (the mayor's official residence). David Dinkins had climbed the quadrennial barrier and was less than two months away from being given the keys to the mansion and a seat at the table of power in the city. Although Dinkins did not possess Koch's penchant for theatrics, the primary winner was a Democrat in a Democratic city. Democrats had a 5 to 1 registration advantage over the Republicans. Black politicians reasoned that because they had supported white liberals for mayor, it was now time for payback.

In order to beat the Republican candidate, Rudy Giuliani, Dinkins needed to persuade New York City white voters of two things: that he was competent and that his election was not a black takeover. In addition he needed to increase the numbers from the 29 percent white voters he received in the primary. In a poll of Koch voters, six out of ten stated that they would vote the Republican candidate or stay at home.[44] Although Dinkins had spoken in general terms, minorities read their own interpretation into his words. For his black and Puerto Rican constituencies, Dinkins had to keep faith with the promises he had made in the primary.

Candidate Dinkins said, "[T]he question is not so much is the city ready for a black mayor but is the city ready to accept an African-American who can persuade them that he cares about everybody in this town?"[45] In order for Dinkins to win the campaign, staff had to produce a large turnout of black voters. This meant getting more blacks to register. Therefore, Dinkins needed to mount a citywide vote campaign, which could not be seen as a black campaign. Although no one expected him to win the Queens and Staten Island boroughs, he had to campaign there. This is a prime example of a deracialized campaign.

The General Election: Party Loyalty and Cross-Pressures

Generally speaking, middle-class, white New Yorkers regard themselves as progressive and urbane. Non–New Yorkers see themselves as provincials. Many took pride in New York being the largest state to back Michael Dukakis over George Bush in 1988. During that election, the city Democrats voted overwhelmingly for their party presidential nominee. The Dinkins primary victory posed several cross-pressures for New York City voters. Some lifelong, white, ethnic Democrats found it difficult to vote for Dinkins because of his race.[46] Moreover, the Republican candidate was not attractive enough to generate a massive crossover vote for him. Liberals who thought the former federal prosecutor was the best candidate did not feel strongly enough to launch a crusade on Rudolph Giuliani's behalf. Italian Americans, many of whom were lifelong Democrats, were even more cross-pressured.

Democratic political activists and regulars wanted to protect their political turf more than they valued electing a guy from the other party and then trying to negotiate with him. Conservative Republicans were not enthusiastic about having a so-called liberal Republican as the most visible elected officeholder in the state.

Dinkins versus Giuliani (1989)

Dinkins' primary victory caught Republican strategists off guard. Rudolph Giuliani had spent the majority of his time running against Koch. Throughout the 1987 race, the former Republican prosecutor had been leading Koch in the polls and had prepared a general election campaign. Dinkins was black and considered a nice guy and very different from Koch. Moreover, Dinkins' record as borough president was not very amenable to attacks. Hence, Giuliani turned to Dinkins' personal finances, particularly to a questionable deal where he transferred stocks to his son. The charge of financial misconduct continued to haunt Dinkins throughout the campaign. The flap over his financial transactions may have led to a drop in the polls late in the month of October. Dinkins' lead over Giuliani was only four points in a *Daily News* poll.[47] The second strategy was to portray Dinkins as a clubhouse politician who was not good with details. This was an attempt to pin the political hack tag on his opponent and raise questions about his competence. Giuliani also ran an ad in the Yiddish weekly newspaper *Algemeiner Journal* linking Dinkins to Jesse Jackson. He went on to attack the people around Dinkins. First was Jitu Weusi, who was charged with anti-Semitism because of a poem he read in the 1968 school decentralization struggle. Weusi resigned from the campaign. Roger Ailes, Giuliani's media man, also ran campaign commercials that implied that the controversial black nationalist Sonny Carson was blackmailing Dinkins' campaign and was paid off. The aim of such advertisements was to raise questions about Dinkins' character.[48] However, this strategy failed to move Giuliani ahead of Dinkins in the polls. Giuliani's campaign was further damaged by a remark by Jackie Mason, a Jewish comedian, who claimed that "some Jews vote for black candidates out of guilt." He referred to Dinkins as "a fancy shvartze with a mustache."[49] The Jewish-black split would not go away. The *Jewish Daily Forward* endorsed Dinkins, in part, because he had condemned Jesse Jackson for the "Hymietown" remark, Dinkins' campaign promises, and Giuliani's tactics to scare Jewish voters.

Dinkins' strategy was to concentrate on getting the black and Latino voters out and relying on party loyalty among regular Democrats to win the race. He also wanted to associate Giuliani with the Republican positions on civil rights and liberties. National Democrat Senator Kennedy and former Massachusetts governor Dukakis came to New York to campaign for him. Many Broadway and Hollywood celebrities made appearances and raised money for Dinkins. Despite charges and countercharges, the campaign issues never led to a serious debate about the future of the city. It came down to a choice between a black politician that everyone knew and liked and a white politician who touted law and order. Many New Yorkers must have felt that in light of racial tensions, the choice was simple. The *New York Times* endorsed Dinkins, asserting in an editorial,

> What no one disputes is his most evident characteristic. New York knows David Dinkins to be, above all, a conciliator. If he sometimes takes forever to make up his mind, his ultimate decisions are generally prudent. His instinct is to unify. . . . This decency can help the city confront its biggest foreseeable problems: a sagging economy and tension between the races. The two go together. . . . Mr. Dinkins seems better qualified to persuade all New Yorkers to share the burdens ahead.[50]

It is interesting to note that "conciliator" appears again. Obviously this word was being incorporated into Dinkins' image. By August *New York Times* reporter Elizabeth Kolbert questioned that characterization of Dinkins. She wondered if Dinkins was a "conciliator or hesitator."[51] She also used "vacillator." Although her article reported competing views of candidate Dinkins, the consensus was that he was a "nice guy." She reported a long statement from Dinkins which included the following:

> The point is that I have a feel for all people, and I'm very comfortable with them. I don't care whether I'm down in some board room on Wall Street or in Queens with some Asian group or up in Washington Heights with Dominicans. I'm really very comfortable with all kinds of people, because I genuinely like people.[52]

The city was ready for a conciliator and "nice guy" after Mayor Koch. Dinkins received the endorsement of *Newsday* and the *Daily News*. He won the race by 47,080 votes, the smallest margin in eighty years. Despite losing 10 percent of his

Table 2.1. General Election Results, 1989

Candidates	David Dinkins (Dem)	Rudolph Giuliani (Rep)	Ronald Lauder (Cons)	Henry R. Hawes (Right to Life)	Rudolph Giuliani (Liberal)
Boroughs					
New York	225286	142042	1701	3025	15643
	58%	37%	0.44%	0.78%	4.03%
Bronx	172271	93401	1139	2571	6399
	62%	34%	0.41%	0.93%	2.32%
Kings	276903	224855	2328	4140	12977
	53%	43%	0.45%	0.79%	2.49%
Queens	190096	267210	3062	5647	17556
	39%	55%	0.63%	1.17%	3.63%
Richmond	22988	87878	1041	2077	2502
	19%	75%	0.89%	1.78%	2.15%
Total	917544	815387	9271	17460	55077
	50.56%	44.93%	0.51%	0.96%	3%

primary voters to Giuliani, Dinkins was able to hold off the Republican challenger.[53] Election returns illustrated that he got few votes in the white ethnic strongholds of Staten Island and Queens.

Dinkins lost in two of the five boroughs. The shortfall in Queens was higher than expected. Many white voters knew little about Dinkins except that he was black yet felt Giuliani ran a poor campaign. In an interview with a publisher of a major newspaper, one political observer said that Giuliani was "green as a politician."[54] Political Scientist Basil Wilson traced Giuliani's image problems back to his primary fight with Ronald Lauder. Lauder' campaign ads undermined Giuliani's image as a tough federal prosecutor. Wilson concluded, "The savagery of the media attack tarnished the immaculate image of Giuliani."[55] Others had doubts about Giuliani's national Republican connections. The fact that Ronald Reagan was never popular in New York was driven home when Dinkins declared during a campaign stop, "There will be no Republican beachhead in New York City."[56] Giuliani was simply not able to overcome party loyalty, nor was he able to parlay his liberal party endorsement to deliver more voters as Lindsay had done. Old fashioned fusion politics was not as available in post-Lindsay New York City. After the Dinkins victory, Mollenkopf reported in the newsletter of the Urban Section of APSA:

> Once more, the organizational ability of the Dinkins campaign and a substantial core of white liberals make the difference. White Protestants and more secular liberal white Jews stood by Dinkins despite widespread defections. Areas like Chelsea, the Village, SoHo, and Park Slope in Brooklyn all gave Dinkins two-thirds of their votes. Blacks turned out in record numbers for a general election, particularly in the Central Brooklyn areas of Bedford-Stuyvesant and Crown Heights.[57]

Mollenkopf claims that Dinkins won the votes of women and Latinos. Supported by the powerful public employee unions and liberal reform clubs Dinkins managed to assuage white fears of a black takeover. Yet the ethnic cross-pressures for Italian Catholic voters and the racial identity issue caused Dinkins to lose Queens and Staten Island by huge margins. Dinkins got very few votes in white strongholds such as Carnarsie and Bensonhurst.

Another factor in the Dinkins victory was the development of black politicians within Queens and the stabilization of black political organizations in that borough. The emergence of black activists in Queens drew some of the attention and pressure off the Brooklyn/Manhattan rivalries. It must also be remembered that Puerto Rican politicians had become a force in city politics, particularly in the Bronx. The decision to suspend the competition between blacks and Puerto Ricans helped Dinkins to win the Bronx. Charles Brecher and Raymond Horton concluded,

> The significance of race endured through the general campaign. Dinkins continued to draw strong support from black voters, but white Democrats who supported Koch shifted to Giuliani in large numbers. Dinkins's victory placed control of City Hall in the hands of a man whose supporters gave him a mandate to pursue positive measures to enhance the integration of minorities into the local political structure, but this constituency consisted of only a plurality of voters. Many, if not most of the New York City electorate did not

(Left to right) Fred Ferrer, David Dinkins, Jose Serrano, and George Friedman. © Copyright Fred W. McDarrah.

support Dinkins because they did not share his views on race relations; this suggests that the issue will remain the critical dividing line in future contests.[58]

To the surprise of many, David Dinkins became the 106th mayor of New York City. Dinkins was elected the same year as Michael White in Cleveland and John Daniels in New Haven. Douglas Wilder was elected as the first black governor of Virginia. Why was Dinkins so acceptable to New Yorkers? Does Professor Kilson's commentary about weak incorporation still hold true? As we have shown, Dinkins' election represented a contextual victory, not a systemic one (that is, a natural step in ethnic succession). Black and Latino voters could not elect him alone; Dinkins needed the votes of white supporters. In many ways his electoral coalition resembled the one that elected Tom Bradley in Los Angeles.[59] Accordingly, his administration may or may not have facilitated black political incorporation. First there was the problem of integrating 25 percent of the population, many of whom are poor, into any governing coalition. The voting power of Dinkins's basic constituency is neither large nor consistent

David Dinkins on election night (his father is on his left, holding a cane). © Copyright Fred W. McDarrah.

enough to provide leverage for him to use in dealing with economic power wielders. In 1990 it was not clear whether he could have used his role as party leader to facilitate much change in the system. The 1991 expansion of the City Council to fifty-one members provided more opportunities for minority politicians but did not necessarily create the conditions for a strong political incorporation. Dinkins inherited a serious fiscal problem. Maggie Mahar, a reporter, outlined the fiscal problems as shrinking revenues and mounting expenditures. For her the problem was how to reconcile the mild image of Dinkins with the need for bold and innovative fiscal management.[60] Revenues from personal income tax had dropped 25 percent, Wall Street was on one of its layoff binges, and the mayoral aides claimed the city was in a $1 billion hole. New York seemed to be on the verge of repeating the events of 1975.

If this was true, then the carefully constructed and preferred self-image of Dinkins was at variance with the needs of the city. Dinkins was a mediator, not a fiscal manager. Could Dinkins stretch his image to include the skills of a fiscal manager and economic developer?

The Emerging Public Image of David Dinkins

When Koch's name was booed at the primary victory celebration and Dinkins responded, "[N]o, oh no, we're all together now. All together now. Remember me? I'm the guy that brings people together,"[61] no one knew what a telling moment that was for Dinkins. In his attempt to cut short the tension released by Koch's defeat, the Democratic standard bearer was trying to carve out a middle ground for himself in race relations. Reporter Scott McConnell identified "healing" as the central theme of the Dinkins campaign.[62] Later racial incidents proved how difficult being a healer could be. This was a guy who had limited ambitions, not lofty strategic plans. Yet Dinkins' preferred image of a gentleman who would be mayor for all the people got off to an ambiguous beginning.

At the launching of the Dinkins administration, the mayor received several days of news coverage about an expensive cherry-wood headboard he ordered for Gracie Mansion.[63] The headboard, built by a carpenter employed by the city, was billed at

David and Joyce Dinkins on election night.
© Copyright Fred W. McDarrah.

$11,500. Despite Dinkins' reassurances that it would be paid by private donations, the story was framed as a careless black man with expensive taste. *Daily News* reporter Andrew Kirtzman put it in terms that working-class New Yorkers could understand. He claimed that headboards could be purchased at P&G Furniture in Bay Ridge, Brooklyn for the cost ranging from $99 to $350. Kirtzman also wrote that the mayor had come under criticism for his "fondness for tuxedoes,"[64] and that he had also leased a 1990 Cadillac with fancy chrome. This article suggested that the mayor had highbrow taste and was juxtaposed with that of the proposed fifteen thousand layoffs and a cutback on city services. *Newsweek* reported the stories as examples of what it called "a mayoral administration in deepening disarray."[65] The subtext was that of a man losing control in a short time.

Dinkins' press secretary, Albert Scardino, saw the headboard incident in different terms. He claimed that a reporter had warned him that a story was developing, but he would not tell him what it was about. The reporter just said, "It involves his bedroom."

> Later that day I went to see David. I told him that a reporter came to me, but he didn't tell me what [it] was about. A lot of reporters [are talking] about your bedroom life. Is there anything I need to know? Are you having affairs with somebody? (There were all sorts of rumors going in the campaign.) I don't want to interfere in your personal life. I appreciate it, so I can get ready for it.
>
> He pulled from his pocket his schedule and held it in my face. "Where in the world would I get the time?"
>
> I said I don't know what this is all about.
>
> The next day the big story broke about an $11,000 headboard made for his wife. The story became a national and international story.
>
> How do you predict that? It was unbelievable to me that it became a national story. For somebody who didn't want a headboard. It was not his fault. Somebody in the historical preservation in Gracie Mansion said that you should have a headboard in this style. You couldn't get it from the furniture store because they don't make it anymore. We have to get one of the city carpenters to make it.
>
> He [Dinkins] said if it is for Gracie Mansion, that's fine.[66]

The story took on a life of its own, suggesting that Dinkins was a man of taste that first of all was outside his background and second that would cost the taxpayers. This compromising of Dinkins' preferred image was just the beginning of a slow remaking of the mayor.

More negative press came when, in the metropolitan section of the *New York Times,* the mayor was taken to task for flying first class to a meeting. The headline read, "Dinkins' $2000 Lesson: City Officials Fly Coach." The mayor had to reimburse the city. Dinkins had served for a month and a half in office when he announced,

> I don't propose to change the guidelines. I do propose to travel first class whenever first class accommodations are available, because it is more comfortable. You get more work done and I put in seven days and pretty long days. So as long as I or some campaign fund or somebody other than the city picks up the differential, I'm confident that the people of our city will be pleased that their Mayor is able to work in greater comfort.[67]

For people who are forced to fly coach, Dinkins' social accounting may have seemed inadequate and self-serving. The image of a man with expensive taste was sinking into the electorate mind. However, it was playing tennis that framed his prevailing image. It would also receive considerable and incessant coverage. Even after Arthur Ashe's exploits on the tennis court, a black man in white shorts, playing tennis, was seen as incongruous to a working-class, white constituency. Being photographed with his racket may have suggested that he was not paying attention to his job.

One reporter could not resist an opportunity to make a reference to that image in a story about the Happy Land Social Club fire. He remarked that the mayor was wearing an oversized fire hat and coat. "It was perhaps his first public appearance as Mayor in anything other than a tie or tennis clothes, and he seemed self-conscious."[68] Here the reporter seems to be sharing an insight with his readers. These stories were carefully modulated to create the image of a man ill suited for his job. Photographs portray a man constantly under stress, as the perspiration on his face indicated. Rather than projecting Dinkins as a

David Dinkins and Nelson Mandela. © Copyright Fred W. McDarrah.

concerned mayor, a reporter reminded readers that he was obsessed with his appearance even at a scene of tragedy. Leland Jones, the mayor's press secretary, agreed that the press was promoting the idea that Dinkins was a "man who lives according to his schedule and was consumed about appearances."[69] Joe Klein made a similar observation: "All too often, he allowed himself to be photographed in a dinner jacket and shades, an unfortunate image that reinforced some prevailing doubts about the man: As mayor, Dinkins dressed too well and saw too little. The glasses came off soon, but the image remained."[70] From an editorial in *The New Yorker* came, "[T]here are few occupations in which charm is a drawback. Rock star, Mayor of New York, that's about it."[71]

The image that emerged portrayed Dinkins as clubhouse politician, a possible closet black nationalist, a tax cheat, and a poor manager. Noting the mayor's excessive attention to his appearance reinforced the dandy image. Dinkins' relationship with Sonny Carson and the Red Apple boycott fueled suspicion that Dinkins was a "closet black nationalist." The tax cheat theme was used by Giuliani to discredit Dinkins in the general election. The poor manager theme emerged early as the mayor began to have staff problems (see chapter 4). These initial forays into Dinkins's character set up the reader to expect negative and unacceptable behavior either in the campaign or in office. The message was that Dinkins, although a nice guy, was a flawed man waiting to implode. During the campaign there were repeated references to Dinkins' failure to pay federal income taxes and the disorganization of his campaign staff. The limited education that Dinkins received as a clubhouse politician did not prepare him for the media onslaught.

James Q. Wilson, the political scientist, once called the New York white reform club oriented activists "amateur democrats." These activists were involved in city politics to change the policies of the Democratic Party. Black political clubs such as the George Washington Carver Democratic Club (now merged with the Tioga Democratic Club) and the Martin Luther King Democratic Club were training grounds for political activists and would-be political candidates. Political clubs provided forums for candidates, circulated candidate petitions and did the "nuts-and-bolts political work."[72] The Carver Club recruited David Dinkins and taught him the ways of New York City politics.

Maggie Mahar outlined the constructed stereotype of Dinkins as a "consummate pleasant pol."[73] *Time* magazine called the new mayor of New York a "classic clubhouse politician," someone who was "seemingly content to forge a career more on amiability than activism."[74] Could such a person handle a job that is perceived as "second in importance only to that of the President of the United States"?[75] Would Dinkins stand up to the pressure? Maggie Mahar, in an essay entitled "Mr. Dinkins's Dilemma," outlined the city's growing fiscal problems and asserted that Dinkins was not elected for his "financial acumen" but rather as a "centrist who moved slowly and deliberately."[76]

The borough presidency had exposed Dinkins to Manhattan-wide politics but not citywide politics. In fact Dinkins was never considered for mayoral prospects until the late 1980s. He had not received much publicity until the mid-1980s. In October 1985, Dinkins, then the city clerk, made news by criticizing Minister Louis Farrakhan. After he called Farrakhan's statement about Jews "blatantly anti-Semitic," Farrakhan responded by including Dinkins among "those silly Toms." He asserted, "I am saying, brother and sisters, the reason why a David Dinkins . . . would do that is because they don't fear us. They fear white people. When the leader sells out to people, he should pay a price for that. . . . Do you think the leader should sell out and then live? We should make example of the leaders."[77] Some people regarded the statement as a threat. Mayor Koch offered Dinkins police protection. For a brief moment Dinkins was a hero disagreeing with the Farrakhan rhetoric.

Dov Hikind of Brooklyn, a Democratic assembly member and leader of Orthodox Jews, reportedly declared Jesse Jackson represented a danger to Israel and American Jews.[78] In the general election Hikind supported Giuliani over Dinkins. *Daily News* reporters reported a spirited exchange between a rabbi and Dinkins over his relationship to Jesse Jackson. Dinkins admitted to being a friend of Jackson before a Forest Hill Jewish center. He asserted, "Jesse Jackson is not running for mayor—I am. Should he get life in prison, or what?" A rabbi's response was if you want to be mayor of the Jews, we deserve a better answer than . . . we should put (him) in Jail." Dinkins' response was "You want me to denounce Jesse Jackson and I'm not going to do it. I do not believe Jesse Jackson to be an anti-Semitic—and if I did, I wouldn't support him. When he said Hymietown, I condemned it publicly and loudly and (was) among the first."[79]

Dinkins believed that the way he comported himself mattered. He believed that if he conducted himself with civility that spirit would emanate throughout the government. He did not like the brash way Koch conducted himself in office. He asserted, "I ran because Koch was the way he was."[80] Dinkins sent several messages about changing the tone of government. In an interview with former Deputy Mayor Steisel, he stated,

> Koch had this hard edge to him. . . . David wanted to set a different tone. One, he wanted to be perceived as a conciliatory figure. He wanted to be far more civil. If he couldn't accommodate the views of his opponents, he wanted to create forums where they could be discussed rationally and without heat. And people could make judgments about what needed to be done or what was the right way to go. All facts were on the table. Everyone presented their analysis or point of view, which make for better decisions. . . . He felt that part of Koch's problems and city problems it was kind of one-man rule and you didn't hear other voices. . . . Their views would be balanced with competing views. That is how he decided he wanted to govern."[81]

Many people who worked for Dinkins shared the aforementioned characterization of the mayor. Dinkins wanted to be as unlike Ed Koch as possible. Professor Herminia Ibarra's work suggests that an individual's adjustment to a new role is a matter of "negotiated adaptation." She believes that "people adapt to new professional roles by experimenting with images that serve as trials for possible but not yet fully elaborated professional identities."[82] She called these identities "provisional selves." Dinkins was searching for the right image as mayor, while the press was trying to adjust to someone who wanted to be as different from Koch as possible. Ibarra continues: "People make identity claims by conveying images that signal how they view themselves or hope to be viewed by others. By observing their own behavior as well as the reactions of others, who accept, reject, renegotiate these public images, they maintain or modify their private self-conceptions."[83] Most new mayors engage in this self-examination and experimentation. They ask themselves what type of mayor can I be? What type of image will the public accept? If the new mayor had defeated an unpopular mayor, then he might be persuaded that the people were looking for a different type of leader. Having run as an anti-Koch candidate, Dinkins became convinced that was the type of mayor the voters wanted. Ken Auletta wrote a critique of the candidate podium performance during the campaign. He stated, "This Dinkins was the ecumenical man who disagreed with blacks who said it was racist for a white opponent to criticize him, or who said it was wrong to stereotype all Bensonhurst as 'racist.'"[84]

Deracialization and Dinkins

Peer and Ettema believe that news accounts of mayoral election campaigns work as ideology in three ways: "by framing the campaigns in terms of racial strategy, by naturalizing racial difference and division, and by positioning citizens as having a civic identity based solely on race."[85] In the 1990 race Dinkins faced an important decision, to run as a racial candidate, or as a candidate who just happened to be black. Given New York City's demographics and political culture, the first choice was not available. The second choice fit his personality and his political instincts. Although Dinkins had encountered racism, he believed that he could win the white vote by presenting himself in nonracial terms.

Political scientist Nayda Terkildsen's research suggests that white voters are not always persuaded by this appeal.[86] These same voters would say they do not vote on the basis of skin color, but in reality they do. Terkildsen contends that these voters engage in self-monitoring that allows them to appear to be race neutral, yet in the privacy of the voting booth, skin color decides their vote.[87] If the black candidate is conducting a deracialized campaign, then he is downplaying his blackness. The Dinkins campaign-organizing theme was inclusive politics. Not only would it win him white voters, but it was consistent with how he saw the world. Deracialized campaigns as an election strategy are credited with allowing minority politicians to be more successful in mixed constituencies.[88]

If black politicians are concerned with winning elections in districts where whites make up a large percentage of the electorate, then such strategy is rational. Interestingly, candidates who conduct deracialized campaigns may or may not follow through with deracialized policies. As political scientist Charles V. Hamilton suggested, there must be "continued diligent political mobilization" to insure that these candidates follow through with deracialized policies.[89] Can it be demonstrated that whites that vote for deracialized candidates do so because they expect deracialized policies (race neutral policies)? Black and white voters may interpret the concept of deracialization differently. White voters may interpret a deracialized campaign as assurance of the status quo, and for blacks it may be read as a harbinger of evenhanded policies. In any case, the campaign strategy that Dinkins employed was only partially successful. He was elected, in part, because the media framed Dinkins as a safe choice, but this framing eventually eroded his standing as a leader.

Summary

Dinkins' name was suggested as a possible mayoral candidate in the 1989 elections because he was the borough president of Manhattan, a position some black politicians considered to be a steppingstone to candidacy for mayor. His precampaign images were mixed. He was part safe black candidate and part tribune for progressives. Charles Bagli and Michael Powell described him as "a cautious son of traditional machine politics and a member of Democratic Socialists of America. Dinkins is an unlikely blend of the progressive and the pedestrian."[90]

During David Dinkins' first campaign, the *Christian Science Monitor* published an article headlined "Real Estate Men Favor Dinkins." Being thought of as the housing industry candidate was at variance with his progressive credentials.[91] Reporter Jim Sleeper also linked Dinkins with real estate interests. He asserted that "his vote for the Times Square plan marked but one of the many occasions over the next few years when housing advocates felt Dinkins had gone over to the developers; he moved comfortably among them, playing tennis regularly with Koch's housing commissioner, Anthony Gliedman, who would become Donald Trump's executive vice-president."[92] *Monitor* reporter Anne Colamosca argued that real estate people felt that they needed a coalition politician and a Democrat who would persuade an overwhelmingly new city council to make a concession to that industry. The article quoted Sid Davidoff, a lawyer and an active Dinkins supporter: "We've taken some tough fights with Dinkins over the last couple of years. But we have seen that there is some middle ground with him. He can be reasonable."[93] The article quoted an unnamed developer as saying, "We have no idea in the world what Giuliani would do if he became mayor. We have no relationship with him at all. Dinkins, we know, can be open to discussion and is a reasonable man."[94]

Dinkins' image as a "reasonable man" was enhanced by his comments on the Tawana Brawley case. Many whites read his comments as those of a man willing to stand up for what was right. Blacks may have read it as what may be called "gratuitous endearing."[95] This occurs when black leaders engage in soft bashing of other blacks to endear themselves to whites. Dinkins' letter to the editor was written, in part, to offset that type of interpretation by his black constituency.

Clearly image making starts before an individual reaches city hall. New York had experienced several racial incidents such as Bensonhurst that were handled badly by incumbent mayor Ed Koch. There were also major city scandals that happened during

Koch's watch. Dinkins had built a reputation as a congenial man and as a race mediator. A *New York Times*/WCBS-TV poll that was taken six months after Dinkins came into office showed 66 percent of whites, 83 percent of blacks, and 64 percent of Hispanics approved of the way he handled relations between races.[96]

The problem with the regime that Dinkins inherited was that it was a centering coalition fighting the forces of a decentering region. When David Dinkins became mayor in 1990, the media made sure to assuage white fears that his election represented a black takeover. Reporters attempted to educate New Yorkers about Dinkins' story. A close reading of the early media coverage reveals condescending statements and implicit stereotypes. The tabloids constantly sought the "real story" on Dinkins. No black politician could possibly be free of flaws. More important, the people needed to know for whom they were voting. Reporters constructed an image during Dinkins' primary campaign that linked him to Rev. Jesse Jackson's politics. Jackson, a former presidential candidate and famous civil rights leader, had been represented as a reckless anti-Semite to raise doubts in the minds of the city's important Jewish voters. Dinkins was never a Jackson-type politician. If anything, he was a true believer in New York City liberal ideology.

Phillip Thompson claims that a Dinkins-led Jackson campaign exposed the soft underbelly of the quixotic crusade, the lack of an organized, black, grassroots mobilization capacity.[97] Dinkins did little to inspire such a mobilization. Hence there was no black citywide organization left after the 1988 Jackson race upon which to build a citywide campaign. For the 1989 mayoral race Dinkins relied on name recognition, his centrist race reputation, and the old liberal/labor coalition.

Harold Lasswell, a famous political scientist who was trained in the psychoanalytical approach, saw political personalities in Freudian terms.[98] He believed that politicians seek power as compensation against deprivation. In other words, politicians are trying to overcome their low self-esteem by asserting themselves in the political arena. They want to change themselves or the environment in which they function. Many reporters have adopted this view and applied it to the new black politicians. Accordingly, they see black politicians as the progeny of the generation of status deprivation, which supposedly explains their predilection for narcissism or self-aggrandizement. Political deprivation causes an obsession not only with the uses of power but also with the trappings of power. Reflecting their sense of insecurity, black politicians search for fulfillment by becoming the center of attention. Reporters repeatedly mentioned Dinkins' passion for playing tennis and wearing formal attire, which became a running gag. At a party, Dinkins joked about it and pledged, "Read my lips, No New Tuxes." One reporter suggested that the mayor should have said, "Don't need any more/Already got four."[99] Much was made of Dinkins' choice of words during crises and his unwillingness to speak extemporaneously. In his inaugural address, Dinkins called New York City a "gorgeous mosaic." Several reporters used that phrase to criticize Dinkins.[100] During his last year in office, the Patrolmans' Benevolent Association bought a full page add in the *Post* to outline how the mosaic was "shattered."[101] The press also made much of the fact that Dinkins was slow to anger. One reporter characterized the mayor's persona as "angry civility."[102]

Explaining black politicians in these quasi-psychoanalytical terms plays into the prepackaged image of black people held by some whites. Such characterizations pander to white readers and viewers who believe that white elected officials are better adjusted, qualified, and altruistic than their black counterparts. The negative images of African American politicians make their electoral competition with European American politicians more difficult. Dinkins soon discovered this in his ill-fated bid for reelection. The initial questioning of his ability and judgment began with his selection of a staff and aides.

CHAPTER THREE

DAVID DINKINS AND REGIME CHANGE

Since the publication of Wallace Sayre and Herb Kaufman's 1965 classic study *Governing New York*, the city had become a very different place. The ensuing thirty-five years had produced a generational change not only in political leadership but also in economic conditions. The city that David Dinkins had chosen to lead had acquired internecine multiracial divisions and daunting financial challenges. What is more important, New York City had more economic competition on the world stage. As we suggested in the last chapter, the election of Dinkins was a combination of unelecting Ed Koch, quelling racial tensions, and putting New York in the ranks of those cities that had elected a black mayor. The tantalizing question was, did the 1989 election represent the same coalition that had governed the city for twelve years (albeit with a different face), or did it represent what Clarence Stone calls a "regime change"? (A regime is a working coalition of political and economic leaders centered around *social production* goals.) Stone has identified four different types of regimes: caretaker; economic development or growth-oriented; middle-class progressive (that is, with liberal goals of environmental protection, historic preservation, affordable housing, and so on); and lower-class opportunity-expansion.[1] In each type, there is a different demand for available public resources. This chapter analyzes some of the elements that made up the prevailing regime by examining changes that gave hope to a possible transformation.

Under Ed Koch's leadership the New York City regime was an upfront, progrowth operation. His tough-on-crime and antiwelfare rhetoric fortified his right-leaning coalition. Koch was proud of his $2 billion tax abatement program to keep businesses in New York. He defended his record in the campaign and predicted that the tax abatement program would ultimately yield $23 billion in tax revenues over twenty years.

Campaigning two years after the 1987 Wall Street crash, Dinkins suggested that the city economy should be less dependent on Wall Street, which accounted for 5 percent of the city job base, but 20 percent of its income.[2] He talked about more support for small business. He thought that the tax abatements were made to businesses that had never intended to leave the city. Of course this was a candidate talking. Now that he was in office, what were the political messages that the regime wanted delivered? At one of his first interviews about the budget crisis, Dinkins asserted, "I know one thing, you can't raise taxes. It is not desirable to raise real estate taxes. It is counterproductive. Realistically, City Council will not even pass a real estate tax."[3] He indicated that his strategy would be to trim city expenditures.

Dinkins said repeatedly that he was not Koch. Of course it would have been difficult for a black man with a progressive reputation to promote a right-leaning coalition and get elected. Accordingly, Dinkins had to distinguish himself from Koch and try to put together a regime that at least looked different. Given the fact that the city was at the dawn of a new decade, and there was a lot at stake, one would think that a different theme was indicated. Needing to communicate their goals of the nineties, the stakeholders had supported a man they thought could appeal to a wider constituency. As we saw from Dinkins' rhetoric, he intended to be the mayor of all the people. This translated into a fusion regime that included all the coalitions Clarence Stone had identified.

The 1975 fiscal crisis had shaken the city's belief in its financial invincibility.[4] The city had been in virtual receivership and continued to be monitored by the state. The intervening Koch years were part recovery and part symbolic reassurance. The Koch interregnum did not preclude the fundamental changes taking place in the city's life. Between 1980 and 1990 the city experienced significant demographic, economic, and structural changes. Although much of Manhattan, the heart of the city's economic profile, looked the same, there were several significant shifts in the way the rest of the city looked and functioned. A sharp new separateness had griped the city. This separateness manifested itself in an overall decline in white residents, an increased number of black and brown residents, and a more visible contrast between the haves and have-nots. The racial flare-ups during the latter years of the Koch administration were, in part, a reaction to this change.

Demographic and Economic Changes

New York City's population grew from 7,071,639 in 1980 to 7,322,564 in 1990, making it one of the few large cities that saw a population increase. Since 1980, 1,515,101 immigrants moved to the city. New York's black population increased slightly from 1,701,880 (24 percent) in 1980 to 1,847,195 (25.4 percent) in 1990. The Asian population also grew slowly from 274,560 (4 percent) in 1980 to 489,851 (7 percent) in 1990. In 1980 the Latino population was 1,406,389 and by 1990 it had grow to 1,783,511. Latinos represented 24.4 percent of the city's population. Of that number, 50.3 percent were Puerto Rican, 18.7 percent Dominican, 3.5 percent Mexican, and 27.5 percent other.[5] In 1990 whites represented 43.2 percent of the population and had become a minority in the city.

Between 1989 and 1990 the city had lost more than 370,000 or 8.7 percent of its jobs. In 1991 Samuel Ehrenhalt, regional director of the U.S. Bureau of Labor Statistics, pointed out that the city held 43 percent of the state's private-sector jobs, and it generated 53 percent of the $100 billion earnings. Manhattan alone accounts for three-fourths of that amount. There were fewer private-sector jobs in Manhattan in 1990 than there were in 1980.[6] As Carol O'Cléireacáin observed, "As Wall Street profits go, so go New York City's incomes."[7]

Was New York City dying? Had the forces of economic dislocation and population dispersal rendered this once proud retail, manufacturing, and distribution center obsolete? These two questions must have crossed the minds of New Yorkers in the late 1980s and early 1990s. When David Dinkins came into office, both the nation and the city were in a deep recession. There was a lot of pessimism in the air. The first sentence of a *New York Times* editorial read, "New Yorkers are losing heart." It went on to describe signs that indicated that the city was "disintegrating," and services were suffering. It concluded, "At a time when we crave strong leadership, Mayor Dinkins has been disheartening passive."[8] The purpose of the editorial was to root out the pessimism and defeatism that seemed to be gripping the city. Although the editorial also criticized Governor Mario Cuomo and the state, it was clearly aimed at city hall.

The recession came at a time when the nation had undergone a profound socioeconomic transformation and had transitioned into a service economy. *Deindustrialization* became the favorite term used to describe what was happening to the city's economy. Reaganomics was fading as President George H. W. Bush was struggling to upright the sluggish economy. Although Reagan and Bush never had a strong following in cities, it appeared that Washington had abandoned the city.[9] New Yorkers remembered the 1975 fiscal crisis and all the uncertainty it created. A *New York Times* editorial sought to disabuse readers of an analogy with the 1975 crisis. "One can blame the Reagan and Bush Administrations. A steep withdrawal of federal payment to cities has deprived New York of billions of dollars. But this crisis is not nearly as severe as the one that brought the city to its knees in the 1970's."[10] The editorial admitted the current economic problems of New York were closely linked to the nation's overall economic future.

In his campaign David Dinkins had talked about how great the city's future looked. He was clearly the optimist in the general election against Giuliani. For him the city was not dying—it was just undergoing yet another social metamorphosis, a mosaic. The *Times* editorial listed four overlapping crises facing the city: a budget crisis, the overall national economy, a social crisis, and a morale crisis. It cited a poll that showed that blacks were somewhat more optimistic that whites.

Historical evidence supported Leibnitzian optimists. New York survived as it had throughout its three distinct periods of development: preindustrial, industrial and postindustrial. In the preindustrial period, the city mainly functioned as a trading center for nascent merchant markets. In the industrial period, manufacturing became the primary engine behind the growth of the city. The aggregation of workers and production in cities such as New York made sense. Great waves of European immigrants came to work in the factories. Transportation cost was low, and the economy of scale served the interest of producers. The central business districts of the city could easily house all retail and personal service functions.

In the current postindustrial period, the economy has shifted from a manufacturing to a service base. It is now cheaper to decentralize production. Indeed, many manufacturing jobs have been moved to low-wage international labor markets. Production is no longer restricted to a central place. Transportation cost is even less of a restraint, so people can live farther and farther from their places of work. Interstate commuting has become commonplace. The leaders of cities can no longer promise jobs to their residents, so workers everywhere compete in the world labor market. This explains why New York City cannot compete with garment manufacturing in the third world.

New York City has also lost some of its retail functions to suburban malls; professional office space to regional office complexes; and middle-class residents to New Jersey, Westchester, and Long Island. Companies have become increasingly nomadic, since satellite cities were above making lucrative offers for company headquarters (for example, Stamford, Connecticut's offer to Morgan Stanley).

Was New York still the most important city in America? Despite New York City's reputation as the place where many of the world's financial decisions are made, it seemed to be in a lot of trouble at the beginning the Dinkins era. The job market was shrinking at a time when the demographics were changing. Although African-Americans and Latinos had slowly become the dominant ethnic group in the borough of the Bronx, the governing elite had failed to figure out how to feature this population as a magnet for new business.

Since 1960 companies that felt an urgent need to locate in New York no longer had to do so. Policy analysts Stephen Moore and Dean Stansel pointed out that since 1965 more than fifty of the Fortune 500 companies had left New York City.[11] In the late 1980s Exxon and J.C. Penny moved their headquarters from New York City to Dallas. Fleeing the high cost of rental space and occupancy taxes, these companies decided they no longer needed to be physically in the city. Improvements in communications and transportation enabled them and companies like them to be anywhere at any time. As writer William Knoke predicted in *Bold New World*, we are moving toward a placeless society. He asserts,

> I define the Placeless Society as the awakening omnipresence that will allow everything—people, goods, resources, knowledge—to be available anywhere, often instantaneously, with little regard for distance or place. . . . Everywhere, people, money, goods and knowledge flow so effortlessly from point to point that place becomes an irrelevant concept. The world is becoming placeless.[12]

Just as the economic function of cities such as New York has changed, the lifestyles of Americans have changed. Big cities such as New York are no longer preferred places to live. Why? Claiming more private space is more important than proximity. Careers and schedules are more uncertain. Americans attach status to exclusive and prestigious living arrangements. The rich can create an inaccessible residential area and live apart from the masses. This inclination to separate from the less fortunate has caught the fancy of the white middle class—manifested in gated communities, time-share vacation homes, and private security guards.

Structural Changes

The political structure of New York City government described by Sayre and Kaufman was a very different one from the one Dinkins inherited. There had been two charter changes since 1965. The 1977 charter revision added more new auditing and accounting procedures to the city's budgetary process and reduced the mayor's control over the budget. In 1986 the city's political structure changed dramatically when a federal district court abolished the Board of Estimate, one of the last remaining bicameral municipal legislative systems in the nation. Under the old board of estimate system the city counsel president, elected citywide, like the mayor, had two votes, and borough presidents had one vote, even though the actual populations of the five boroughs varied markedly. The finding was that the Board of Estimate violated the one man, one vote principle first articulated in *Baker v. Carr* (1962). The U.S. Supreme Court upheld *Morris v. Board of Estimate* (1989), and Mayor Koch appointed a charter commission headed by Frederick Schwatz. The fifteen-member commission recommended redistribution of the powers of the old board of estimate among the mayor, the new, expanded city council (from thirty-five to fifty-one) and a reconstituted planning commission. The office of city council president was abolished and replaced by a public advocate (ombudsman). The public advocate would be in the line of succession for mayor if there were a vacancy between elections.

Although new city charter referendums are relatively subdued, they do disrupt the various power arrangements, called "functional islands of power" by Sayre and Kaufman, that had become so institutionalized in the city. The new council gained power over zoning and land use and became the new arbiter in the budget. This meant that it had to approve a general budget for city contracts. (The city purchasing contracts involve many billions of dollars of goods and services.) The mayor retained the power to select the contractors. The new charter required the creation of a procurement policy board. The new city council also took over the authorization of franchise awards, but borough presidents still selected the companies that received the franchises in their boroughs. This meant developers had to deal with a different group of people to get things done. The new charter advocate estimated that 40 percent of the council members would be minorities. This was promoted as including more minority representatives in city affairs. Overall the new city charter was supposed to make the mayor more accountable to the city council through the budgetary process. In order to make that happen, the new charter also created the Independent Budget Office (IBO) that would provide the borough presidents, council, public advocate, and comptroller with expert advice.[13] The director of IBO was to be chosen by a special committee to serve a four-year term. The new charter also established an advisory committee to IBO. The members would be appointed to staggered five-year terms and are required to have experience in fiscal matters.

Mayor Dinkins, as a former borough president, was described as a "reluctant" supporter of the replacement of the Board of Estimate. He observed, "I think it needs to be remembered that this Board of Estimate helped build this city, which I still say is the greatest urban center in the world. Like many, I'm sure that we hope that they haven't thrown the baby out with the bath water."[14]

Another change came as a result of a state court ruling that city officials could be barred from holding political party offices. Brooklyn borough presidents such as Howard Golden served as both party leader and elected head of the borough. The court upheld the new charter provision barring high-ranking city officials from holding party positions. This was designed to prevent another political empire such as that held by the late Donald Manes, a powerful leader in Queens, who was involved in one of the city's scandals.

Economic Changes

Generally speaking, New Yorkers regard their city as a national resource capable of survival under the most extreme economic conditions. Indeed its downtown space includes some of the leading financial institutions of postindustrial capitalism. Michael Smith and Joe Feagin designated New York as one of the "command cities of the world economy."[15] They also include London, Hong Kong, Paris, and Tokyo. The elites in such cities make the financial decisions for the globalized economy. The city's openness to immigrants promotes its increasingly transnational character. Sociologist Nathan Glazer observed,

> We know that the headquarters of most large companies have already moved from New York. But that has been going on for decades. We also know that the banks, law firms, and accounting firms that deal with, as well as the people who design their new out-of-town headquarters and logos—in short, the entire multifarious system of support for business—remain centered in New York. The city also contains the major centers of mass media and the major cultural institutions that the rich and powerful will want to group around them—or group themselves around. All these are part of what makes a world city.[16]

For all the international money that passes through the city, there has been difficulty generating enough low-skilled jobs for its newly arriving blue-collar and minority immigrants. New York City relies primarily on service jobs to support this new wave of immigrants but will need more manufacturing jobs to sustain the economic uplift it provided to previous immigrant groups. New York has been forced to expand its economy into the blue-collar sector, particularly personal service occupations. Nevertheless, it remains a city dominated by white-collar service jobs. Mahar, in her article in *Barron's*, makes this point at the beginning of the Dinkins administration. She quotes Jane Jacob in saying that the New York economy is "too specialized—built on a narrow base."[17]

Yet in the midnineties, people talked about a New York miracle. Fred Siegel and Joel Kotkin questioned the New York miracle in a *Wall Street Journal* op-ed editorial. They claimed that the city is dangerously dependent on its financial sector. They asserted that "although the number of people working in the financial sector has actually fallen to 150,00 from 163,000 in 1987, they now account for 17% of personal income in the city, up from 12% a decade ago."[18] Some of the effects of this weak economy surfaced during the Dinkins years and played a critical role in his tenure.[19]

The weak economy does not entirely discourage local real estate transactions that play an important part in the city's economy. The "buying and selling" of places to live and work is a major cash producer for the city. Some people contend that the real estate industry actually runs the city. Founded in 1896, the Real Estate Board of New York has over five thousand members,[20] including property owners, managers, lenders, brokers, and developers. They are clearly the movers and shakers of New York City and have even created a hall of fame for themselves, the Creators of New York Hall of Fame. This shameless selling and buying of property and buildings in New York is the principal way money circulates in the city. Transactions about the "built" environment are primarily a Manhattan game, but increasingly the other boroughs (such as Brooklyn Heights and Park Slope) have been caught in the inflation of residential properties.

Residential development is essentially about land use. Accordingly, the New York mayor's job is to assuage public concern and discontent should they arise in the economic decisions concerning the real estate industry.

The Mayor as Salesperson

Part of the mayor's job is to sell the city to investors, tourists, and potential residents. Since the image of the city is crucial, the image of a competent mayor is a necessity. Dinkins was well aware of this when he asserted in a new conference for the Urban Summit of Mayors, "We're in a global competitiveness mode, and we had better get our act together in this nation because we have to compete with Tokyo and London."[21] If a mayor's image is tarnished, it is a crisis for the governing elite. The choice is not to support the incumbent for reelection or to help the mayor repair his or her image. Journalists are often enlisted to shape this decision, because whether they like it or not, journalists and mayors are partners in storytelling and image making. Publishers and owners are aware of this relationship, but their main interest is in selling newspapers or increasing the ratings. They worry about advertising revenues and let their trusted editors supervise reporters.

In promoting the city, New York City elites have been particularly adept at controlling public discourse. Economic elites' messages are flexible or contain ambiguous references to their interests, and contrary to social scientists' characterization, New York elites are very indulgent of dissent. Accommodating dissent was built into the planning of projects such as the renovation of Times Square.[22] Dissent came from preservationists, citizens' groups, and crusading writers.[23] But after some adjustments, elections, and co-optation, New York developers intended to return to their economic agenda, in spite of the obvious demographic and social transformations taking place.

Social Separateness

Douglas Massey and Nancy Denton called this social separation "American Apartheid," that is, the segregation of the races and housing.[24] They found that blacks and other minorities were

(Left to right) Raymond Flynn, Tom Bradley, Richard M. Daley, and David N. Dinkins, all mayors of U.S. cities.
© Copyright Fred W. McDarrah.

isolated from whites,[25] in some cases hypersegregated in some of the nation's largest and most prestigious cities. One reason that races and classes are so separated is that the low cost of transportation has worked to downgrade residency inside the city.

Aside from the economic changes, the face of the city has changed. Turn of the century buildings have been replaced by giant, rectangular glass office buildings reaching thirty to forty stories high. Most people who work in them do not live in the city proper. They live in spread city, edge city, and exurbs. Robert Fishman suggested that these "new type[s] of cities" have changed life in America. White-collar workers can now enjoy all the technological innovations of modern civilization while sleeping in a place that resembles the country.[26] He proclaimed a new relationship of cities and physical structures. Downtown becomes empty at night and retail stores close after the noncity residents leave. Fishman observed, "The downtowns provided a counterpoint of diversity, a neon-lit world where high and low culture met, all just a streetcar ride away. By comparison, even the most elaborate mall pales."[27] Crescents of white suburbs have surrounded the old inner-core neighborhoods, making cities racially divided living spaces.

Even after electing its first black mayor, race continued to be a problem even as New Yorkers become more tolerant and sophisticated. As blacks and Latinos move into the cities, whites move out. The new immigrants now occupy venerable neighborhoods such as Brooklyn Heights that once housed ethnic whites. Whites who left claim that poor schools and high crime rates drove them out. Others ran to escape the declining property values. Still others want more space and less noise. Only a few will admit that they did not want to live in racially mixed neighborhoods.

From Realpolitik to Pseudopolitics

One of the consequences of these social and economic changes is that residents adopt an "us against them" mentality. Cultural and ethnic issues become more salient and often distract from the serious politics of economic development. Politics revolves around recognizing identity groups. The poor become disconnected from the ongoing economy and less connected to the economic order. William Wilson called this group the "truly disadvantaged."[28] The postindustrial realities made bringing the "great mass" of unskilled workers back into the economy more difficult. The city government had to decide what to do with immigrants from India, the Caribbean, and China.

Were the early 1990s an urban apocalypse? Granted the social ills of New York were more visible and daunting than ever before, there seems to be more resignation. Statistically speaking there were more poor and unemployed people in the city, and their life chances were more problematic than those of their counterparts in the previous two decades of city development. Fuchs concluded,

New York's Mayor Dinkins, who ran on a platform of improving the quality of life for all New Yorkers, began his first term in 1990 by calling for an austerity budget to fend off an impending budget deficit. Dinkins's fiscal problems continued to escalate as he faced a $732 million shortfall in fiscal 1991's budget and a possible takeover of city finances by the state FCB. His "doomsday" budget for fiscal 1992 included drastic cuts in social services, parks, and libraries, as well twenty thousand municipal employee layoffs.[29]

The situation of the minority poor was particularly grave during Dinkins' tenure. The mismatch between the skills of inner-city residents and jobs grew more apparent. In a knowledge-intensive economy, unemployment among these groups had become the norm. This is not to say that the city did not try to intervene in this job-skill mismatch. There was a plethora of job training efforts, both private and publicly funded. Curtis Skinner's study of the decade before the Dinkins administration raised questions about the "efficacy of public policy efforts in New York and elsewhere that concentrate almost exclusively on labor supply-side measures (strengthening basic literacy and vocational training) to improve wages and employment outcomes for workers with less than a college education."[30] According to Skinner the city's effort should be directed at increasing the supply of midskilled jobs. In order to create more midskilled jobs, the city would have to attract manufacturing industries. However, manufacturing industries refused to locate in the city because of the high cost of labor.

Journalist Ken Auletta popularized a new term for people caught in this economic dislocation-the *underclass*.[31] They were written off as beyond the ability of the new economy to engage them. No longer counted in the unemployment statistics, they became economic untouchables. Even more important, there was no overall organization linking these individuals into a group. Since they were not organized, they were unable to state their case. Establishing a lower class opportunity-expansion regime for this group was easier said than done.

The Myth of the Quick Fix Solution

In refurbishing the facade, New York City, with its entertainment and tourism industries, became a city built for a visitor class.[32] Jobs for the poor and work for minority contractors are supposed to be generated from these efforts. In 1992 Dinkins announced the Minority and Women-Owned Business Enterprise Program

(M/WBE). Of the ninety thousand city contracts let in that fiscal year, M/WBE companies only received 7 percent of the $2.3 billion of the business. These M/BE firms represented 25 percent of the business community, and Dinkins wanted to raise their share up to 20 percent.[33] After study by the National Economic Research Association, Dinkins confidently said, "The statistical evidence paints a clear picture of exclusion."[34] With this inclusion ideology one should expect more demands for big development projects. In the name of the city image and what Clarence Stone calls "small opportunities," economic development is facilitated.[35] Dinkins saw his opportunity to demonstrate his economic stewardship with the threat of losing venerated New York institutions such as Morgan Stanley, the Girl Scouts, the U.S. Open, and the United Nations. He recalled, "We didn't want them to leave New York. . . . We met in the office of . . . it wasn't a government building. We had both U.S. Senators, the Cardinal and an awful lot of other people. That shows you the level of the meeting. We won and kept them here."[36]

Although these institutions did not leave the city, keeping them was a holding process, not a job-creating one. Besides, Morgan Stanley, with its four thousand jobs, did not hire many poor people, the group Dinkins wanted to help. Nevertheless, Dinkins was most proud of his effort to save the U.S. Open tennis tournament. He claimed that the U.S. Open generated more revenue than all other sports events combined.

> We needed a new stadium. They wanted a new stadium.
>
> We cut a new deal with the U.S. Tennis Association. We built a new $300 million stadium with their money.
>
> One of the complaints [of the association] was the [noise from] planes that flew over it [the stadium], so U.S. Open insisted on a fly over penalty provision. If the city didn't keep the planes [from flying over] during the period of the tournament, there will be fines. We struck a deal with the FAA to alter the flight patterns of the planes during that time. The pattern they took was a more safer route. You just piss off a different group of people.
>
> . . . Around the world, people said, "You are the mayor that moved the planes." This was very important to the economy of the city, more actually, the city treasury.[37]

Saving the U.S. Open was an important victory for Dinkins, but it did little to shape his prevailing image of being marginal in handling the massive economic turnaround needed for the city. If Dinkins, an avid tennis player, had not been so associated with the sport, the impact might have been different. Simply put, this feat did not resonate with enough voters.

During the 1993 reelection campaign, the deputy mayor for finance and economic development, Barry Sullivan, produced a report entitled *Strong Economy, Strong City*.[38] The report called for a four-year strategy to create jobs and improve the city's position in the global marketplace. This plan and his efforts to keep business in the city did not provide enough heroic moments to transform Dinkins into the economic savior of the city.

Keeping the mayor's image concurrent with the positive image of the city is what consultants are paid to do. In a 1991 op-ed piece, Anna Quindlen makes a similar observation about the linkage between the mayor's image and that of the city. She claims that the job of mayor entails more than "wrestling the city to a draw but giving it a human face, of developing an image that shows what we are made of." She goes on to say, "Mr. Dinkins has failed to do this. He has developed a persona by default; part tuxedo and tennis togs, part fiscal victim, his image is of a man none of us know very well, an Abe Beame of the 90s."[39]

Summary: The Larger Context

The purpose of this chapter was to examine the social, structural, and economic challenges facing the New York City Dinkins inherited. Dinkins' greatest supporters, blacks and Latinos, thought that his election heralded the start of a lower class opportunity-expansion regime. Clarence Stone points out, "An opportunity-expansion regime involves a very heavy resource demand, including a strong grassroots foundation. As a financially constrained city, especially with its lower SES population only weakly organized, New York could not realistically be expected to go very far in that direction. The resource match is not there."[40] It is possible that some New Yorkers may have thought that Dinkins' election would be a catalyst for such grassroots organizing and progressive taxation. As borough president, Dinkins was described as taking "positions that were to the left of anyone else on the Board of Estimate."[41] One of his advisors described him as the "tribune for the underclass."[42] Such talk did not escape the economic elite. During the 1989 election *Christian Science Monitor* interview, a senior vice president of a large real estate firm asserted, "David Dinkins is a lovely man, but his advisers are remarkably ill-informed on most economic issues. From what I hear, a number of people around him are from the radical left. New York City could go the way of Montreal economically if it is led by a strong clique like those in Quebec who essentially are anti-growth. Congressman (Charles) Rangel, in my book, is the only Dinkins' advisor who even comes close to knowing anything about economic reality. Despite these misgivings, I have contributed to the Dinkins campaign. [The real estate industry had better] 'find a way to provide some access to City Hall or we're doomed.'"[43]

Dinkins appointed Sally B. Hernandez-Pinero (his former deputy Manhattan borough president) as his first deputy mayor for finance and economic development. This was a signal that minorities would be represented in the economic decision circles of the city. However, there is no evidence that she had any significant impact on development policy, and in 1992 Dinkins replaced her with Barry F. Sullivan, former chairman of the First Chicago Corporation. David Rockefeller and the business community were involved in the recruitment of Sullivan. At a press conference, Sullivan asserted, "[T]he Mayor is saying that the private sector is important to the city and if I can get a business expert who also understands the city, I can get a bridge between the two that I don't have today."[44]

Two years into the Dinkins administration, it became clear that there was no bridge. The resources for a fundamental transformation of the economic arrangements were not in place. As anxiety about economic growth increased, a change in the leadership of economic department was indicated. Did the Sullivan appointment mark the end of the fusion coalition? The appointment of Hernandez-Pinero was an important symbol, but the recession and the budget crisis precluded much effort on behalf of the economically disadvantaged. As discussed in the previous chapter, the election campaign concentrated on Dinkins' character and his plans to defuse racial tensions, not economic policy options facing the city. Members of the development regime got multiple reassurances that his administration did not represent any curbing of developmental efforts. As we shall show in the next chapter, staffing is a way to signal the varied constituencies of a new administration.

As it is for any new administration, the task for the new mayor is to separate myth from reality. Although elected to return civility to the city and mend its racial fences, the myth was that the Dinkins fusion mandate could work and that developers would not consider it a zero-sum game. It is not surprising that Dinkins wanted to help the development regime. H. V. Savitch and Paul Kantor concluded,

> The right-leaning coalition was replaced during the David Dinkins's single term. Elected as the city's first black mayor in 1989, Dinkins tried to rebuild something like the old Lindsay coalition. Dinkins did, however, take pains to maintain a tight alliance with the city's business leaders who supported him in order to defuse the racial tensions. While Dinkins pursued pro-business policies, his presence provided powerful symbolic assurances to black voters. Despite his efforts, Dinkins's coalition proved unstable, and conflicts over race plagued his administration.[45]

In New York political folklore, the Lindsay administration is often referenced as the path of good intentions as well as maligned as a road to failure. Not only did the Lindsay coalition have more resources than Dinkins, but its goals also seemed more sweeping. Yet Lindsay was not able to produce a durable regime. In our interviews, Dinkins never indicated that he was trying to replicate the old Lindsay coalition even though he supported expansion of economic opportunities. Nonetheless, fifteen years after the 1975 fiscal crisis, the city's fiscal trap preempted any lasting regime-building efforts on his part.

Progrowth coalitions have always enjoyed support from the city's mayors because they had done an effective job of linking their interest with the overall employment interest of the poor. Projects such as Times Square Redevelopment and Grand Central Terminal improvements are vetted through what Kevin Cox and Andrew Mair have called a "redemptive ideology of locality."[46]

Progrowth leaders used such terms as *crime, downtown eye sore,* and *abandoned atmosphere* to engage the public's identification with the projects. The discourse is that we must struggle to keep our city attractive; we are all New Yorkers, and we shall overcome; and somehow the improvement of these areas will benefit all. Obviously if this narrative holds, the material winners in these economic schemes will be the investors, but even they need to convince the public that all are symbolic winners.

The progrowth coalition access is augmented by a small number of high-power lobbying firms such as Davidoff and Malito. Sid Davidoff, a former aide to John Lindsay, emerged as the most successful lobbyist. Since 1989 his law firm accounted for 20 percent of the lobbying fees paid by contractors.[47] Steve Spinola of the Real Estate Board of New York (REBNY) and John Gilbert of the Rent Stabilization Association (RSA) were officials during the Koch administration and continued to play roles in the property tax fights during the Dinkins years.[48] These lobbyists were high-ranking ex-city officials and knew members of the Dinkins administration personally. Lobbyists represented clients doing business with the city and those who wanted contracts with the city. Despite the requirements that lobbyists register with the city clerk, there is little regulation of their activities. In fact, the chummy relationship between lobbyists and Dinkins aides was a not secret.[49] Unfortunately, there is no comparable lobbying group that represents neighborhood interests on a full-time basis.

The nominal voice of the people, the city council, does not have the leverage or resources to produce an alternative narrative about economic development nor to act as a facilitator between the public and developers. The council's Economic Development Committee does conduct hearings about a variety of economic issues, but airings of views do not always translate into a veto over economic policy. The council seems to work best when it supports the progrowth coalition. When it appears to be at variance with the coalition, it gets bogged down in turmoil. Although most of the antidevelopers' speeches are aimed at the members' constituencies, in the end they usually support the developers. An example is the 1993 brouhaha over extending tax abatements to builders of large highrise apartments in Manhattan. They supported the measure in December after the mayor's reelection defeat. What is more important, during the Dinkins era, the new fifty-one-member council itself was in the process of development.

The question was whether Dinkins' team at city hall fully understood these structural and economic contradictions in the scaffold the mayor was using to build a fusion regime. As I shall discuss in the next chapter, his choice of staff members was payback for disparate members of his constituencies. The people Dinkins selected to help him implement policy would play a key role in determining whether his election represented a regime change or politics as usual.

CHAPTER FOUR

THE STAFFING OF DINKINS' CITY HALL

avid Dinkins was trained as a city politician, not a municipal administrator. The staff chosen by his administration would become a part of the *ecological* image constructed by the media. Mayors need help making and explaining decisions, and a new mayor must find people who can read numbers (those associated with the budget and polls), understand municipal department culture, and link him to the various constituencies. One of the first stories reported during a new mayor's transition concerns the staff chosen for administration. Most incoming mayors try to promote the idea of an open and collegial staff. However, since mayors are politicians, their first instinct is usually to survive. Picking the people who will make them look good should be the first priority. Some incoming mayors are often unaware that staff appointments can affect their images. Fewer of them are aware how aides will react to newly acquired power and status. As we shall see in later chapters, the names of staff members surface as the media tries to sort up a crisis.

Selling a public image accelerates during the transition period. Journalists are aware that much knowledge can be gained by analyzing the staff appointments. The *New York Times* assigned several reporters to write brief biographies on the Dinkins appointees. They assumed that readers wanted to know who was selected for what departments and which individuals would be on the mayor's personal staff. "Mayor watchers" see the appointments as cues for understanding a mayor's judgment and values. Words such as *diversity, inclusion, professionalism,* and *experience* are woven into our lexicon and become a part of the new administration's story. New names and management themes are introduced during this period of transition.

This chapter will discuss the appointments of Dinkins. Appointments act as (a) public image builders, (b) signals for policy, and (c) reassurances for members of the permanent bureaucracy (the civil service). In this arena campaign promises and the biography of the candidate's close advisor are important. If the mayor stresses the need for personnel or policy change in the campaign, then an effort will be made to appoint outsiders or proven administrators to head a troubled permanent bureaucracy.

With every change in each administration, there are payoff appointments. Most politicians can identify individuals who are their career facilitators. Reporters try to separate the traditional patronage appointments from the obligatory managerial appointments. Patronage appointees are usually longtime friends, supporters, and associates. Mayors use such people as personal and liaison staffing and as such are rarely given management responsibilities in city departments. Other mayoral appointees are party loyalists who are hired to work in the city departments. These appointments are a way to repay a mayor's debts to volunteers, supporters, and fundraisers. The managerial staff members organize the mayor's office, lead departments, and carry out administrative duties.

In 1964, Theodore Lowi's *At the Pleasure of the Mayor* suggested that New York mayors had little control over appointments.[1] This tradition can be traced back to the Tammany Hall era, to the infamous New York City political machine. Mayors who were elected on so-called fusion or reform tickets were also constrained by political considerations. These politicians understood the nature of their political obligations. Lowi asserts that the "Mayor is not a mute pawn, but neither is he a free agent."[2] Mayors have to consult with party leaders before making appointments. Because there are so many positions and so few political activists with appropriate credentials, the new mayor is forced to look outside the immediate circle for talent.

Lowi characterized these appointments as having "indexes" or "tracer elements" that identified the composition of the city power structure. In other words, various interest groups wanted to have their members represented in the newly formed government. Few self-starters get mayoral appointments. The old Chicago political machine adage "We Don't Want Anybody Anybody Sent" applies to some extent in New York. In order for one to acquire a top-level job, one needs a referral. The individual who makes the referral must have a political account with the newly elected mayor; otherwise it becomes less likely for an applicant to get a job.

The examination of the rise and fall of patronage in New York City illustrates a difference between old-style petty and more modern grand patronage. Petty patronage includes low-skilled, blue-collar city jobs such as maintenance/service employees and low-level clerks. These jobs are now a part of the civil service. Today, there is more grand patronage—a wide variety of white-collar jobs and contracts. The new saying is that you can not get a job at city hall without a college degree. Indeed the U.S. Supreme Court drove the final nail in the petty patronage coffin with the 1974 *Elrod v. Burns* case.[3] The Court ruled that the Sheriff of Cook County could not fire nonconfidential employees simply because of their party affiliation. With this ruling all public employees have due process rights regardless of how they were appointed. Justice Lewis Powell, in a dissent, argued that this was the end of local political parties and was right to a certain extent. Local political parties are no longer regarded as the primary candidate recruitment pool. Professional networks have replaced the parties for high-level appointments. Organized interest groups provide the political context of modern appointments.

The Context of Mayoral Appointments

As suggested earlier, mayors make appointments in an environment of competing interests. Allocating patronage must be seen as being fair and representative. Political activists may like to be asked to serve, although some cannot afford financially to do so. For many political activists, a mayoral appointment is considered a career enhancer. The appointment process is made more difficult when a particular interest group sees itself as directly responsible for the election of the mayor. For them, election is a collective victory. Now is the time to collect. These groups are quite verbal about what they expect from the mayor. Referring to the Dinkins victory, City Councilman Archie Spigner (D. Queens) reflected this view when he asserted that, "when you win the general election by 47,000 votes, you owe everybody."[4] Dinkins' view was that "we in New York are proving by example that we can form a government representative of all the people."[5]

Lowi's 1960 book on New York politics says that the mayor governed with "competing demands and expectations." Thirty years later the mayor is still dealing with competing demands and expectations. A mayor still has to decide who gets what and when. If it appears that the mayor has delegated patronage-allocating responsibility to others, party regulars regard this as reneging on a promise. Often groups and individuals who feel unrewarded go to the press with their stories.

A new mayor is allowed some leeway in personal patronage. She or he is expected to reward loyal campaign workers, contributors, and longtime supporters. One of the goals of a newly elected mayor is repaying those he or she owes. Mayors are expected to appoint "buddies" or "cronies" as long they do not have much political baggage. These appointees are considered the "comfort ones" for the mayor. Some old "buddies" will settle for a sinecure, but a few want substantive jobs. For Dinkins, the latter included the people who had worked for him in the borough president's office. As one former high-ranking Dinkins aide put it, "This was their day in the sun now that David had won." They were regarded as advocate groups. Most of these appointments do not become problems for reasons we will discuss later.

In this postmachine politics era, interest groups rather than party regulars are rewarded with high-profile jobs. Individuals are appointed as representatives of their interest group. An individual may be referred to as "coming from" labor, consumer movements, the gay community, or the reform clubs. These are purely political appointments. In the Dinkins administration, African Americans Ron Gault, an investment banker; Earl Graves, publisher of *Black Enterprise Magazine*; and Ed Lewis, publisher of *Essence* magazine served on high-profile mayoral advisory committees. Rarely are these individuals allowed to roam into managerial turf.

It is also traditional that a big city mayor appoints at least one department head from the "national roster" or the professionals with national reputations in municipal management areas described by Nathan Grundstein as "nationals" as opposed to "locals."[6] These individuals are referred from a mayor's external networks and associations. They are useful appointments if the mayor wants to send a message to the permanent bureaucracy.

Dinkins' Staffing

Mayor Dinkins appointed a so-called blue ribbon transition team. The purpose of such a committee is to *associate* the mayor's name with the leading figures in the city, to inflate the status of the mayor. Dinkins' committee included people familiar to New Yorkers, such as Basil Paterson, Felix Rohatyn, Nathan Leventhal, Carol Bellamy, Geraldine Ferraro, Hazel Duke, and Thomas Stoddard. Former mayors Lindsay and Beame were also listed as special advisors. Mayors generally create a commission to write a report during the transition period to define their administration.

Dinkins' effort was entitled "The Reform and Renaissance of New York City Government" and outlined fifty-one separate initiatives designed to restructure the way New York did its business. The mayor pledged to report each month on the progress of these initiatives. After a year, a former member of the mayor's Office of Operations reported to the media that the initiatives were a success.[7] However, the mayor's monthly reports did little to enhance Dinkins' reputation as a manager or dispel claims that his appointments were politically inspired.

After the inauguration, Dinkins appointed another blue ribbon committee, the Committee on Appointments, to screen and make recommendations on appointees. The committee members included Liman and Victor Alicea, June Jackson Christmas, Ronald Gault, Nathan Leventhal, Kenneth Ong, and Martha Wallau. Floyd Abrams was chair of the committee. This group was commissioned to screen resumes.

The actual appointments by Dinkins were done the old-fashioned way through political connections. Under the city charter, the mayor appoints deputy mayors to help him manage the city. The Dinkins transition had few surprises. However, sexual harassment charges were filed against Randy Daniels, the public relations man and Dinkins' choice for deputy mayor for community and public affairs. Gail Collins called him a "stupendously ineffective Deputy Mayor for Image Enhancement."[8] She also accused Dinkins of having prior knowledge of the charge and took former borough president Andy Stein as a source for Daniels' credibility.

During the Beame transition, Dinkins had been offered a position as deputy mayor, but he rejected it after the media published the fact that he had not paid income taxes. This revelation, which almost destroyed his career, presented a crisis for the new Beame administration and portrayed Dinkins' as a man who was overwhelmed by his job. Therefore, Dinkins was determined to shore up his image, which had been damaged by those revelations and subsequent ones involving the transfer of stocks to his son. He needed to appoint people with credibility. Appointees with political baggage could be a loadstone on Dinkins' image.

Deputy Mayors and Representation

New York City has a structured deputy mayor system. Each deputy supervises a set of departments and reports to the mayor. The first deputy position is often considered as prime minister of the city government. To the surprise of many, Dinkins appointed Norman Steisel, a man who had served under Beame, Lindsay, and Koch as first deputy mayor. Steisel was trained as an engineer and an expert on economic modeling; he was also assistant budget director and sanitation commissioner in the Koch administration. Steisel described himself as the "chief operations officer and a part of the permanent government."[9] Despite tending to the details of operation, Stiesel was also the lightening rod for several interest group complaints.

The next in line of authority was the deputy mayor for intergovernmental affairs. Dinkins appointed his campaign manager, Bill Lynch, the "rumpled genius" to this post.[10] Lynch had considerable labor credentials and had worked with Dinkins in the borough president's office. A former radio commentator and political director for local 205, day-care workers, Lynch was seen as a powerful figure in the Dinkins administration. In charge of government and community relations, he also supervised the Community Assistance Office, a city-state and federal lobbying unit. Lynch quickly began to emerge as the central figure in

Dinkins' media relations and patronage appointments in the black community. Lynch also acted as a liaison to a variety of political groups in the outer boroughs. As we shall see later, Lynch became Dinkins' point man during a series of racial conflicts.

Dinkins appointed two women to his immediate staff. Sally B. Hernandez-Pinero (the deputy Manhattan borough president under Dinkins) was appointed as the new deputy mayor for finance and economic development.[11] Pinero's portfolio consisted of the Public Development Corporation, the Department of Business Services, and Taxation and Finance. She was subsequently transferred to the Housing Department.

The second highest-ranking female in a high-visibility position was Deputy Mayor for Policy and Planning Barbara Fife. She had been involved in city government for a long time and had worked in the borough president's office.

Barbara Sabol, a former states Social Services commissioner and an African American, was appointed head of the Human Resources Administration. Robert Little (brother of Malcolm X) was appointed head of the Child Welfare Administration. The New York City Department of Health was headed by Dr. Woodrow Myers, also an African American.

Two other deputy mayors were appointed. Milton Mollen, a retired judge, was named as the deputy mayor for criminal justice. He had experience with the Fire, Police, and Correction Department. As we shall see later, Mollen became a central figure in the Safe Streets, Safe City campaign and in the investigation of corruption in the New York City police department (NYPD). Cesar A. Perales was appointed as the deputy mayor for health and human services. He supervised the Health and Hospital Corporation, the largest such agency in the nation, and the Human Resources Administration. Billy Jones, mental health commissioner, later became head of the Health and Hospital Corporation. Leressa R. Crockett, an investment banker and vice president at Salomon Brothers, was appointed commissioner of the Financial Service Corporation.

The personal staff of the mayor included his press secretary, Albert Scardino, a Pulitzer-prize winner Italian American, and former *New York Times* business reporter. The role of press secretary is critical to the mayor's image making. He or she not only makes announcements and hands out press releases, but also explains the mayor's actions to the media. Scardino asserted "The mayor of New York is terribly important, because New York is the media capital of the world, and the media amplifies everything the mayor says. Dinkins, who is starting with immense good will in spite of some problems, has an opportunity to influence public discourse everywhere."[12] On another occasion Scardino opined, "If the job of a mayor is to provide bread and circuses, then I would agree that Ed Koch provided an enormous number of circuses and very little bread. Whether or not the Mayor provides the circuses, circuses have to be provided for the press to survive. Circuses aren't David Dinkins' long suit."[13]

His former colleagues had heavily criticized Scardino because he had helped Dinkins in his mayoral campaign. Scardino also got off on the wrong foot with some of the reporters in the press room. One reporter who was interviewed recalled that Scardino "lectured them" about referring to the new mayor as either "Mr. Dinkins" or "Mr. Mayor." Reporters were accustomed to calling Mayor Dinkins "Dave" during the campaign. It is traditional to call the mayor a nickname in the print media. One bureau chief reported, "He [Scardino] thoroughly alienated the press. He was a problem for Dinkins from day one. . . . Dinkins' honeymoon lasted about six months." The media's dislike for Scardino "was transferred to Dinkins."[14] Sam Robert agreed. He stated, "As a lightening rod, Mr. Scardino may have offered himself as a human sacrifice, but the static he attracted also burned the mayor." [15] Scardino ended up being the first casualty of the nascent administration. Scardino believed that the immediate cause of his downfall was a letter written by Todd Purdum. Scardino recalled,

> What happens was Todd Purdum, who was a reporter at the *New York Times,* wrote David Dinkins a personal letter, a handwritten letter, in which he said that the *New York Times* could not believe the mayor's press secretary. If they can't believe the press secretary, they would not believe the mayor. This was going to interfere with the mayor's relationship with the *New York Times.*[16]

Dinkins and his counsel, Victor Kovner, called Scardino in and asked, "What do you think we should do?" Scardino believed Purdum was suggesting "that the *New York Times* wants you

[Dinkins] to fire me." Dinkins did not fire him immediately as Scardino tried to ascertain whether Purdum's letter reflected the official view of the *New York Times*.[17] He asked the publisher (Arthur Sulzberger) to verify if this was the *Times'* official view. Through a relative, Sulzberger communicated to Dinkins that this was not the case. Scardino also allowed that Dinkins was not satisfied with his work. Scardino observed, "David felt that my relationship with the press was so at fault, it was so tense because every time I said something it was misinterpreted one way or another.[18] A month later Scardino offered to resign, and the mayor accepted his resignation.

Other appointments also proved to be controversial. Dr. Woodrow Myers, an African American and former Indiana health commissioner, was appointed to head the city Department of Health. Since Myers had advocated quarantining those who knowingly spread the AIDS virus, he was considered controversial. AIDS activists opposed the Myers appointment, but a *New York Times* editorial supported it. [19]

The highest ranking Puerto Rican in the Dinkins administration was Fire Commissioner Carlos Rivera. He was a career firefighter and the second minority to head the fire department. Philip Michael, former executive director of the New York State Financial Control Board, was appointed budget director. Eric Schmertz, a labor management arbitrator and former dean of Hofstra University, was appointed commissioner of the Office of Labor Relations. As the mayor's chief labor negotiator, Schmertz would be the spokesperson for the mayor and his relations with the unions. Schmertz, a Republican, had been fired from an arbitrator job by former Mayor Koch.

A review of these appointments demonstrates how important race, ethnicity, and gender were to the public image of Mayor Dinkins. Black mayors have traditionally hired white press secretaries, and Dinkins continued this tradition. Part of the reason lies with the predominately white press group and the lack of strong black or minority figures in the local media. For some mayors using a white face to explain administrative actions means a built-in apologist for the administration. None of the appointments, save that of Schmertz, was thought initially controversial. These appointments suggested that Dinkins was a cautious man trying to satisfy the representative needs of all groups.

Writer Joe Klein thought that Dinkins' management style was a model of order and rectitude. It was made up of a board of directors with five deputy mayors, a press secretary (Albert Scardino), a corporation counsel (Victor Kovner), and Dinkins' personal counsel (George Daniels). [20] However, Klein concluded the structure was "a bit cumbersome."[21] Not only was it "cumbersome," but it also was ineffective in promoting and preserving Dinkins' image.

The Meaning of Appointments

Political appointments not only are rewards to supporters, but they are signals to public interest groups and to the permanent bureaucracy. As I will discuss later, Lee Brown was a signal to the minority community that Dinkins was committed to changing the relationship between the New York Police Department and the minority community, as well as the permanent police bureaucracy. Signals are "statements or actions . . . issued mainly to influence the receiver's image of the sender."[22] Dinkins was signaling the relevant actors in the city. Accordingly, each high-profile appointment was aimed at improving the political image of the mayor. High-profile city departments such as the police, school, and health departments (especially in New York) are critical to a mayor's transitioning into power.

During Dinkins' campaign, he announced his intention to appoint Victor Kovner as his corporation councilor. Kovner, a very prestigious Jewish lawyer, was a signal to the business community. Ruth Messenger, a veteran city politician and former Manhattan borough president, stated that this appointments was a signal that whites would play a major role in the Dinkins administration. "It was clearly done because it is was a way of saying that whites would carry significant responsibility."[23] Arnold H. Lubasch, a *New York Times* reporter, stated, "The choice was meant to signal the city's Jewish liberals and legal community that Mr. Dinkins is a mainstream Democrat."[24]

Thirty years earlier Wallace Sayre and Herbert Kaufman had found that the organized bureaucracies were persuasive participants in the New York appointment process:

Their basic aspiration in the appointment process is, it would seem, to confine all such appointments to their own members, invoking for that purpose the values of "career service," "promotion from within," "nonpolitical appointments," and other doctrinal formulae for controlling the discretion of the appointing officers and limiting the intervention of other competing participants in the appointment process. To these appeals is frequently added an emphasis upon the risks and costs of appointing an outsider whom the staffs will allegedly resist.[25]

Dinkins' transition team recommended individuals for a variety of jobs. Although the mayor did appoint a career firefighter to the fire department, he choose Lee Brown, who had been a police chief in Atlanta and Houston to be police commissioner. The so-called organized bureaucrats continued to have a substantial influence in appointments "to such subordinate positions as deputy commissioners, division director, or bureau chief."[26] These important concessions to the permanent bureaucracy are rarely covered in the media.

One of the perennial problems for a new staff is how to accentuate the mayor's image and subjugate their own identities. Attributing all the successful outcomes to the mayor's leadership skills and taking the blame for things that go badly is very difficult for some staff members. In the 1930s, the famous Brownlow Committee Report advised future presidential aides to acquire a "passion for anonymity." Anonymity can be extremely difficult for some staff members who have high visibility separate from the mayor. In New York, being a high-ranking city official can gain citywide visibility, but it is very important for an appointee to stay on the same page as the mayor.

There is always the propensity for appointees to go native, i.e., putting the department's interest before the mayor's political interest. This can be a serious problem when disputes between the mayor and his appointee become public. Dinkins' City Hall aides apparently thought that fire commissioner Carlos Rivera, an appointee, had "gone native" when he sought to promote publicly the interest of the department at the expense of the mayor's overall policy. Such behavior by a patronage appointee is rarely tolerated. The fact that Rivera was a Latino did not exempt him from removal for violating this policy.

The increasing demand for diversity in mayoral appointees reflects the representational demands of the city's population.

Mayors are now expected to appoint women and minorities to high positions in government. As Professor Andrew Hacker put it, "They kept a little color card. How black is the Administration going to be?"[27] Dinkins appointed Sally Hernandez-Pinero to be the deputy mayor for finance and economic development. The appointment of Sally Hernandez-Pinero, Carlos Rivera, and Victor Alicea to top positions caused quite a stir. At first glance, these were Latino appointments, but Hernandez-Pinero was not a referral from the elected Latino political leaders. Reporters openly asked if Alicea would be the last Hispanic appointment. Many reporters were aware of the growing competition between Latinos and African Americans for political empowerment. They interpreted the Latino appointments as playing the Latino card.

On the surface, one would think Dinkins had done well in appointing women and minorities to high-profile positions in the administration. However, the pressure was on during the early days of his administration, and Dinkins' numbers were disputed. Press Secretary Scardino claimed that Dinkins had appointed one-third women. In an article in *Vanity Fair,* Marie Brenner alleged Scardino made some racist comments about the Dinkins selections. Scardino allegedly said, "City Hall is no longer run by a bunch of tired old Jewish men," and, "most white people in [New York] have had no experience with blacks," and "they think that black men are felons and black women are maids."[28] Scardino denied the Brenner quote and stated, "Mary made up the quote and put it in my mouth."[29] In a highly volatile city such as New York, any quote that implied anti-Semitism received an immediate reaction. Dinkins and Scardino called a press conference to deny the allegations, calling them "manufactured."[30] The Brenner interview hurt Dinkins' image as a man who recruited people based on ability, and it further undermined Scardino's credibility with his former colleagues. For a man who considered himself a radical on racial matters, this left the public with an erroneous opinion of Dinkins. He lamented that in the minds of some, he [Scardino] "became one of the world's greatest anti-Semites as a result of that comment."[31]

The Media Role in Appointments

When a new mayor is elected, the media engages in speculation about who will be appointed to what jobs. Reporters collect information during the campaign, and names and positions are leaked to the media often to test public reactions. Once an appointment is announced, the media launches a biographical examination of the appointees. The so-called quick analysis of an appointment includes examining the educational background and the government experiences of the appointee. This is what Sayre and Kaufman call the "distinctive function" of the media in the appointment process. The press provides visibility for the process and thus becomes part of it, highlighting appointments that seem unusual and precedent breaking. The media either approves or disapproves of candidates for certain positions.

> In their usual participation in the appointment process, the communication media tend to reveal several consistent attitudes: implicit hostility (often made explicit) toward party leaders as participants; friendliness toward civic, professional, and business groups as participants; aloofness toward labor union, ethnic, racial, and religious groups as participants; and susceptibility to the claims of the bureaucracies for "career" appointments.[32]

Since the 1990s, mayors have been more sensitive to gender and minority representation. As was suggested earlier, appointing a female deputy mayor is almost obligatory. Moreover, a cabinet that represents both genders is now the norm in big cities. When Dinkins appointed a Puerto Rican to the fire department, which was considered a white, male enclave, the appointment was newsworthy. The same is true for holdovers (such as Norman Steisel) from previous administrations.

Was Dinkins' appointment of Norman Steisel a reassurance for party regulars? Some pundits perceived Steisel as a white knight in the administration. He was part of the coterie of former mayor Koch. Many minority activists considered the Steisels of the administration an alien power bloc within the Dinkins administration. "They were running a piece of the government."[33] Many black politicians and members of the progressive community were not pleased with the Steisel appointment or any of the so-called Koch people. One prominent black politician found him to be arrogant and thought Steisel's enemies were "transferred to Dinkins."[34] The *New York Amsterdam News* also questioned the appointment of Steisel as the first deputy mayor. Some political pundits had used the phrase "the best thing to happen to the City since sliced bread" to describe Dinkins' appointment of Steisel as his chief aide. The *News* editorial entitled "The Best Thing for New York since Sliced Bread"[35] was a sarcastic rejoinder to Dinkins and the pundits." The editorial asserted, "we respectfully beg to differ from your assessment, Mr. Mayor." The editorial raised questions about appointing Koch loyalists to the Dinkins administration. It named names and ended with "We do not wish to believe that a 'shadow government' is being built within your administration."[36]

This controversy about the former Koch people did not help Dinkins' image in respect to being in control of his administration. Jim Sleeper said the many Koch people "littered" Dinkins' staff.[37] Dinkins never explained the appointment of the Koch holdovers. However, the selection of controversial appointees was a windfall for story-hunting reporters. Delving into the political motives of a mayor who flaunts warnings about individuals can become a good story. If the mayor is secure enough to appoint strong aides, the media will give a new mayor high marks, but few are forgiving for controversial aides.

Eric Schmertz was one of Dinkins' most controversial appointments. Mark Voorhees concluded, "Schmertz' Achilles heel is not that he's too soft but that he's too cocksure and convinced of his rectitude." Voorhees quoted former Mayor Koch, now a columnist for the *New York Post,* as saying, "Schmertz is the archetypical fox given the duty of watching the chickens by the foolish farmer"[38] As we shall see later, Dinkins' relations with labor were not helped by the Schmertz appointment.

Mayoral Images and Advice Taking

At first glance, it appears that the mayor relies primarily on his staff for advice. But a new mayor soon discovers that there are a variety of individuals who want to act as advisors, such as journalists, who often try to advise in their columns. Dinkins received a great deal of advice when he attended community meetings. In most cases staff advice is taken on political issues.

Whether advice is sought depends upon the mayor's definition of the solution. If the mayor defines it as a technical issue, he will rely on staff members who are considered technicians.

Mayors are not restricted to advice from staff members. Dinkins appointed a Council of Economic Advisors consisting of Felix G. Rohatyn, David Rockefeller, and Joseph Flom. Felix Rohatyn of Lazard Freres and Company, played a major role in the 1975 fiscal crisis. Acceptance of an appointment to a blue ribbon mayoral committee is often a matter of noblesse oblige. As individuals members may give overall advice, but not on day-to-day operations. They seek ways in which they can be helpful to the mayor, and vice versa.

Exit, Voice, and Loyalty

Most politicians understand that staff turnover is inevitable. The pay is not outstanding, the hours are long, and ones' privacy may be diminished. Appointees are often surprised at the difference between government work and the private sector. Most are surprised that the media does not hold high opinions of their work. Among the first to leave are often staff members on loan from businesses who have standing offers to return. For example, Leland T. Jones replaced Press Secretary Albert Scardino. Peter Sherwood (of the former NAACP Legal Defense Educational Fund) replaced Victor Kovner as corporation counsel. Dinkins also made changes in his personal staff replacing Ken Sunshine. John Flateau, an African American was made chief of staff and cabinet member. Flateau was his deputy campaign manager and a key proxy for the central Brooklyn political base.

Eric Schmertz was fired on March 9, 1991, after he got into a public argument with the budget director, Phillip R. Michael. Michael had sent a confidential letter to Moody's Investors Service Inc., reporting that the city was negotiating with unions to defer 1.5 percent of the recently won wage increases. Michael claimed Schmertz had prepared an outline for the letter, and Schmertz claimed otherwise. However, Michael subsequently produced Schmertz's handwritten note. Resolution of the episode revolved around whether the note implied negotiations were underway or that such negotiations would take place at an appropriate time.

Labor leaders were furious with Schmertz and demanded that he be fired. Dinkins sided with Michael and replaced Schmertz with James Hanley. The appointment was greeted by enthusiasm among labor leaders such as Barry Feinstein, but Schmertz claimed that "what they intend to do is put the blame on me. I refuse to be the scapegoat. If this is the way that the mayor is going to resolve it, I don't want to be part of it."[39] In a *Newsday* interview, Schmertz claimed that the real reason was that Michael "was encroaching too much, too often on my jurisdiction."[40] For him the Moody note incident was the last straw. A *New York Times* editorial reacted to the Schmertz termination with the following observation.

> The Michael-Schmertz dispute is only the latest in a series of less-publicized problems at City Hall, where internal bickering has become the norm. Commissioners contend they cannot get the Mayor's attention, outsiders complain they cannot get a decision because they don't know who is in charge, and reports of paralyzing feuds between deputy mayors are so common that nobody bothers to deny them.[41]

In 1993 Michael was accused of showing favoritism in his handing of a $150 million contract to Lockheed Information Management Services, a parking fines collector. The *Village Voice* wrote a series of articles about the company that prompted a review by the Department of Investigation, and Dinkins had to dismiss Michael.

High-profile turnovers, even the less contentious ones, were a problem for the Dinkins administration. Any change in top-level personnel had the potential of being read in different ways. When Dinkins replaced Sally B. Hernandez-Pinero, his deputy mayor for finance and economic development, with Barry F. Sullivan, some read it as a concession to the business community. Hernandez-Pinero was subsequently appointed to the Housing Department.

There were a variety of reasons people left the Dinkins administration. Some left to return to the private sector, others left because they wanted a change, and still others left because the administration was having problems. A few left because they were pushed out.

Economist Albert Hirschman's *Exit, Voice and Loyalty* analyzes reasons individuals leave organizations. According to Hirschman, organizational loyalty is tested when organizational performance does not meet the member's expectations. Hirschman is concerned with repairable lapses or temporary deterioration of an organizational performance.[42] Some members will respond to these lapses in management or as a way to exercise their exit options, they resign. Others take the voice option defending the organization. These members try to reform the organization from within. Hirschman observed that some individuals exercise both *exit* and *voice* options. These are individuals who will speak out and leave.

High-Profile Exit and Dinkins' Image

The first Dinkins election sparked a sense of entitlement among blacks and Latinos. None of the top Dinkins Latino appointments were considered grassroots or borough politicians "people." So far as the "Latino politicians, David didn't give them anything."[43] Conversely, the black appointments were better known, and the grassroots organizations felt that they had a voice, whereas many Latinos apparently felt that they were deprived of a voice.

Ten months into the administration the first Latino appointee decided to leave the administration. After the city closed his illegal social club in East Harlem, William Nieves resigned as the director of the mayor's Office of Latino Affairs. Nieves claimed he did not have access to Dinkins.[44] Nieves' resignation fed into the perception that Dinkins took the Latino support for granted. Meanwhile, Dinkins was trying to transfer him to assistant commissioner for intergovernmental affairs with the Community Development Agency. However Nieves resigned before the transfer was made. The media described the attempt to remove Nieves as botched.[45] Marlene Cintron replaced Nieves. Later Carlos Rivera's departure became a significant exit for the Dinkins administration. In an interview with Steisel, he described his version of events leading to Rivera's departure.

> We [the administration] had had enormous problems with the Fire
> Department. We had serious reservations about the way it was

managed. . . . The new commissioner [Rivera] seems reluctant to implement [budget changes]. . . . We had severe deficits in the immediate budget and the city's financial plan. . . . There was a real need to have a discipline from a managerial point of view implement cost saving kind of approach. . . . Rivera just dragged his feet. Unions got into the way to slow the thing. It became clear that the commissioner was helping them behind the scene. Dinkins was not happy about this. The word got out. I [Steisel] knew a lot about the Fire department. . . . We [Rivera and Steisel] went at it hammer and tong. Talking about the using of the press. The press fomented the white/Latino thing. . . . He [Rivera] was clever enough to call up city councilmen. He quit in a huff and supported Giuliani.[46]

This quote suggests that city hall concluded Rivera was identifying too closely with department interest and was now at odds with Dinkins. Arguably, the Rivera resignation and subsequent endorsement of Giuliani was not a turning point in Dinkins' reelection campaign. Dinkins downplayed it by stating, "I don't think it hurt at all. There is no ill treatment of Latinos in this administration."[47] Reporters tried to make a subordinate ambush story of it. Rob Gurwitt, a guest writer from the *Governing*, suggested, "It wasn't so long ago that you could have gotten a good chuckle out of any politician in New York by suggesting that its first black mayor might lose his seat to a white Republican challenger riding a wave of Hispanic support. . . . In the urban political deck of the 1990s, the Hispanic vote is the wild card."[48]

Another exit was the head of the Health and Hospital Corporation, J. Emillio Carrilo. Steisel asserted, "He had difficulty managing this retrenchment program. He was the center of a major controversy for the mayor. We had to let him go."[49]

Summary

The old adage that the staff can make or break a mayor is not necessarily true. A mayor can make bad appointments, appoint the wrong people into office, and still survive. It is relatively easy to push someone out if that person is generating a lot of bad publicity. However, a mayor can make good appointments, appoint competent people into office, and not survive reelection. Dinkins' appointees may have hobbled his administration because they were not sure what he wanted to do. Lacking an overall vision, subordinates resorted to an every-man-for-himself strategy. Besides, many of them were in the queue for the revolving door that would lead to a future lobbying job.

Obviously, Dinkins did not anticipate that the Lynch and Brown appointments would be the most important to maintain his preferred image. In a later chapter I will discuss why these two men were key actors in the two major racial crises of the mayor's tenure. Otherwise the press kept revisiting the theme that Dinkins was not a "hands on" mayor. This is why the media found incessant turf battles among the deputy mayors and even some commissioners so intriguing. After one year in office, reporter Todd Purdum reported bickering and disarray in the mayor's inner circle.[50] Some appointees had public profiles before they joined Dinkins and what one top official called an "affinity for the media (loving the limelight)."[51]

When it became obvious that some appointments were not working out, the changes Dinkins did make sent a signal to the constituency that their representative replacement was a political necessity or that some appointees were simply not up to the job. Replacing Albert Scardino with Leland Jones as press secretary was a both a signal and a concession to unhappy city hall reporters. Replacing Sally B. Hernandez-Pinero with Barry Sullivan consolidated his relationship with the business community. Replacing Lee Brown with police insider Raymond Kelly was a signal to police bureaucracy.[52] Replacing Eric Schemetz with James Hanley, a signal to the labor community, was not well received, nor was keeping Norman Steisel and replacing Carlos Rivera. The latter two actions sent the wrong signal. In retrospect, Mitt Mollen never provided the gravitas that Dinkins had hoped, nor did he become a major player in the racial disturbances.

Reporters Charles Bagli and Michael Powell traced his appointment problems back to his electoral coalition. This coalition was a mix of old guard and African American activists. They concluded that Dinkins' "initial appointments reflected the Dinkins dichotomy: Political office would be shared by the different factions within his coalition, but the established power brokers would, initially at least, hold the upper hand."[53] Sites, a political scientist, suggested that at least with housing policy, the real estate industry was able to keep the upper hand until the end of Dinkins' administration. The slumping economy precluded the establishment of a progressive regime in housing.[54]

Yet Dinkins remained proud of his selections and their tenure. In an interview he asserted, "I used to say fondly of my staff: We had some of the finest people that ever served in the municipal government. I would stack them person to person against any people that ever served."[55] Yet the press stayed with the appointment story throughout the Dinkins tenure. As Hacker put it, "it was as if he [Dinkins] was on probation. Other mayors knew where to get a corporation counsel, etc. They [reporters] behaved as if Dinkins had not lived in the city."[56] Noisy exits are a problem when they involve high-profile minority staff such as Rivera. Two of Dinkins' high-profile Latinos turned out to be bad choices. In the end, their departure managed to create more doubts in the minds of Latino voters about the mayor. Unlike his predecessor's appointees, Dinkins' were more likely to make public statements or have a willing media anxious to print their comments. The New York media seemed to be convinced that there was a plethora of side stories within the Dinkins inner circle. The press was especially interested in the management style and policies of Lee Brown. As a famous and successful police officer, he made for a good story line. The police's permanent bureaucracy's instinct was to resist outsiders at the top of the force, but it turned out that Brown's changes were not at variance with the extant organization. Most of his deputies were career people in the department. As discussed in a later chapter, Brown's management style and Bill Lynch's negotiation style were questioned in the fallout from the Crown Heights incident.

Advising a mayor, especially one who has spent years in city politics, is not always easy. Aides can offer advice, but it is the mayor who makes the final decision. Different aides have the mayor's ear at different times. As stated earlier, the media is not above trying to advise the mayor by dropping hints in editorials and columns. Most mayors read newspapers and watch television news programs. They often feel obligated to respond to media reports. Dinkins seemed too amenable to advice from a variety of sources.

It was unrealistic to expect Dinkins, a quintessential regular Democrat, to refuse to appoint members of his staff who had worked for former Mayor Koch. People such as Deputy Mayor Norman Steisel are a part of the so-called permanent government of New York City. These individuals are recyclable in any Democrat administration. Failure to appoint these individuals would have been seen as a plan to change the way the city is run. This may have upset Dinkins' new colleagues in the governing coalition. As he made the transition from a borough politician to a citywide one, Dinkins did not want to alarm them.

Finally, the nascent image of Dinkins emerged in the early days of his administration. Dinkins' appointments came under constant media scrutiny, yet he seemed oblivious as to whether his aides were undermining his preferred image. Some of this attitude was reflected in the discretion his aides enjoyed during public crises.

CHAPTER FIVE

RACIAL EVENTS, DIPLOMACY, AND DINKINS' IMAGE

Since the 1970s survey researchers have been tracking the impact of the election of a black mayor on trust in city government. Some scholars believe such elections would decrease white trust in city government, while others believe it is blacks who undergo an opinion change. The question is whether the trust in city government is related to a more generalized reservation about government. Opinion polls consistently show deep levels of cynicism regarding politicians in general and a lack of trust in the government among Americans.[1] If the public shows a lack of trust and respect for an elected official, it is difficult for him or her to govern.

As early as six months into Dinkins' term, the *New York Times*/WCBS polls showed that blacks gave higher approval of Dinkins' performance in the office than whites, 77 percent to 46 percent.[2] The same poll illustrated that both blacks and whites were pessimistic about the economy. After nine months in office, a Gallup poll conducted by *Newsday* found that 38 percent of respondents approved of Dinkins' performance, and 43 percent did not.[3] This poll suggested that Dinkins began losing support soon after taking office. Abney and Hutcheson's early 1980s study of Atlanta's first black mayor, Maynard Jackson, highlighted the importance of building trust through performance. They concluded,

> [T]he election of a black mayor does not appear to have precipitated a decline in trust among whites, but seems to have forestalled such

a decline among blacks. Additionally, the leadership image projected by Atlanta's first black mayor seems to have decreased perceptions of preferential treatment among both blacks and whites. Yet perceptions of the personal characteristics of public officials are consistently more closely associated with trust in government than are perceptions of government policy. These findings, then, support the view that leaders may be significant agents of opinion change simply as a result of the images they project.[4]

In each case, the office of mayor works best when the incumbent is trusted and when his or her constituency believes he or she is governing in the public's best interest. Mayors are expected to be accountable and trustworthy, and those who are deemed untrustworthy find it difficult to lead their city.[5] This does not mean that a mayor must be beyond reproach. This chapter examines the critical role the media plays in the social construction of mayoral trust and mayoral accountability.

Robert Bies defines a social account as "a verbal strategy employed by a person to minimize the apparent severity of the predicament or convince the audience that the wrongful act is not a fair representation of what the actor is 'really like' as a person."[6] In periods of diminishing public images, social accounting is critical to image repairing. To govern effectively, one must explain oneself effectively.

Mayors face a variety of image-threatening decisions, some of which may temporarily upset their image and others that may permanently undermine it. In order to prevent the latter, mayors seek to impose their interpretations on events. Successful mayors fashion "constituency-specific" messages to propitiate acceptance of their interpretations of events. This requires rhetorical skills that will resonate with the audience's views about their political reality. Accordingly, a mayor must understand the fears and aspirations of his/her constituents. A mayor must also understand and meet their needs, therefore communication is essential. In other words, the audience members must be able to translate some of their personal reality into the mayor's characterization of events.

A questioning and otherwise critical media can complicate the communication process between a mayor and his or her constituencies. A nonsupportive media can obscure or skew a mayor's messages. Indeed, Jeffrey Pressman has argued, media support is a precondition for mayoral leadership.[7] Providing the public with information about mayors and city politics accords reporters a considerable opportunity to dominate the discourse. According to Robert Stalling, "by selecting events to report, by interviewing and quoting experts who interpret those events, and by assembling and distributing news products, news organizations create an important component of public discourse referred to as media discourse."[8] As the principal intermediary and storyteller between mayors and the public, print reporters have become an important part of the imaging-making and governing process.

This book contends that Dinkins faced a series of political events that were amenable to a variety of interpretations. If Dinkins could not impose his interpretation on such events, he could lose the framing contest and watch the media or other actors impose alternative explanations, as an enterprising reporter can seize the opportunity to challenge the mayor's framing of events. Because mayoral images are defined by events, evaluation of performance is an ongoing process. Some events are more important than others, and a mayor can often count on the public's remembering the most recent set of events.

The goal of any political evaluation is to hold the mayor accountable. In a democratic society, all elected officials must account for the disposition of the tasks for which they have taken responsibility. If they make mistakes or bad decisions, do not explain them cogently, or fail to compensate for their actions, then the public has good grounds for withdrawal of support and removal from office. The media plays a critical role in determining the extent to which a mayor can effectively present his interpretation of events. When and if the mayor's interpretation can be folded into ongoing discourse between the media and their audience, then everything runs smoothly. When the mayor's views do not fit, then problems arise. Some problems require the mayor to invest time and energy offsetting the media's negative interpretation. In most cases, the social construction of a mayoral image relies upon elements of his or her personality and themes from the political culture. On occasion, an unanticipated crisis can throw the whole process off track. To understand how these constructions are made, a brief review of social constructionism is necessary. Andrew Valls summarizes the basic premise of social constructionism.

> The fundamental premise . . . is that reality is constructed and comes to be shared in language. On this view, language does not merely reflect the world, but actively structures our vision of reality through the categories it contains and the meaning it embodies. Perception and thought do not take place independent of language, but are structured by the language used. This active role of language in shaping reality implies that meanings are not fixed, but are subject to change and variation. This variation is found at many levels, from cross-cultural differences in views of the world, to small changes in meaning within a particular context through re-description of a situation.[9]

Race relations is one of those areas where language is crucial. One ambiguous or confusing statement can generate an unending controversy. A poor choice of words can undermine an individual's image and create a situation where apologies are not accepted. Accordingly, the language that a journalist brings to an event does matter. It is not as if the journalist can divorce him or herself from the event and point to the actors as the culprits. Journalists become a part of the event. Nowhere is that more apparent than during the media coverage of spontaneous racial conflicts.

During times of racial disturbance and natural catastrophe, decision makers rely on the competency of subordinates to address the crisis. Each person with responsibilities is assumed to be competent to do his or her job. Researchers Sue Newell and Jacky Swan suggest that competence trust is critical within networks of responsibilities. They state,

> Competence trust is based on an attitude of respect for the abilities of the trustee to complete their share of the job at hand. The truster feels that they can rely on the trustee. The development of this form of trust thus relies on perceiving the competencies of the other partners. . . . This type of trust can therefore develop much more swiftly but it is also likely to be more fragile since, if the trustee does not quickly demonstrate the competencies that were expected, the trust breaks down.[10]

In politics all trust relations are fragile ones that can be easily developed and just as easily broken. Elected officials, particularly mayors, are rarely accorded unconditional trust.[11] They have to build trust and maintain it during crises. Racial disturbances and disputes are particularly difficult because of their potential to escalate quickly. Two racial incidents show how prior social constructions shaped the public view of each situation. The Crown Heights and Red Apple (sometimes called the "Church Street" situation) incidents in Brooklyn demonstrated how reporters framed events in ways that challenged the mayor.

Blacks, Koreans, and the Red Apple Boycott

New York City is a political environment replete with socially isolated ethnic groups. Groups usually come into contact with each other in the commercial realm, and retail sales has been the theater for this encounter. This is how the Chinese met whites and how Jews met blacks. Usually the buyer and seller enjoy a limited and peaceful transaction, but occasionally there is a misunderstanding that leads to conflict. An incident may start as an individual conflict then can escalate into a confrontation of imagined and real competing group interests. When that happens, a simple misunderstanding or conflict can take on a larger meaning and may require a third party (presumably a neutral individual) to resolve it.

The premise of Dinkins' campaign was that the city needed a mayor who could resolve these recurrent racial/ethnic conflicts. The Bensonhurst and Howard Beach incidents had convinced many New Yorkers that the racial situation was getting out of hand. Dinkins portrayed himself as the man who could create a political environment in which such conflicts would be unlikely and as a man who could anticipate these racial incidents before they occurred and resolve them once they did.

The test of Mayor David N. Dinkins' ability as a healer and a conciliator came early in his administration. Ironically, the test was not a black/white conflict but a black/Korean one. The conflict started at Bong Jae Jang's Red Apple (produce store) in Flatbush, Brooklyn. On January 18, 1990, shortly after Dinkins' inauguration, Giselaine Fetissainte, a Haitian immigrant, accused Mr. Jang and two of his employees of assaulting her for allegedly stealing. They denied the charge and claimed that she became angry when asked to pay for some produce.[12]

There are different versions of what happened, but the incident sparked a boycott by Flatbush residents against Red Apple, led by Sonny Carson, the activist whose connection to the Dinkins campaign had been so controversial.[13] The boycott also included the Korean-owned grocery store across the street, Church Fruits. The protesters wanted the employees of Red Apple to be arrested and prosecuted for assault. Furthermore, protesters also wanted both stores (since the owners were closely tied to each other) to be put out of business.

Howard Kurtz of the *Washington Post* claimed that the incident was a minor altercation that escalated. Then, strangely, the *New York Post* began covering the boycott and openly criticized the rest of the press for ignoring it. Slowly, the other news organizations descended on Church Avenue. The television crews showed up, giving Carson and his followers an audience of thousands. Suddenly Dinkins was being denounced for failing to end the boycott. But the minicams never pulled back far enough to show that there were only a few dozen chanting protestors or that some blacks in the neighborhood thought the boycott was unfair.[14]

A week after the boycott started, Brooklyn police commanders attempted to arrange a meeting with community leaders, which turned out to be unproductive. The protesters and their leaders were not ready to negotiate. The New York City Commission on Human Rights tried "quiet diplomacy" with the groups involved,[15] but this also failed, creating pressure for direct involvement by Mayor Dinkins.

The leader of the Korean Produce Association (KPA), Bo Young Jung, stated in a March 1 letter to the mayor, "[Y]ou are looked upon by many New Yorkers as a healer. It was under [that] premise that you were elected to lead our great city. What better opportunity to show your strength and ability."[16] This invoking of Dinkins' preferred image was designed to force the mayor to get more personally involved in settling the dispute. Meanwhile, the media stayed with its racial conflict frame.

Claire Kim's *Bitter Fruit* outlines the press narrative as a scapegoating story in which the blacks lashed out against the hard-working and thrifty Koreans whose success shows up black failures.[17] She saw the enfolding of events as an example of racial ordering, locating Asians above blacks but below whites. For her, the Red Apple coverage used all of the stereotypes of Asian Americans to undermine the community control aspirations of blacks. A Russell Baker article in the *Christian Science Monitor* supported this view. He observed, "Of 200,000 businesses in New York City, Latinos own a whopping 40,000. Combined, other recent immigrant groups—chiefly Koreans, Arabs and Indians—own about 18,000 businesses. By the year 2000, that should top 30,000. Blacks, however, may own as few as 1,500 enterprises."[18] The article goes on to discuss high unemployment among blacks and their lack of capital to start businesses but the point was that blacks were clearly at the bottom rung, lagging behind immigrants.

Kim asserted that "the quieting of Black collective action against Korean merchants ritualistically affirms the American racial order: Blacks are confirmed as the pathological underclass; Korean merchants as the hardworking model minority; Whites as neutral enforcers of colorblind justice."[19] However when one adds a black mayor who aspires to be a deracialized one, perceptions become more complicated.

The presence of Robert (Sonny) Carson, one of the leaders of the boycott, made settling the controversy even more difficult. Carson had been identified by the media as a former Dinkins campaign worker and convicted kidnapper. They quoted him as declaring himself "anti-white."[20] Carson wanted to frame the boycott as a racial affront to the black community and to expand the boycott to other boroughs. Carson was a self-styled grassroots leader who had been banished from the Dinkins campaign and was now resurfacing in this crisis. He reportedly said, "In the future, there'll be funerals, not boycotts."[21] A May 8, 1990, *New York Times* editorial reported this statement and attacked the so-called quiet negotiation tactics used by Deputy Mayor Bill Lynch. The editorial ended, "[I]s that all Mayor Dinkins can think of to do? Racist fires are alight."[22] The mayor's office tried to get more involved in April after Deputy Mayor Bill Lynch met with Korean leaders. The mayor's office formed a "fact-finding" committee of Koreans and blacks to continue to engage in "quiet negotiations." But progress was slow, and the situation was not helped by comments made by former mayor Ed Koch in a *New*

York Post column. The essence of the Koch comments was that civic and religious leaders should condemn racist remarks by demonstrators. He reasoned that black leaders should be on the side of the storeowners. Koch wrote, "If I were mayor and I was dealing with an extortionist . . . a thug like Sonny Carson . . . I would go out there myself and I'd cross the picket line and I would buy all the fruits and vegetables Gracie Mansion needed for that week."[23] Dinkins responded that he would "go today or tomorrow if I thought a trip at this time would solve the problem."[24] Sam Roberts responded with an article in the *New York Times* entitled "Which Mayor Knows Best on the Boycott?" Roberts agreed that bigots, regardless of color, should be denounced. Although Roberts criticized Koch as a less than ideal messenger, he pointed out that "at some point, [Dinkins'] failed diplomacy may be perceived as weakness."[25]

Dinkins criticized protesters, saying "[A] large mountain has been made out of a very small molehill," and argued that the protesters' demands "'have expanded this beyond reasonableness." More important, he sought to explain why he did not criticize Sonny Carson by name.

> I have in the past spoken out, sometimes pretty much alone, and sometimes expressed myself in disagreement with those who are African-American. Now it seems to me that either I have some credibility [on such subjects] or I don't. Now people can disagree with my methods and that's fine; I think that's fair game. People can say, "Dave, if you were to go out there and stand on your head, it would resolve it. If you just simply went out there and said please go home, it would resolve it." They're entitled to those views. But I don't want to exacerbate the situation. I don't want those who are there picketing to figure that I'm telling them that they have no right to express dissent.[26]

On May 10, 1990, State Supreme Court Justice Gerald Held urged both sides to negotiate and ordered the boycotters to stay at least fifty feet from each of the two grocery stores. However, police officials appealed and refused to enforce the fifty foot rule because it would force demonstrators to gather across the street in front of a church, which might cause more violent confrontations.[27] Judge Held also said that he "regrets the failure of the

Mayor of the City of New York to personally intervene and use the prestige of his office and his high standing in the community to convince the parties to bring a suitable end to this dispute."[28] In reaction to the judge's criticism, Dinkins said, "One, I'm pleased that the judge feels that I have a high standing in the community. That's nice. Two, to personally intervene, without knowing what his definition of personal intervention is, let me hasten to say that I have personally intervened. . . . If the time comes when it appears that would be helpful, I'm certainly happy to do."[29] Dinkins had said earlier that "whether it would be resolved by me appearing on Church Avenue is highly problematical. I may have an adverse impact."[30]

The city also argued that police officers were not obligated to enforce court orders in civil cases between private parties and that they had exclusive discretion in law enforcement. On June 26, 1990, the judge held that the police department was not enforcing his order and ordered them to do so. Eight months later, a unanimous appellate court ruled that the NYPD had to enforce the court order.

Mayor Dinkins claimed that the parties were close to settling the dispute but that the media attention had exacerbated the demonstration. The mayor's initial tactic was to use quiet negotiations" with his aides.[31] Some reporters expected more from the mayor because of his reputation of building a "gorgeous mosaic" and because he was New York's first black mayor. Sales and Bush concluded that in practice the mosaic "meant a continuation of clubhouse loyalties and an unwarranted concern for the sensibilities and agendas of powerful white ethnics, while muting the demands of his poor Black and Latino supporters."[32] Mayor Dinkins said, "Some people think that confrontation is superior to conciliation. I disagree."[33] Some considered the mayor's use of conciliation an excuse for inaction. Others believed that Dinkins was working hard, only behind the scenes.

In response to accusations of not being vocal enough, Dinkins gave a speech on May 11, 1990, at city hall saying, "We gather tonight, here at the seat of the government, to reaffirm our commitment, to renew our mission and to reassert a simple truth: All of us want to live our lives in peace and dignity, free to walk any street and shop in any store, at any time, in any neighborhood, without fear of force or violence."[34] In his speech, Dinkins

Mayor David Dinkins, daily press briefing, City Hall.
© Copyright Fred W. McDarrah.

also said he would stiffen penalties for hate, foster tolerance, teach merchants about consumer rights, and help small businesses. Dinkins also said "My administration will never lead by dividing. At the same time, and in the same spirit, we will never allow any group or any person to turn to violence . . . no matter how legitimate their anger or frustration may be."[35] The *New York Times* editorial praised the speech and read it as evidence of "leadership."[36] Reverend Al Sharpton felt the speech did not address the substantive issues: "It was more like a James Brown record—talk loud and saying nothing."[37]

Todd Purdum's first article in the *New York Times* about the speech proved important for its references. The article stated that speechwriter John Siegel drafted the Dinkins speech, with contributions from Andrew Cuomo, Norman Steisel, and Ken Sunshine. Four television networks carried the twenty-five-minute speech live, and it got the biggest applause when the mayor asked the media to join in the effort to foster race tolerance. Purdum also suggested that the speech was delivered in anticipation of the Bensonhurst case verdict. The article also quoted Dinkins as saying,

This was a crime committed by individuals. All of Bensonhurst did not commit this crime; rather, a few people committed this crime in Bensonhurst. We must absolutely, categorically reject the notion of group guilt. We abhor those who preach it, and we must be mindful that predictions of violence and anger tend to self-fulfilling. But whatever the outcome, as we have so many times over so many years, we must repress our rage, channel our energies and come together to make this tragedy transforming."[38]

Purdum characterized the speech as "Surreal Air at City Hall" and quoted the "we must repress our rage" statement. Dinkins condemned the boycott of Red Apple and asserted, "I oppose any boycott based on race."[39] He called the boycott inappropriate and offered himself as a mediator, even though earlier, he had stated that picketing was "as American as apple pie."[40] Purdum ended the article with supporting quotes from politicians, blacks, and labor leaders. Reporter Jim Sleeper offered another view of Dinkins' behavior.

What accounted for Dinkins's bizarre indulgence of Carson and his crowd? The answer may lie, paradoxically, in the mayor's determination to transcend the politics of race without transcending the politics of the establishment. It may be that his embrace of the permanent government's fiscal-crisis politics left him feeling morally vulnerable to the militants' attack.[41]

Korean Americans realized the lesson of the boycott, which was their relative marginality in New York politics. Just giving money to political campaigns was not enough. The boycott caused them to attempt to mobilize for integration into city politics. Thousands of Koreans rallied outside city hall in September 1990, promoting racial harmony. The crowd booed during comments made by Mayor Dinkins, expressing disappointment at how he had handled the boycott. A couple of days after the rally, Dinkins showed his support for the merchants by going to the Red Apple and purchasing ten dollars worth of fruits and vegetables. This gesture may have taken the oxygen out of the protest, but it did little to rebuild Dinkins' image as a mediator.

The boycott did spur Korean Americans to form the Korean American Civil Rights Committee of the Korean Association of

New York. The association intends to advocate for Korean American interests in matters related to business, discrimination, and voter registration.

Sung Soo Kim, a Korean American business owner and the founder of the Korean American Small Business Service Center in New York said, "Before they can have a real impact on the city's political scene and begin electing their own candidates, Korean-Americans will have to broaden the issues that concern them."[42] On May 30, 1990, Bong Jae Jang announced that he was selling his store. Dinkins expressed his regrets. In August *Times* reporter Don Terry's article questioned Dinkins' quiet tactics, and he observed, "[T]hat dispute appears no closer to resolution today than when it started in January, 1990. The city's inability to settle the Church Avenue conflict has been politically embarrassing for Mr. Dinkins. And as it has dragged on his critics have attacked what they say is his slow and overly cautious style."[43] A committee of black and Korean leaders appointed by Dinkins criticized Brooklyn District Attorney Charles Hynes for moving too slowly in prosecuting in the Church Avenue case.

Two years after the incident, the U.S. Civil Rights Commission issued a report criticizing the way Mayor Dinkins had handled the boycott. The report constituted a small section of the federal agency's two hundred-page study of increasing acts of bigotry against Asian Americans throughout the United States. Mayor Dinkins stated in 1992 that "the reason Church Avenue did not get resolved more quickly is because there were people involved who did not want it to be resolved."[44] Dinkins' response to the report was that it was Monday morning quarterbacking.

Given time, the mayor's office did help improve communication between blacks and Koreans. In 1990 and 1991, the city helped organize goodwill missions to Korea. Only black ministers attended the first mission, but the second included a cross-section of community leaders. The missions also led to the formation of the Ethnic Committee for Racial Harmony and Outreach (ECHO), which promotes dialogue between blacks and Koreans. The boycott also mobilized and politicized the Korean community in New York. Pyong Min, a sociology professor at Queens College, suggested, "This is the beginning. They [Koreans] do it, and in the future they will stand upon that collective mobilization more often."[45] Min, along with others, formed the Korean American Civil Rights Committee of the Korean Association of New York.

The Red Apple incident allowed the media to challenge Dinkins' public image as a mediator in race-related disputes. The media saw the case as a test of Dinkins' mediating skills. Larry Simonberg, a press aide to former mayor Ed Koch, wrote a full-page opinion, admonishing Dinkins not to oversimplify racial tensions. Simonberg asserted that Dinkins' statement during the campaign that "the climate is set at City Hall" led people to believe that he could wipe out deep-seated causes of racism. "You are now expected by many to be able to end the boycott of Korean stores in Flatbush by simple fiat. The lack of progress damaged your reputation as a conciliator." Simonberg concluded by saying, "Don't play weatherman again and don't let others issue such a glib forecast."[46]

The Red Apple conflict faded away once the protest limits were enforced. The sight of a black mayor crossing the picket line to buy produce robbed the protesters of some of their racial claims. Because Korean Americans were a small minority group with no political organization, the Red Apple incident represented an opportunity for Dinkins to show his conciliatory skills. If he stumbled in this situation, then a future racial incident could sink his image. The incident in Crown Heights did precisely that, triggering the unraveling of Dinkins's prevailing image.

The Crown Heights Incident

August 19, 1991, will live (to borrow a phrase) in infamy. At about 8:21 P.M., a car driven by a Hassidic man of the Lubavitcher sect, named Yosef Lifsh, ran a red light to keep up with his colleagues, swerved, and jumped a curb, striking two black children, Gavin and Angela Cato, cousins. Gavin was killed, and Angela was badly injured. Lifsh was part of a three-car convoy led by an unmarked police vehicle that served as an escort for the Grand Rebbe Menachem Schneerson, the leader of the Lubavitchers. Police escorts for the rabbi had been policy since the Koch administration. There were two immediate questions. Did the car actually run a red light? Second, did the Hatzolah ambulance ignore the injured children and instead take the Hassidic driver away?

Rumors spread that a Hatzolah ambulance immediately tended to the slightly injured men, instead of the grievously injured black children. A crowd began shouting, "Kill the Jew." Police Commissioner Lee Brown told the press that the Hatzolah ambulance and the emergency service ambulance arrived "almost simultaneously." Police asked the Hatzolah ambulance to remove the driver of the station wagon "in the interest of preserving the peace as the crowd was becoming increasingly violent" [47] Dinkins stated that the rumor that the Hatzoloh paramedics had ignored the children was false. He stated, "That's just inaccurate because I spoke to the father [of the one of the children]."[48]

In the evening, blacks assembled and pelted Jewish homes with stones in the Crown Heights section of Brooklyn. Later that same evening, at approximately 11:15 P.M., a gang that allegedly included Lemrick Nelson Jr., stabbed Yankel Rosenbaum, an Australian seminarian student. (Nelson was later tried for the murder.) *Daily News* reporter Dean Chang described police as saying that a "separate band of black youths roamed Crown Heights seeking revenge."[49] Pictures of blacks turning over a car and rampaging teens supported a *New York Post* article by Mike McAlary. McAlary tried to be evenhanded in the assignment of blame for the riots, and he cited name calling by both sides. In addition, McAlary worked the names of Sonny Carson and Leonard Jeffries into his piece: "They have their audience, and moved a hateful group to the street."[50] Dinkins' slow reaction to the chain of events seemed to have made the situation worse and further damaged his image.

Just as he did during the Red Apple incident, he assigned the management of the crisis to Bill Lynch. Lynch established a city hall presence in Public School 167, where he attempted to bring together Jewish and black leaders to defuse the situation. A two and half hour meeting with sixty leaders and police brought about no progress. There was too much anger and too many rumors, to come up with a resolution.

Dinkins went to the Crown Heights neighborhood and also visited the victim in Kings County Hospital, where Dinkins recalled, "I visited him (Rosenbaum) in the hospital. We were told he would be OK, but the doctors overlooked the wound, even though the ambulance attendant had indicated to them that there was more than one wound. So he died."[51] The death of Rosenbaum further eroded the competence trust in Dinkins, not the hospital.

The mayor became embroiled in an endless explanatory and social accounting fiasco as reporters kept seeking information. Dinkins was quoted as saying "There's an awful lot to suggest he [Lifsh] did go through the red light. We are in a tense situation. We've had a tragedy. There are at least two deaths, and it's painful. We ought not to have further injury."[52] Dinkins attempted to frame the incident as an accident, the subtext of which was that the lead police car was responsible. He suggested that the police cruiser heading the convoy was responsible for keeping it together. Dinkins then proffered a story: "Part of what I did in the Marine Corps was to drive convoys. What you do if folks get ahead, you've got two options. The one behind to speed up or the one ahead to recognize it and slow down."[53] Obviously, this framing did not work.

For reporters and the general public, the Jewish-black tension story offered more possibilities. The rioting lasted for several hours. Blacks appeared at the Lubavitcher synagogue chanting, "No Justice, no peace." One headline stated, "Anarchy Grips Crown Heights."[54] Jimmy Breslin, a famous columnist for the *Daily News*, was actually pulled out of a cab and robbed.

During the disturbance, Dinkins used a bullhorn, declaring, "I care about you. I care about you very desperately. I too want justice, and we will get justice but we will not get it with violence." However, Dinkins was greeted with boos and soon became a target for flying rocks and bottles as he tried to enter a building on President Street. Dinkins recalled, "I was personally in Crown Heights ducking bricks and bottles. Not the behavior of someone that needed to be sheltered and hiding some damn where."[55] Again Dinkins had put his skill as a race mediator on the line and was attacked. Dinkins claimed the media distorted the situation.

> The media stated that Crown Heights was a situation of rioting for several days culminating in the death of Yankel Rosenbaum. That is just factually inaccurate. . . . The accusation was that I had held back the cops. That was not true. [And] that we [his office] had

permitted blacks to attack Jews. That was not true. In fact, for several days we had rioting, [but] not continuously every minute of every day.[56]

Bill Lynch also agreed that the press "missed the boat on the coverage. You would think there [were] weeks of riots. It only happened two days."[57] Yet many people criticized Mayor Dinkins' handling of the black rioters. The press asked Dinkins why he did not take a walking tour, like John Lindsay had done in the 1960s to calm down Harlem. Dinkins did walk through the neighborhood to no avail. Dinkins' press secretary, Leland Jones, responded by saying "We'll be very careful in choosing when the mayor goes there."[58] Bill Lynch commented, "We're not sitting here wringing our hands. It's not easy where there are people who are hell-bent on confrontation, the thing is quote-unquote out of control."[59] Dinkins' "increase the peace" theme was ignored, and he was called a traitor. The angry crowd shouted, "The Mayor is not safe."[60] It was reported that Dinkins aborted the walking tour.

The press began framing this most recent disturbance as the result of a long-standing and growing tension between the two groups. *Daily News* reporter Don Singleton asserted that from the outside the neighborhood looked like a melting pot, but "bubbling just beneath the surface is a long history of conflicts and uneasiness between the area's Hasidic Jews and blacks."[61]

By the next day this incident had pushed a story about a coup in Russia and President Mikhail Gorbachev off the front page. The *Daily News* headline read "Streets of Rage."[62] However, each group saw the latest incident differently. The Hasidic Jews saw it as a continuation of anti-Semitic persecution. For some of them, the riots evoked memories of Czarist pogroms and the Nazi Holocaust. They saw their black neighbors as intent upon destroying them as Jews. Blacks saw the incident as yet another example of the arrogance of the Lubavitcher community. They also feared the violence caused by the Hasidic vigilante patrols.

Bob Herbert, a respected black reporter, wrote a *Daily News* column entitled "Blood Feud in Crown Heights,"[63] in which he compared the Hasidim to the Hatfields and the African Americans to the McCoys. "The African Americans felt that the Hasidim got preferential treatment. The Hasidim get too much in the way of police protection. Some African Americans believe their own community is being denied police protection that could be directed at drug dealers."[64] The editorial page of the *Daily News* called for a permanent neighborhood council to facilitate communication between the two groups.[65]

The events surrounding the Crown Heights incident may remain in dispute. The week after the riot and before the trial of Lemrick Nelson was a time of hyperbolic rhetoric. Earl Campbell wrote an op-ed editorial entitled "The Fire Next Time Is Alarmingly Near." Taking off on James Baldwin's book, Campbell characterized the black youths as being out of control with no values. "That was the future Dinkins got a glimpse of when he visited Crown Heights. He was staring at the fire next time. Not even a police bodyguard will protect him from those flames."[66]

Dinkins' problem worsened as Reverend Al Sharpton and Alton Maddox, an activist lawyer, organized a march in the Crown Heights neighborhood days after the incident. Maddox threatened to make a citizen arrest of Lifsh, the driver of the car that hit the Cato children. Dinkins tried to dissuade people from marching but failed, and the march went on the next day. An estimated two thousand people peacefully participated in the demonstration. Dinkins himself participated and laid a wreath at Gavin Cato's and Yankel Rosenbaum's death sites.

In a related effort to repair his image, Dinkins gave a speech at the First Baptist Church of Crown Heights to a mainly black audience. The speech went well. Dinkins asserted, "Today our mosaic stands badly incomplete. Now two of its brightest and most vibrant tiles have been lost. We can never bring Gavin and Yankel back, but we can let their deaths serve as the catalyst for meaningful changes that will prevent other deaths."[67] The next day reporters felt it newsworthy to report that Dinkins had decided to watch the US Open in Flushing Meadow in Corona Park.[68] It was a small article, but it brought the readers back to the tennis theme. In addition, the *Daily News* editorial stated that the crisis was not over yet.[69]

Several months later a jury found Nelson not guilty, prompting a *New York Post* editorial writer, Eric Breindel, to use the pogrom references to attack the way the Dinkins administration handled the incident and the trial. In a *Wall Street Journal* editorial Eric Breindel claimed that the Nelson supporters signaled "a

sense of triumph," and the police were relieved at Nelson's acquittal. He even suggested that Dinkins tried to mislead the
public by focusing on the few city hall marchers with signs that
said: "Wanted for Murder: David Dinkins." This rambling essay
successfully managed to link the Korean boycott, black anti-
Semitism, and white middle-class flight. For the latter he
claimed that the "message was plain: New York no longer welcomes them."[70]

New Yorker writer David Remnick called the language used by
the Hassidic community and its supporters consistent with the
Hassidic sect's apocalyptic culture and "tragically overblown rhetoric." Remnick asked, "Who really believes David Dinkins is a 'Jew
hater'? Is New York in 1992 really worse than Nazi Germany?"[71]

Orthodox Jews created the Jewish Action Alliance to stop
anti-Semitism. They attacked a WLIB radio talk show because
the callers were using anti-Jewish rhetoric. They also attacked
Lee Brown, Dinkins' police commissioner. Some people believed
that Dinkins had ordered the police to go easy on rioters. Several
journalists made a connection between Dinkins' handling of
Crown Heights and his chances for reelection.

The Crown Heights incident incorporated all the features that
a reporter needed: a race riot that could be compared to others,
a city with its first black mayor, and a conflict between Jews and
blacks that left the police baffled. Every move that Dinkins made
could be analyzed and second-guessed. Dinkins was aware of
this situation when he told a reporter that "for me, it's a lose-
lose." You're damned if you do and damned if you don't."[72] Dinkins outlined the dilemma he was in:

> Some would like to say, I hereby denounce Sonny Carson, I hereby
> denounce Al Sharpton, I hereby denounce Al Maddox and on and on.
> And the same reporters put to me the question. "But are you doing
> all you can Mr. Mayor. Are you reaching out to these people? Have
> you sought them out"? And I would like to know, do you want me to
> denounce them just before or just after I sit down and meet them.[73]

This exchange with a reporter is both interesting and revealing.
Dinkins saw himself in a bind with reporters and actors in the
Crown Heights incident. The entire Crown Heights incident was

particularly frustrating for the mayor because it involved two groups that he had been closely associated with, blacks and Jews. Now both groups were criticizing his handling of the situation.

Village Voice reporter Wayne Barrett suggested that Dinkins passed up an opportunity to transcend the death of Yankel Rosenbaum and the Lemrick Nelson acquittal. Barrett suggested that Dinkins should have been more enthusiastic about a federal probe and waited too long to support the Justice Department investigation. Barrett also said that the statement issued by Dinkins after the Nelson verdict read "an endorsement for the flawed outcome."[74] Barrett suggested that the "mayor could've found language that put perceptible distance between himself and the acquittal, questioning it without denouncing it; he has instead very consciously chosen not to—an invitation to anger."[75] Furthermore, Barrett felt the mayor should have appointed a commission that would have preempted the state's investigation, which he predicted would be critical of the mayor's reactions to the events in Crown Heights.

Governor Mario Cuomo created a special investigation group to review the accusations and allegations surrounding Crown Heights. It was a classic example of state encroachment into a local matter. Richard Girgente, state director of the Criminal Division, held hearings and produced a two-volume report. The four-hundred-page Girgente report did not directly criticize the mayor's handling of the situation, but the implications were clear. However, the report did target the breakdown in the police leadership hierarchy.

On July 21, 1993, the *New York Times* headlined "Crown Heights Study Finds Dinkins and Police at Fault in Letting Unrest Escalate."[76] Dinkins' press secretary, Leland Jones recalled, "We got no advance copy of it as it was being handed in. We got no tip from Cuomo."[77] The lack of a strong rebuttal to the report further racialized the incident and supported the press' characterization of Mayor Dinkins as "incompetent." In response to the report, *New York Amsterdam News* reporter Herb Boyd published an article entitled "Crown Heights Report Exonerates Mayor Dinkins from Any Blame."[78] An editorial written by Wilbert Tatum, the publisher, attacked the report as being biased toward the Jews and redundant.

Following the lead of a White press corps in New York City that had already made it clear that Blacks were the culprits in this drama and that they would brook no interference with their interpretations and conclusions about events, no matter what information to the contrary was unearthed and presented by those who would share credit or blame for the "Report."[79]

For some in the press, Dinkins' performance in the Crown Heights incident was further evidence that his skills as a racial conciliator were lacking. The report also pointed out that a "leadership vacuum existed at the highest level."[80] This was clearly a reference to Commissioner Brown and Mayor Dinkins. The effort to repair Dinkins' image was doomed. Bill Lynch was correct when he stated that "this is not like Bensonhurst."[81] In the end, this situation got out of control.

The Rosenbaum murder turned the issue into more of a racial one, and the Lemrick Nelson acquittal brought outrage from the Jewish community. Dinkins' speech in response was entitled "Reason, Respect and Reconciliation in New York," and apparently he thought it to be an act of "social accounting" that would calm down the situation. The *New York Amsterdam News* ran the entire speech as an op-ed page. During the speech the mayor returned to his themes of reason and racial unity, while asserting that he was not responsible for the verdict in the Nelson case.

> Astonishingly, a few people even sought to blame me for the verdict reached by the jury in the Rosenbaum case, even though I had nothing to do with his prosecution or his defense. The mayor has nothing to do with the operation of any district attorney's office.
>
> . . . I'm proud to be accountable because the buck does stop here at this desk. That's why there are more cops on the beat. That's why crime is down across the board for the first time in almost 40 years.
>
> . . . I have never nor will I ever pander or cater to one group to gain an advantage over another group.
>
> . . . Unlike some before me, I will never use code words and subliminal message to create mistrust between groups.
>
> . . . If we trust in the truth and in each other, then the cement that binds our gorgeous mosaic will remain seamless and strong.[82]

The language in his speech was intended to repair his public image. However, emotions in the city were too high, and the speech could not reframe the events or make an effective "social accounting." *Village Voice* reporter Michael Tomasky compared Dinkins' speech to the inadequate response President George H. W. Bush made after the Rodney King verdict. Tomasky thought the mayor was not reacting from the "gut."[83] Part of the public's problem was Dinkins' communication skills. Senior *Times* reporter Sam Roberts talked about his frustration when covering stories involving Dinkins. Roberts asserted, "He spoke in this baroque grammar. If you listen to his locution, he had these convoluted sentences. He didn't speak declarative sentences. He never said anything directly. He had this ambiguous way of talking."[84] In other words, Dinkins lacked the communicative skill necessary to reframe the Crown Heights incident.

Media coverage of the Crown Heights affair contributed to the transformation of an accident and a murder into a black-Jewish conflict. The framing is critical to understanding this particular incident. Carol Conaway, a political scientist, faulted the reporters as framing the Crown Heights event as purely a racial incident. She suggested that if the media divided the participants into African American, Caribbean America, and Lubavitch Hasidim, the incident would have been properly framed as a conflict of both culture and religion. In other words, the reporters were framing it as a racial incident, while the antagonists characterized it as an anti-Semitic incident. Conaway saw the incident in anti-Semitic terms.[85] She argued that all incidents between whites and blacks do not have to be framed as racial ones.

The reaction of the Crown Heights incident would not go away. In November 1992, the *CBS Evening News* reported that tensions remained in Crown Heights even after Dinkins had denounced race baiting in Crown Heights. The *Evening News* showed a clip of Dinkins commenting, "I will never, nor will I ever, tolerate or sanction or allow disorder or lawlessness by any group toward any other. By the same token, I cannot allow a quiet riot of words and epithets to poison our citizenry."[86] CBS reporter Jacqueline Adams, an African American, responded, "Not surprisingly, few in Crown Heights were impressed." The clip also showed a statement by a resident of Crown Heights. Adams ended the piece with "hyperbole and high drama are the norm in this city. What mayor could permanently put an end to racism? Still, unless David Dinkins came up with a bold program to bridge the city's racial divide, many activists believe the tension between blacks and Jews would only worsen."[87] This news clip haunted Dinkins' remaining tenure in office and was used as a major factor in the mayor's reelection bid. In fact, it would take many years to close the book on this incident, since the Nelson case dragged on.

As is the case in most racial disturbances, rumors played a big role in making the settling of the incident more difficult and lengthy. It has been said that nothing is more inviting to the media than one racial group claiming another racial group has done something wrong. Proclaiming innocence is a natural refuge for both races. The question is why? Is it a matter of framing or a difference in crisis management style?

Summary

Were the Red Apple and Crown Heights incidents caused by a failure to communicate? Or was the latter a case of a middle-aged politician trying to persuade and assuage West Indian youths? Were the so-called black nationalists leading the disturbance, or were they appropriating it to get attention from the city leaders and the media? There were certainly a lot of things said and done, none of which seem to improve the situation. There were a variety of messages in both incidents. As mayor, Dinkins needed to trump all other attempts to frame the circumstances surrounding the events and to impose his own criteria for success. In other words he had to communicate well at every opportunity that became available. This was particularly true in the media. In many instances what one says is enhanced by how well one uses language. Scardino, Dinkins' first secretary, agreed with Sam Roberts' assessment of Dinkins' speaking style.

> He [Dinkins] didn't have the best media presence in the world. Because he unfortunately spoke in a sort of rich nineteenth-century Victorian stylized manner in which he used what he thought and what he had grown up with, was appropriate and proper English. But he used a lot of "One would have thought

that" kind of expression[s] instead of being more blunt and direct the way Ed Koch had been. It was very difficult to convey what he was trying to communicate.

He was often misinterpreted by the media because he was not particularly comfortable with television. His language and the depth of his feeling and philosophy was a very very poor match for TV and for tabloid journalism. I think as a result he was not able [to] communicate himself and his message [as] effectively as others might have.[88]

The two racially charged incidents illustrate how important it is for the mayor to win the contest of words that follow controversial events. If one has difficulty communicating, then one runs the risk of being misunderstood and possibly alienating both groups. In each situation, quick and coherent social accounting is critical to assuage the combatants. Social accounting should attempt to convert a faulty anticipatory response into a socially acceptable or corrective one.

On the national television show *McNeil/Lehrer Newshour* Dinkins complimented the media coverage of his speech on race regarding the Red Apple or Flatbush incident.

Let me say the media has been enormously helpful and the electronics media, especially by giving the time they gave on Friday. We had no way of knowing whether on not that would be forthcoming. The decision to do the speech on Friday was made on Thursday. We figured we could do it on WNYC, the public radio, the city station, and hopefully some of the other stations would carry some of it. We assumed the print people would cover it, but there's a big difference to have that live on television in prime time, so that was very useful.[89]

A supportive press can help convince the public that the mayor did the right thing or that he intended to do the right thing. If the mayor is to be successful in selling his version of political events, he needs a sympathetic press. Dinkins did not get that support, and his prevailing image collapsed.

The Red Apple and Crown Heights incidents had a profound effect on the image of Mayor Dinkins. The Red Apple boycott was a classical framing struggle, with Carson's group defining it as a discourse about racial injustice, the Korean merchants and activists vying to make it a conflict between a hard-working minority (Koreans), and its nonworking, whining minority counterparts (blacks), and Mayor Dinkins attempting to contain the conflict as the simple boycott of a retailer. Russell Baker's article in the *Christian Science Monitor* supported this construction.[90] The media accepted some of the merchants' framing but also were intrigued by Dinkins' bungling of what they viewed as his first opportunity to show off his mediating skills.

Political Scientist Claire Kim interpreted the overall Red Apple conflict in a broader context. After interviews with several participants, she concluded that the conflict was part of a racial ordering that pitted minorities against each other in the service of preserving the notion of race. She believed that the colorblind rhetoric was a tool to promote cleavages between the two groups and reproduce the racial order.

There is no evidence that Dinkins saw the conflicts in those complicated terms. He contended that these were easily solved disputes that were confounded by the personalities involved and seemed comfortable with assigning his expert Bill Lynch to manage them.[91] Dinkins' Red Apple speech reflected his views. Despite Todd Purdum's point that the speech was written by his white aides, the speech followed Dinkins' overall civility themes. The text included the sentence "I opposed any boycott based on race," but few picked up on the meaning of that statement. The black response might have been, "I can't believe he said that." The entire Montgomery Bus Boycott was based on race. Was the mayor engaging in some "gratuitous endearing"?

Dinkins claims that initially he thought the Red Apple incident was similar to two others involving a Korean merchant and a black consumer in Queens and Brooklyn, respectively. They were solved in two days. He asserted, "[They were] solved by the same people who worked on the Red Apple, Bill Lynch. In the Red Apple, we had some folks that did not want it to be resolved. Some blacks that didn't want it resolved."[92]

There is no evidence that Dinkins had any relationship with the Korean community prior to the incident. Furthermore, the Korean community had little, if any, political profile. Dinkins should have been able to impose his frame on events. Why? Claire Kim, a political scientist, concluded,

Of course, as both the direct beneficiary of and supposed antidote to the resurgent Black Power movement, David Dinkins was between a rock and a hard place from the moment he was elected. The ambiguity of his "gorgeous mosaic" campaign promise had helped him to walk the tightwire between Black and White expectations into Gracie Mansion. But the Red Apple Boycott brought his balancing act to an abrupt halt.[93]

The attempt at quiet negotiations failed, and Dinkins was forced to renounce his "erstwhile allies in the name of colorblindness."[94] Apparently, he did not regard it as a test of his image. He could not have predicted this would become a national story. The CBS program *48 Hours* did a story about the boycott with reporter Bernard Goldberg interviewing people on the picket line. Goldberg wanted to know what the mayor thought of blacks calling Koreans "yellow monkeys." He asked the mayor if he had been called a "nigger"? The mayor admitted that he had been called the "n" word "many times" but responded philosophically to name calling, "I don't think that you ought to burn the flag, but our Supreme Courts of the United States says that's freedom of speech. Because I don't agree with what one says doesn't mean that I don't feel they have a right to say it."[95] This was vintage Dinkins, making what he thought was an appropriate response but losing the opportunity to use the moment.

In retrospect Dinkins' decision to delegate the mediation was a mistake. Although Bill Lynch tried to take the blame for the Red Apple debacle, he acknowledged that the incident tarnished the mayor's image. He stated, "Yes my soul is bleeding, for the Mayor and this trying year. When there's a mistake or a miscue, if we don't do something, it ends up at his [Dinkins] feet."[96]

Dinkins' image as a race mediator was seriously damaged by the Red Apple incident, and his prevailing image was so weak that he had little to draw on in the Crown Heights incident. Even the small *News/India-Times* carried an editorial that scolded the Indian community for its silence on these two events and condemned Dinkins' reaction to them.[97] The events of Crown Heights took on a life of their own, and there was limited room for intuitive intervention. Although not a national issue in the beginning, Benjamin Hooks of the NAACP said, "Crown Heights is being politicized by the minute. And that means that the chance that this will spill over grows by the minute."[98] Simmering turf issues between blacks and Jews complicated Dinkins' strategy of careful reengineering of civility. Although Dinkins had been a member of the black Israel support group and had traveled to Israel, his preferred self-image of even-handedness was forgotten during the Crown Heights controversy. Dinkins misread and seriously misjudged the volatility of the situation. In our interview Dinkins repeated his statement about his obituary. "When my obituary is written, they already have a boilerplate. In the first paragraph, it will read the first black mayor of New York City and [then] the next sentence will be about Crown Heights."[99]

Dinkins' prediction may come true, but he also admitted that the Girgenti report was "one of the reasons we did not succeed."[100] Martin called the Girgenti report "a scathing portrait of ineptitude and miscommunication" on the part of the Dinkins administration. The choice of "ineptitude"[101] reminded readers of the subtext of Dinkins' competence as a crisis manager. This report was released at the beginning of the Dinkins campaign for reelection. Wayne Barrett of the *Village Voice* suggested that Governor Cuomo was the ghostwriter for the report.

> The best evidence of the governor's hand is what is not in the generally thorough report. As telling as much of what Girgenti found out about the mayor's miscalculations and indecisiveness is, not all of the hard facts surrounding these horrid events were allowed to fall where they might. The Cuomo Report is so focused on David Dinkins as to resemble another assassination analysis. Substituting a single culprit theory for a single-bullet fantasy.[102]

An alternative explanation for the reactions to the incident was that Dinkins tried to be neutral in the story. If Dinkins had supported the Jewish version of the story, he would have lost all credibility in the black community. If he had supported the black version, he would lose credibility in the Jewish community. Dinkins may have thought that race neutrality was a possible safe compromise, but it was not. Obviously some blacks did not realize the unfolding of events would result in destroying Dinkins' image. For many of them, the situation offered an opportunity to vent their anger toward vigilantism and arrogance on the part of the Hasidim. It is doubtful whether the curious history of the Lubavitchers was known.

However, it was assumed that Dinkins had some credit with the Jews. He did, but only with the liberal and secular Jewish activist community. Unlike Koch, who provided police protection for Rebbe, Dinkins had never "tipped his hat" to the Hasidic community. Reporters played up the racial angle and framed the story as a lack of leadership, which led to a misjudgment by the mayor. Former *New York Times* reporter Paul Delaney reminds us that editors tell the reporter how to pitch the story. "The editor's ideas are planted. You start from a premise. The Mayor blew it on Crown Heights. Tell us how he blew it."[103] David Dinkins seemed to be aware of this when he observed,

> Too often reporters will make a judgment what they think is the case and then they will try to substantiate it. As opposed to analyzing, investigating and reporting their findings. They start out with a conclusion and try to justify it. I can't say all reporters do that. I think too many do. I think we are afraid to complain because to complain is to blame the media for your failures. That is a lot of damn nonsense. It really is.[104]

The Crown Heights event was a turning point in the history of the Dinkins administration. During the crisis Dinkins attempted to take a centralist position, which won him little support from either group. Dinkins even made an appeal to the Council of Jewish Federation General Assembly. He asserted that "no member of the African-American community has spoken out more forcefully and consistently against anti-Semitism than I."[105] Yet his "social accounting" of the situation was not effective. The *Amsterdam News* blamed Rabbi Avi Weiss for the escalation of the Crown Heights situation and printed letters from Jews supporting Dinkins.[106] David Saperstein wrote an editorial in the *Jewish Telegraphic Agency* that asserted,

> Media coverage, obsessively fixed on the negative aspects of our relationship, feeds the suspicion and mistrust, which often plague our communities. When, in the very early days of the Crown Heights crisis, black leaders first gathered at City Hall to condemn

the violence, there was virtually no coverage—leaving Jews to feel a sense of betrayal by the silence of old friends. When, recently, Rev. Calvin Butts and Rev. Jesse Jackson raised serious concerns about the justice system in the wake of Lemrick Nelson's acquittal, there was no virtually no coverage."[107]

Although the New York Board of Rabbis joined the African American clergy in commending Dinkins for his effort to bring peace to the areas, doubts about the mayor's actions were carried over into the reelection campaign. Crown Heights became a subtext of Dinkins' 1993 reelection bid.

Herbert Daughtry, a minister and a social activist in Brooklyn, suggested that the Crown Heights incident caused the defeat of Dinkins.

> The 1993 defeat of David Dinkins for a second term as New York's first Black mayor was one devastating result of the Crown Heights episode. Dinkins was blamed for the continued violence and rioting in Crown Heights, specifically for not applying greater police action. In fact, the Mayor was accused of restraining the police in the community.
>
> There were two coded messages communicated in the accusation: *Dinkins deliberately handcuffed the police because the rioters were Black. Therefore, this Black mayor must be removed.*
>
> One of the reasons Dinkins had been elected in the first place was to keep Blacks in check; to ease the racial tensions which had reached the boiling point . . . If Dinkins could not keep things cool, he was of no use.[108]

There is no denying that race played a role in the reporting on Crown Heights. Mike McAlary saw it as Dinkins' story. Just as Bensonhurst had sealed Koch's fate, Crown Heights would do the same for Dinkins. McAlary asserted that Yusuf Hawkin and the "divisive politicians hit the payment dead together" and concluded, "In that moment, with the city's racial sensibilities hot to the touch, a peacemaker dared to stand up. David Dinkins declared himself the candidate of healing. He was elected with the sole charge of soothing racial passions. No one hired him to fill potholes. He was hired, instead, to fill a vacuum of sensitivity."[109]

CHAPTER SIX

WHO RUNS THE CITY?

UNION BOSSES OR THE MAYOR?

Who runs New York? Is it the mayor, businesspersons, interest groups, or political parties? Political scientists want to believe it is the mayor. Others see businesspersons as the less visible part of a governing elite. Few people would answer that the political parties run the city. New York still has political clubs, but there is no overall boss of the city. Political parties are not defunct but rather have been downgraded in importance. This explains why some New Yorkers believe that the leaders of the public employee unions control the politics of New York. Presidents of labor unions have replaced the old Tammany Hall bosses. Steven Malanga asserts that "instead of party bosses running City Hall, it is the powerful public employee unions and community non-profit groups living off the government money that control the city's political process and political agenda. Yes, these groups are aligned with the Democratic party, but they are not subservient to the party; the party is their instrument, a tool of their convenience."[1] Regardless of Dinkins' response to questions of who runs New York, the public elected him to "run" it.

Of course, no mayor can run a city alone. The public employee union leaders know it, and that is why they volunteer to co-manage. Since the Wagner mayoralty union leaders have grown in influence. If the union leaders had their way, the politics of the city would be about whether the labor contracts are being faithfully administered. Their political power flows out of their involvement in city elections and their skillful use of the media. Dinkins' dilemma of having to balance the budget and feed the union was not unique. Touted as a friend of labor and supported by union leaders since he came to city hall, the norm of reciprocity hovered over Dinkins' first months in office.

There is a great deal of difference between the textbook and real-life versions of the relationship between the mayor and public employee unions. The textbook version suggests bargaining, making concessions, and outlining expenditures be done in an orderly manner. The real-life version involves more theatrics and chaos. Labor leaders use the media to pressure the mayor and his negotiating team. Colorful language, demonstrations, and job actions (such as not showing up for work, refusing to do work, and sabotage of work procedures) are not uncommon. The media, in turn, focuses on the street antics of union leaders and the mayor's reaction. In this chaos, the mayor's image is fair game. As union leaders are fond of saying, it is not personal; it is all about the money. Since personnel costs can take up to 80 percent of the billon-dollar budget, labor negotiation is a serious business. This is why the media uses its coverage and editorial pages to test, second-guess, and criticize the relevant parties.

Every newly elected mayor steps into an ongoing stream of claims and counterclaims about wages and benefits. Like a river, one cannot step in the same current again. Economic conditions change, contracts run out, and union leadership changes. What one's predecessor settled may become unsettled, and every bargaining session is a new game. Wilbur Rich observed,

> Labor leaders view themselves as brokers. Brokers are agents or middlemen who represent sellers and products. They are authorized by the sellers to negotiate prices and deliver agreements. The higher the price that the broker obtains, the more he or she is seen as competent and tough by those selling. The sellers in this case are the city workers, and the product is their labor. Selling labor is a most difficult task, one that requires the finest thespian skills. The typical municipal labor leader has to sell his product to the city, the negotiated agreement to the membership, and the salary increments to the public.[2]

Mayors often see themselves as accountants. They are expected to protect the fiscal solvency of the city. The worst fate a mayor can endure is to have the city go bankrupt during his or her watch. Union leaders do not want to bankrupt the city, but rather they want the mayor to stretch financial resources so their members can get pay and benefit increases. If that means borrowing against anticipatory revenue and shifting around service and maintenance cost, then so be it. This is a natural position for union leaders to take since they are judged by the contract they negotiate.

The public expects the mayor to stand up to the unions and not roll over in the bargaining process. At contract time, a tough mayoral image is critical. Most mayoral candidates promise to be tough at the bargaining table, but once elected a new mayor faces a different set of pressures. In many cases public employees are among the newly elected mayor's strongest supporters. They expect a quid pro quo. The public expects a mayor to be the sentinel in a struggle against what the media may describe as exorbitant demands of the employee unions. Accordingly, the management styles of the mayor and his labor team can set the tone for good labor relations in the city.

Mayors and the Management Image

Mayors of New York reveal their managerial styles by organizing their government with certain themes and with the people they select to assist them. After the fiscal crisis of 1975, the city of New York wanted a mayor who they believed would be free of the old ways of managing the city, getting along, and going along with the unions. They voted in Edward Koch, a congressman with a progressive reputation, but who espoused a trendy neoconservative message on crime and a tough bargaining stand toward unions. Koch took a tough guy approach to managing the city and wanted everyone to know he was in charge. The New York City voters expected Koch to manage the city by keeping the unions in line. However, after Koch the voters elected, for reasons we discussed earlier, a less confrontational and more conciliatory mayor. They liked Dinkins because he exuded civility. Besides, Dinkins was the union's choice for mayor. The political message was that Dinkins would usher in a new era of management and union cooperation.

Despite differences in mayoral styles, there has been a tendency for each mayor to nurture a managerial image. The theme "We are management and they are labor" had gripped the minds of those in city hall and the city bureaucrats. Post-Beame mayors believed that the excesses of the union contacts were one of the paramount causes of the 1975 fiscal crisis. As a result, there has been a trend toward centralizing labor negotiations. Labor negotiations and budgeting functions are at the heart of the inner circle of the mayor's office.

In most unionized American cities, public employees play a major role in the city's politics. Unlike other interest groups, unions are largely responsible for organizing and mobilizing city voters, for exerting pressures on city council members to block mayoral actions, and for organizing the various viewpoints concerning the direction of city policies.[3] Accordingly, the leadership of public employee unions receives a lot of publicity at contract time and when their members are involved in a controversy. It is not unusual for a mayor to be challenged or to be called names by a union leader. The press reports these stories as if the mayor's job depends on how they react and whether they "stand up" to the demands of union leaders for salary increases. "Standing up" means defending the city's interest against a well-organized group. Mayors rarely want to be perceived as being in the pockets of union leaders. Union leaders are aware of this and often manipulate the situation to make the mayor look like a difficult person to negotiate with.

Collective Bargaining in Theory and Practice

In the public labor relations literature, the bargaining process puts management and labor on opposite sides of the table, each trying to present their case. The theory is that each is under pressure to settle. The union leaders use information picketing and job actions to compel the mayor or chief negotiator to compromise.[4] The mayor uses budget information and the media to force concessions. Each has a bottom line that must be honored, and each must sell a contract after an agreement. The union leader has to convince members that this is all he or she could get, and the mayor has to convince the public he or she has made a good deal.

Raymond Horton's review of New York City labor relations during the Lindsay and Wagner eras, led him to conclude that employee unions have "two bites at the political apple in New York City."[5] One bite comes with collective bargaining, and continuous nibbles are also taken during the day-to-day political process. Although the union's ultimate weapon, the strike, is seldom used, union leaders have learned to feed the media quotable sound bites that make for good story lines. There is always the ubiquitous threat of a job action, even though there are no funds to pay for wage increases for union members. The public does not like to be inconvenienced with job actions by city unions, nor does the public like to see a mayor pushed around by a union leader. When the latter happens, the mayor's image suffers. Most mayors are aware of this possibility and begin campaigning with pledges to be tough with and stand up to unions. After the 1989 election, union leaders took turns receiving credit for Dinkins' victory, but this was not the case for his successors.

Dinkins' First October

In New York, the mayor's relationship with the unions is very public because of the city's history of budget problems and the militancy of the city's unions. New York City is home to some the largest public employee unions as well as some of the most famous labor leaders. The big membership unions include the United Federation of Teachers, District Council 37 of the American Federation of State, County, and Municipal Employees (AFSCME), and the International Brotherhood of Teamsters local. Together these unions represent 237,000 of the 300,000 city workers in New York. Stanley Hill, executive director of the District 37 American Federation of State, County, and Municipal Employees (AFSCME) led a union of 140,000 employees. Sandra Feldman, protégé of Albert Shanker, head of the United Federation of Teachers, led a union of 106,000 members, of which 55,000 were teachers. Elected in 1986 and reelected in 1991, she and her union played an important role in the Dinkins campaign. Although Barry Feinstein, president of Teamster Local 237 (22,000); Phil Caruso, head of the Patrolman's Benevolent

Association (20,000); and James Boyle, of the Uniformed Fire-fighters Association (8,700) controlled smaller membership, they also knew how to demand attention and use their political clout. Not just labor politicians, these individuals are city politicians in their own right, who serve as role models for their national unions. For example, reporter Alessandra Stanley wrote an article carefully describing low-key Stanley Hill and contrasting him with his predecessors and peers. Accordingly, when union leaders negotiated, it was as much for their members as for their standing and reputation in the labor movement.[6]

Unions are on what Llwellyn Touliman calls a "treasure hunt."[7] Because they have long been active in Democratic politics and played a critical role in Dinkins' election campaign, the public assumed that unions would be among Dinkins' staunchest supporters.

After getting Dinkins elected, leaders thought it was time for payback in respect to contracts. In the first budget the unions were allotted an increase of 1.5 percent. Eric Schmertz, the mayor's chief negotiator, supported a generous settlement with the teachers' unions.[8] Schmertz assured the unions that the Dinkins administration would take a different approach to labor negotiation. He asserted, "Mayor Dinkins believes in a different approach from the Koch approach, which was antagonistic, disrespectful, confrontational and abrasive."[9] Again, Dinkins' image as a conciliator was invoked to reassure the public.

Upon assuming office in 1990, Dinkins faced a $1 billion budget gap and a nagging recession.[10] In his mayoral campaign, Dinkins had pledged to hire thousands of new police officers to fight city crime. How could he simultaneously be fiscally responsible, put more police on the streets, and reward his supporters in the unions? Before the negotiation season started, the *New York Times* editorial pages cited rumors that Dinkins was prepared to offer nonuniformed workers a 5 percent raise and opined that "the Dinkins administration is moving toward a settlement with the city unions that New York simply cannot afford."[11] With a huge budget gap and uncertain revenues, the city would have difficulty paying for a raise. The editorial called for the mayor and the unions to moderate their demands. It then reminded the readers that Dinkins had won the election with strong union support. Despite calls for restraint from several sources, Dinkins faced an October negotiation season that would haunt him for the rest of his tenure.

Like mayors before him, Dinkins was threatened with a teachers' strike. Such a strike could be very disruptive and could undermine the new mayor's hopes of winning over individuals who doubted his abilities. The leadership of the teachers' union, particularly Sandra Feldman, the president of the United Federation of Teachers (UFT), had been among Dinkins' strongest supporters in the campaign. Since over one hundred thousand employees were part of this union, a third of the workforce, a strike was the last thing Dinkins needed. Under this pressure the mayor settled with the teachers, first with a 5.5 percent wage increase for one year, which also contained school-based management provisions. This $236 million settlement would be funded by state aid and revenues from the teachers' pension fund.

Even after the settlement with the UFT, the fiscal situation did not improve. There were budget gaps for the current year, and more were on the horizon for next year. Since the city was in a recession, the logical strategy for the Dinkins administration was to engage in "cut-back management." The administration had to do what Joe Klein calls the "root-canal work of politics," layoff and service reductions.[12] The mayor's budget director recommended fifteen thousand layoffs and cut the capital budget by $2.3 billion over the next three years. Joe Klein concluded, "Dinkins, who wafted into the mayoralty on a gust of union support and then dedicated his administration to the city's children, found himself having to choose between the two. He chose chaos, and the union."[13]

The chaos began as the 132 other union leaders wanted to pattern their contracts after the teachers' negotiations. Earlier, Barry Feinstein, president of the Teamsters, had announced, "David is the boss, and the boss is my enemy. The reality is he is management and we are labor. Now we are married, and we may be estranged and fighting as many couples do, but we're not getting divorced."[14] Feinstein called the teachers' settlement "terrific." He stated, "We're ready to justify the 5.5% hike and feel we can be creative and imaginative in outlining ways to finance the package."[15] Dinkins, who took a personal role in the negotiation, announced that "this is a triumph of collective bargaining."[16] (A photograph was published in the *Daily News* with Dinkins, Feld-man, and Fernandez smiling with their thumbs up.)

Dinkins' labor strategy came under intense scrutiny, as he got further into the October negotiation season. An article in the *New York Times* claimed that Dinkins had taken action that committed the city to a costly round of wage settlements.[17] It criticized the planned tax proposal to include a twenty-five-cent surcharge on lottery tickets and $200 million in higher property taxes. More important, the article cited the prediction of the mayor's critics. Raymond D. Horton of the Citizen's Budget Commission, a business-sponsored watchdog group, and Felix Rohatyn, chairman of the Municipal Assistance Corporation (MAC), a state agency, expressed reservations about the lack of a coherent strategy to meet the city's fiscal crisis. Horton told the *Daily News*, "This is the worst collective bargaining settlement since before the fiscal crisis. One would think the city is rolling in money. This must be very embarrassing for city hall."[18] Roha-tyn questioned the settlement, suggesting it "could be terribly destructive and an extraordinary big risk."[19] Rohatyn's concerns about the budget were particularly noteworthy because the press had lauded him as a hero in the 1975 New York fiscal cri-sis. The *New York Times* editorial page echoed concerns about the teachers' contract. Union leaders continued to hail the teachers' settlement. The Dinkins style of avoiding confrontation with unions began to emerge. In *New York* magazine, Joe Klein asserted that style had become the least of Dinkins' worries. "The analogies have moved from Gentleman Jimmy Walker, the playboy mayor of the Roaring Twenties, to Abe Beame, the fall guy of the 1975 fiscal crisis."[20]

In the *New York Review of Books,* an article by Felix Rohatyn charged that the city was "buried by grinding pressures" and called for reactivation of the Financial Control Board. Rohatyn also wanted to defer all wage increases from two to four years. The mayor's press secretary, Albert Scardino, responded by say-ing that the "mayor viewed any reactivation as an attempt by Rohatyn to become the fiscal mayor of New York."[21] At a press stakeout during Dinkins' visit to Capitol Hill, Dinkins was asked if he would seek MAC assistance. He responded, "The people elected me Mayor of our city, and I'm doing that job. I'm governing. And the difficult fiscal times we face are not the fault of this administration or the fashion in which we are administering things."22 Dinkins stated that he would accept assistance but not yield control. He concluded, "There is nothing the Control Board can do that we can't do."

Joe Klein opined, "The FCB became the only thing that mattered to David Dinkins. It would be the white establishment's ultimate victory. It would be proof that the city's first black mayor was incompetent. Words like emasculation and coup and impeachment were tossed about."23 Deputy Mayor Lynch threatened to resign if the FCB was reactivated. "I thought it was a direct slap at Mayor Dinkins. Once you take over the budget, the mayor is just a figurehead."24 Klein claimed that Dinkins was obsessed with that possibility, and it now took precedence over all his other goals.

Three days after the teachers' settlement, veteran reporter Sam Roberts wrote an article raising questions about Dinkins' leadership and his decision-making skills in the teachers' deal. Within the span of a week, the mayor had announced a plan to expand the police force, implement a selective hiring freeze, and possibly layoff 15,000 people. Dinkins proposed an increase in the payroll tax to pay for new police. This proposal that had to be approved by the state legislature was quickly dismissed by the governor's office. Roberts suggested, "He (Dinkins) seems to be leading the city in several directions at once."25 Dinkins' announcements about layoffs caught some labor leaders by surprise and "accused him of betrayal for not forewarning or consulting them."26 Stanley Hill, a black man who was a major player in Dinkins' campaign and the head of the giant public employee union, District Council 37 (140,000 members), asserted this in an interview:

He [Dinkins] lied to the members of this union. The Mayor stated at the first negotiating session that he would not balance the budget on the backs of the workers. He gave us his word, and now that's exactly what he is doing. It is a totally disgusting and disgraceful display of an administration that really undermines the workers who helped put him into office. My executive board is so angry. They have been betrayed by this mayor."27

Barry Feinstein, the Teamster leader, also denounced Mayor Dinkins and asserted, "The Mayor, today, has spit in the face of every city employee. The Mayor has declared war on the unions, and we are prepared to fight the war in every battlefield."[28] Although the mayor apologized for not consulting union leaders, the damage was done. Dinkins had been called a liar by an ally and one of the most powerful black men in the city. Whites who had voted against Dinkins were receiving messages that confirmed their doubts. The mayor was receiving criticism from a variety of sources that condemned him for giving mixed signals and not being on top of his job. Feinstein rallied his Teamsters to authorize a strike against the city in case the scheduled negotiations did not go well. The media coverage returned to the teachers' deal and uncovered the fact that there were disagreements within the administration about the advisability of such a settlement. The point of this discourse was to tell the public that Dinkins was warned of possible fiscal problems.[29] The recurrent theme of the media's discourse was now set: Dinkins was getting conflicting advice, and he was making the wrong choices. The message was that Dinkins was a confused man leading a confused administration. Joe Klein's headline was "Is He up to It?" He asked, "Is this guy overmatched? Does he have the strength and intelligence to meet the crisis?"[30] After one of Dinkins' aides denied that Dinkins' administration was one of "confusion, the press began interviewing other aides and reporting negative comments without identifying their source."[31]

Meanwhile, the city's budget situation grew worse.[32] In an attempt to dramatize the city's fiscal problems, Dinkins announced a personal pay cut of 5 percent and the same for seven hundred senior administrators and staff of various politicians. The move was designed to save $4.5 million. Other elected officials agreed to take a pay cut, but the gesture backfired politically. Feinstein retorted, "This is an administration out of control."[33] Nevertheless, it became clear to Dinkins that he could not approve a 5.5 percent increase to remaining unions without layoffs. Veteran reporter Todd Purdum declared that Dinkins "finds himself the target of labor's scorn and disbelief." He quoted Stanley Hill as saying, "It is a crisis of confidence in the Mayor."[34] Barry Feinstein asserted that the negotiations with the city were "the most inept in my 33 years of dealing with government."[35] One labor leader stated, "They created a politically impossible situation for their labor friends to help them in. If there weren't a teacher contract, the other unions would be out there trying to help Dinkins. Now he's created a series of almost caged animals. They've got no way out."[36] In November, five thousand union members gathered at city hall to protest the deadlocked labor negotiations. David Dinkins, once a friend of labor, was now under siege by his friends (or what Joe Klein called the "pinochle club"),[37] who refused to believe him and did not accept any of his promises.

After October, Dinkins continued to encounter labor controversies during his tenure. Despite settling with District 37 and the Teamsters with a 5 percent pay increase and replacing his labor commissioner, Dinkins' image of untrustworthiness continued. Sam Roberts concluded,

> The ouster of Schmertz, and the agonized balancing of interests that led to that decision, also underscored what may be the most important single fact about David Dinkins: he is a minority mayor. The word resonates on several levels. First, Dinkins is acutely conscious of his precarious position as a black man being judged by a white society. Second, he won the slimmest of victories in the mayoral election by carefully holding together a coalition of minority interests. Finally, he governs a city of minorities, seeking to apportion its diminishing resources equitably among the myriad racial and ethnic group that form the New York he likes to call a "gorgeous mosaic."[38]

At the reopening of contract talks, Dinkins was quoted as saying, "These [labor leaders] are my friends and I don't want to see them hurt."[39] Despite his best efforts to appease labor leaders, they continued to criticize the mayor. In 1991, this criticism was restrained after the mayor and the union leaders signed a $232.8 million, fifteen-month union agreement with Teamsters Local 237 and District Council 37, with a 4.5 percent wage hike. Barry Feinstein and Stanley Hill stood next to Dinkins in a news conference and were given a chance to retract their comments that Dinkins was running a chaotic government. Hill refused and stated, "[T]hat's negotiable."[40] The city was in a recession with a $500 million budget gap. The agreement was not well received, but *Newsday* praised Dinkins' "pragmatism."[41] Klein saw it as feeding the "dinosaurs."[42]

Negotiating in a Fiscal Crisis

The following years were no better for the Dinkins team. A 1991 *New York Times* editorial charged that Dinkins had "no labor policy."[43] It called for trimming the city's workforce of 243,000 and leaving the negotiations to the professionals. In 1992 the Dinkins team negotiated a one-year, 3.5 percent raise deal with the city's 6,800-member Uniformed Sanitation Association. The Citizen Budget Commission (CBC), a public interest group, criticized the agreement because it did not address productivity issues. Raymond Horton asserted, "If the goal was to get a full day's work for a full day's pay, then the city failed miserably in these negotiations."[44] Although Dinkins had negotiated agreement with the Transit Patrolmen Benevolent Association (PBA), the UFT and the AFSCME, he still had to negotiate with firefighters. In September 1992, the city negotiated a 4.5 percent raise for thirty months with the UFA only to have it rejected by members in November.

The fiscal crisis dragged on, and Dinkins decided to unveil a sweeping package called "Reform and Renaissance." The proposal would freeze his salary and that of all additional city workers for one year. A hiring freeze would be instituted with a pledge to shrink his staff. The proposal also called for a reduction of public employees from over 300,000 to 236,000. The state was asked to take over Medicaid. City commissioners were asked to give up their chauffeurs. In a television address, Dinkins declared that, "the changes we begin to institute as a city will, over time, be the most dramatic ever conceived or executed in any American city,"[45] and he offered to listen to ordinary New Yorkers about his proposal for a special office.

Subsequently union leaders' disillusionment with Dinkins was not helped when the city reported a $455 million surplus in the 1992 budget. Stanley Hill held up printed signs at the Labor Day parade to express his frustration with negotiations. "We are going to have about 600 signs that deal with our lack of collective bargaining agreement. . . . Mister Mayor, where is our contract?"[46]

Again, union leaders denounced the mayor for misleading them on the city's fiscal situation and demanded a share of the surplus. Dinkins was forced to enter into an election year without reaching an accord with teachers, police officers, and firefighters. The unions also took out newspaper advertisements attacking Mayor Dinkins. Although the mayor did reach an accord with the teachers' union, it was not enough. He had managed to alienate the United Federation of Teachers (UFT), his closest ally, and thus lose its endorsement for reelection.

At the beginning of 1993 a *New York Times* editorial lambasted Dinkins and his labor policy, saying it was a missed opportunity to restructure the work force and bring about other reforms. It questioned Dinkins' "non-confrontational nature and his politics"[47] and compared him to Philadelphia's mayor, Edward Rendell, who in their opinion had taken on the unions.

Summary

Dinkins' first October provides further evidence of how a simple story can be shaped into a discourse about competency and managerial skills. Dinkins' problems became a major theme for his opponent Rudy Giuliani in the next mayoral campaign.[48] The social constructions of Dinkins as incompetent and even a villain of labor were taking root. Reporters did not have to recount the problems of the recession and the budget deficit; rather they focused on Dinkins' actions that undermined his credibility and trust with labor leaders and subsequently with the electorate. Scardino, Dinkins' press secretary, thought the media was particularly unfair to the mayor. "He got beaten over the head for giving them a 3% [pay raise] instead of being a very successful negotiator. Dinkins proved that he was a fiscal conservative. He got beaten over the head for giving money to his pals in the labor movement. It [the reporting] was just astonishing. . . . It was cheap journalism. It was grossly dishonest."[49]

The racial background of Mayor David Dinkins provided a good mooring from which to anchor the framing of the labor story. The political culture of New York politics is conflictual, and Dinkins was caught in the middle from the moment he took office. Paul Light called this first-year phenomenon the "cycle of decreasing influence."[50] Once a new mayor takes office he or she has a small window of opportunity in which to assert his or her policy initiative without losing it.

Consequently, Dinkins was constructed as an indecisive politician out of his depth. His competence was measured in terms of his ability to moderate the demands of unions in light of the budget exigencies. When his actions did not moderate those demands, and when too much conflict arose between the mayor and the union leaders, reporters were quick to portray Dinkins as losing the respect of his friends in the union, in addition to losing control over the collective bargaining process. The quick and unwise settlement with the teachers' union, coupled with the announcement of layoffs backed up the image of a "confused man" that reporters were constructing in the public mind. The result was that the press coverage of Dinkins reinforced and exaggerated stories about Dinkins' betrayal of his friends in labor. Even after Dinkins settled with the unions, the media was not satisfied. Joe Klein asserted,

> Dinkins is an odd combination of social-work liberal and clubhouse regular. The two are mutually reinforcing; both *thrive* on rules. His blind loyalty to these hidebound traditions has been his greatest failing in office. It was especially striking in his settlements with the teachers. Teamsters and municipal employees: neither the mayor nor his aides appear to have even considered asking for changes in the rules or for anything in return. There was no talk of flexibility, productivity or merit.[51]

First-term mayors such as Dinkins have to demonstrate competency and managerial skills if they hope to get reelected. Voters give them a trial period and then make a judgment. A key element in this judgment is the social construction of competence created by the local media. Dinkins was presented in a negative light and found it difficult to negotiate or overcome the mistakes made by his aides. He faced a difficult test constructed for him in pacifying the unions, and he was not successful. Here it is important to remember Dinkins' second admonition—remember the times. Dinkins was negotiating in a recession. Moreover, the city unions were willing to be good housekeepers as long as they received raises.

CHAPTER SEVEN

CRIME COVERAGE, MAYORAL IMAGES, AND SIGNALING

Stories about the crime rate in New York are not always newsworthy. Crime is a part of city life. However, the number of violent crimes can act as the most important marker of a mayoral tenure. Crime is one of the least understood phenomena in urban life and media discourse. Nothing can focus public attention on City Hall more acutely as in when the evening TV news conducts a live report involving a heinous crime scene, with suspects at large. In big cities, some people feel vulnerable to crime even if they live far away from a reported crime scene. The public wants to be reassured by the police, and even more important, by the mayor. Mayoral candidates are typically asked what they plan to do about crime. Aside from being psychologically reassuring, these proposals about crime (for example, more uniformed officers on the streets, more intelligence units or gang units) also tell us what type of safety compact a mayor plans to impose. A *safety compact* is a putative alliance or agreement that emerges among the mayor, the police department, and the media in the management of street crime. In this chapter I will examine the safety compact of Mayor Dinkins.

During the 1989 mayoral campaign, Dinkins would reiterate again and again, "I intend to be the toughest mayor on crime this city has ever seen." Nine months into his administration Dinkins declared "a war against fear." He asserted, "[W]e are here tonight to begin the long campaign to drive away the fear and crime that has caused it. We will flood the streets with an army of police officers . . . to capture the fear and lock it away."[1] A *USA Today* headline read, "NYC to flood streets with police."[2] To many this pledge had echoes of former Mayor Koch, who made his reputation as being tough on crime. New Yorkers, as Dinkins would discover, are very sensitive to what they perceive as a diminution of their personal safety on the streets. In New York City downtown living is valued and prestigious, and residents wanted reassurance that the city administration intended to be tough on crime.

There are basically two types of safety compacts: closed and open. Although both rely on symbolism to organize messages, the closed safety compact uses more paramilitary rhetoric, such as "flooding the street with uniformed police officers" or "law and order will be maintained at all costs." The message is that criminals will not be coddled, and police officers' hands will not be tied, therefore law-abiding citizens will be able to walk the streets without fear. The closed compact needs media support to make this "tough on criminals" message work.

An open safety compact seeks to convince the public that crime solving involves more than simply arresting criminals. It employs rhetoric that highlights the social pathology of urban life. Aside from community policing, the open regime is designed to protect the civil liberties of the accused and the public from rogue police officers. The message is that the rights of the accused will be respected, police officers will remain within the law, and preventive crime measures are possible. Law-abiding citizens will be able to walk the streets, but a garrison state is not necessary.

The election of a new mayor often presents problems in the coverage of crime incidents as well as relations with the police department and city hall. Newly elected mayors have tried to address these concerns by appointing a respected police officer as commissioner. In 1971, Harrell Rodger and George Taylor suggested that police officers are agents of regime legitimation, and as such they influence the public's perception of a regime's commitment to crime control.[3] If Rodger are Taylor are correct, then the hiring of a police commissioner acts as a signal to the public regarding the administration's intention in respect to crime control policy. The mayor's choice of a police commissioner alerts the police headquarters' staff to the preferred management approach and policing strategy of city hall. For officers on patrol the new commissioner policy preferences can affect how he does his job.

Police Commissioner as a Regime-Signaling Person

Increasingly commissioners of urban police departments have become notable political figures in their own right. Who can forget Eugene "Bull" Connor of Birmingham or Frank Rizzo of Philadelphia? These two men were closely connected with the urban racial unrest of the 1960s and 1970s. Some police commissioners have made their reputations before they entered into police work. When Carl Stokes was mayor of Cleveland, he appointed former air force general Benjamin O. Davis Jr. as police commissioner of Cleveland. His appointment was hailed as a coup by the mass media. However, Davis left the job after a conflict with Mayor Stokes over the type of bullets that would be issued to officers. Some legendary New York police commissioners who made their reputation outside the city include Theodore Roosevelt, William Bratton, and Lee Brown. Roosevelt became president of the United States. Lee Brown became United States drug czar and then mayor of Houston. Frank Rizzo served as the mayor of Philadelphia. Indeed, it is not unusual for a police chief to become a candidate for mayor. This explains why mayors are reluctant to appoint high-profile personalities who will absorb the majority of the credit for stopping crime (such as Giuliani and Bratton).

The media coverage has transformed the role of police commissioners. Indeed, the glamorizing of the job fits well into the symbolic aspects of police work. Policing requires myths and rituals: blue uniforms, badge, loaded weapons, titles (officer, detective, sheriff, marshall), language (suspects, undercover, sting operation), dramaturgy (pretending to be in control of a large bureaucracy), and the rituals associated with the death of an officer killed in the line of duty. Rituals and myths are necessary symbols to reinforce the monopoly of the force held by the state. The commissioner, as head of the department, becomes the trustee of the rituals and myths. The high visibility of commissioners conveys the illusion that crime fighting is a top priority of the police regime.

From Administrator to Folk Hero

Once considered the mayor's contact in the police department, the police commissioner has achieved a separate identity and respectability in crime fighting.[4] The upgrading and featuring of the commissioner is a new social construction and represents a change from the earlier portrayal of the commissioner as the nemesis of the street police. This construction is, in part, a by-product of the entertainment industry. In fact, during the 1990s there was a television show titled *The Commish.* The lead character was a man trying to hold the department together and satisfy his political bosses, while also having a personal life. Occasionally, the lead actor got involved in police work. In real life, newly appointed police commissioners are the subjects of biographical stories in local magazines and guests on talk shows. They visit schools and attend VIP functions. In effect, the police commissioner has become a folk hero. What is the source of this transformation, and what are the implications for this type of mayoral image making?

Part of the reason for the change in the image of the police commissioner is the effort to enlist all members of society in the fight against crime. Crime has penetrated many sectors of the urban community,[5] driving down the reputations of cities, making it difficult to attract new residents or industries to that city. When campaigning for office, a mayoral candidate needs to make a strong case for crime management. During the 1990s, advocates of community policing made increased crime management a major priority.

David Dinkins' Choice

One of the first appointments to the newly elected Dinkins administration was Lee Brown as police commissioner. Brown was a highly educated (PhD) and internationally known and respected African American police chief. He gained recognition for solving the 1980s Atlanta child murders. He had previously served as chief of the Houston Police Department. Yet, despite this impressive resume, many New York City police officers were not enthusiastic about his appointment.

Each community perceived David Dinkins' appointment of Lee Brown differently. It sent three basic symbolic messages. First, an outsider would have a fresh approach to the continuing image problems in the department. Second, the appointment suggested that police leadership would be more humane and be more minority friendly. Finally, this appointment suggested that Dinkins intended to involve himself in police administration. The African American and Latino communities were generally receptive to the Brown appointment. They assumed that a sympathetic person would finally provide much-needed supervision of the police department. Yet the white community was essentially indifferent. Would Brown be an officer's commissioner or a mayor's commissioner?

Because of Brown's close working relationship to Houston's former mayor, Kathy Whitmire, some officers were concerned that he might be a "mayor's chief." A mayor's chief usually sides with city hall in conflicts with police headquarters. Certainly, Brown was well aware of his outsider status and the provincialism of New Yorkers. Brown began his tenure by stating, "I have no mandate to remake the New York Police Department" but then proceeded to outline his "master plan." This plan would get more police officers and detectives out of precinct houses and onto the streets. He also wanted to reduce two-person patrol cars to one person. Moreover, the new commissioner was a strong advocate of community policing. He contended that he wanted the police to be a *part of* the community, rather than *apart from* the community. In an article written for *The Police Chief,* Brown stated, "We defined community policing as a working partnership between police and the law-abiding public to prevent crime, arrest offenders, find solutions to problems and enhance the quality of life."[6]

Community policing has always encountered resistance by traditionalists within the police department. The union and rank-and-file personnel may see it as putting more officers in harm's way or making them into social workers. Such personnel were also opposed to plans that civilianized some police office jobs. A week after he took office, he proposed changing the 911 response system in order to free police for more street duties.

Street Crime and Dinkins' Image

In New York City, the police force is approximately the size of three U.S. Army divisions (over thirty thousand officers). It has more equipment and weapons than some third world armies. Many police officers are highly educated and organized, yet the force is not a very efficient and effective crime fighting operation. Since the Knapp Commission, the New York police department had alternated between two paradigms: the *wayward* paradigm and the *thin blue line* paradigm. The wayward paradigm suggests that police officers are always amenable to corruption since they are underpaid despite the high risks they endure, and they face extraordinary temptations in their jobs. Wayward police officers are thought to be byproducts of a bureaucratic system. Such individuals are what Michael Lipsky calls "street-level bureaucrats,"[7] meaning that they make adjustments to survive and serve their clients.

The thin blue line paradigm holds that police officers are just ordinary people protecting the law-abiding citizens from criminals. This is the image promoted by unions and held by most police officers. For them, crime requires a paramilitary solution, better intelligence units, more armored vehicles, bullet-proof vests, and undercover personnel. The image of the police has been lionized in television drama programs such *NYPD Blue* and *New York Undercover*. It is the image of choice for many police officers and those individuals who want to feel safe within their communities.

Commissioner Brown came to New York at a time when controversy was brewing concerning the number of police needed. In 1990, there were approximately 25,971 police officers in the city. During his first days in office, Dinkins attempted to delay hiring 1,848 police recruits to save money. At the time there was an on-going debate about a merging of the regular police department with the transit police (subway officers). This debate over numbers became a political football. Five months into Dinkins' term, the *Jewish Press* called for his resignation, claiming that Dinkins was "not up to dealing with the criminal revolution that pervades New York City."[8]

Dinkins had run as a candidate who would be tough on crime, but once in office the media began challenging that preferred image. Joe Klein suggested that Dinkins' aides knew about the mayor's image problem early into the administration.

> A common thread runs through the self-analysis by Dinkins staffers: We wouldn't be in so much trouble if the image publishing operation were in better shape. There is probably a fair amount of

truth to this—someone might have told the mayor to take the subway rather than a helicopter to the tennis matches on the day after Brian Watkins, the tourist from Utah . . . was stabbed to death while trying to protect his family from robbers.[9]

A week after the subway murder of Brian Watkins and a rash of muggings and drive-by shootings in New York City, the *New York Post* ran a headline saying, "Dave, Do Something!"[10] The media discourse suggested that the city was indeed in a crime revolution. This headline raised questions about the mayor's control over the police, his overall competence, and his compassion for city residents.

Jerry Nachman of the *Post* wrote a column asking Dinkins to rescue the city from what he called the "Mad Max" nihilism many people feared New York had reached. Nachman attacked Dinkins' style as "measured and managerial" and asserted that the city was at war with crime. "And New Yorkers want Gen. George Patton or U.S. Marshal Dillon leading the charge. . . . It's time for a new style. Right now, scared and forlorn New Yorkers don't want a manager. They want a superman."[11] Philip Thompson concluded, "Dinkins lacked a political strategy for governance."[12] Klein also attacked Dinkins for lacking the "vision thing" "as the city has careened in despair."[13]

> During the mayoral campaign, aides had argued that as a liberal and a black, Dinkins had the political leverage to pull a "Nixon in China"—to say and do things that a white mayor could never get away with—and become "the toughest mayor on crime that New York has ever seen." Dinkins appropriated the line—it may well become his epitaph—but never seems to grasp the substance of what would be required to bring it off.[14]

Dinkins' Grand Plan

Responding to Nachman's piece, Dinkins defended his low-key style. In reference to a combative Ed Koch, he said, "I've seen styles that I don't wish to emulate."[15] Dinkins then declared a "war against fear" and asked his staff to prepare a plan. Dinkins appointed a commission headed by Milton Mollen, deputy mayor for public safety and Norman Steisel, first deputy mayor. The commission included Joseph Fernandez, Philip Michael, Harvey Robins, Allyn R. Sieflaff, Catherine M. Abate, Rose Washington, and Richard Murphy. Dinkins observed, "We did a survey of the police department—it hasn't been done in a quarter of a century. People were yelling and screaming about how many cops I should hire. We went about it in what proved to be the correct way, a logical way [and] . . . we determined we needed some more cops."[16]

The commission produced two reports entitled *Safe Streets, Safe City*. The first volume, 535 pages, was subtitled *An Omnibus Criminal Justice Program for the City of New York Summary*.[17] The overall theme was police officers and children. Dinkins' speech before the Patrol Benevolence Association (PBA) convention dealt with the proliferation of guns and observed that children were settling disputes with guns. "For young people today, guns are as easy to obtain as candy."[18]

The mayor recognized that more police would result in more arrests and the need for more support staff.[19] The Dinkins plan was a four-year proposal that cost $1.8 billion. It called for an additional 3,416 police officers above the 3,063 already in the budget. The cost of the plan would rise from $138 million in 1993 to $644 million in 1994. Half of the budget for additional police officers would come from payroll taxes, which was supposed to generate $339 million. A surcharge on the dollar lottery would generate another $120 million, and another $185 million would come from property tax increases. The plan for raising the money came under immediate attack. This controversy was due to the fact that since the revenue side of the plan needed to be enacted by state legislature, the governor and legislative leadership needed to be on board. However, aides did not consult with state officials.[20] Governor Cuomo stated that he had not been informed, state Senate majority leader Ralph Marino, Mel Miller, and the assembly speakers also claimed they had not been consulted. Yet the *Daily News* endorsed the plan in an editorial. It called the plan "A giant step in the right direction . . . this is a serious business. This is a hard-nosed attempt to make the streets of Kill City, USA safe again."[21] The editorial also challenged Dinkins' critics.

But opponents of the Dinkins-Brown Plan have some heavy responsibility of their own. Those who challenged its scope are ignoring the plainest of facts: New Yorkers are scared—with damned good reason. . . . In any case, Dinkins critics may be underestimating the fear—and will—of the people of New York. New Yorkers know that increased court capacity will hurt them smack in the pocketbook. They're willing to pay the price of safety.[22]

Dinkins slowly began to put his safety compact in place, and the idea of more police officers was well received by the public. A *New York Times* editorial endorsed the community-policing tactics advocated by Commissioner Brown. It also pointed out that the plan depended on Brown's ability to sell it to the police bureaucracy. The editorial concluded by stating, "but the stakes are too high to deny him the chance. Restoring the Police Department's basic working strength and expanding community patrol are the city's best answers to stop street violence. Failure to carry out the plan would signal that City Hall and the State Legislature are prepared to surrender the streets. To do that is to betray the public's trust."[23] Joe Klein was not so sure, as he termed the plan "the political equivalent of Fantasy Island."[24] Dinkins had a different take on why support was so low.

It was an enormously difficult job, but we got it done. You had to first convince the business community in New York and then the city council because you need what you call a "home rule message" to go to Albany to seek legislation and then we did. . . . We fought and lobbied Albany to get it. I was told such things when I complained to one state senator that people were dying in New York, Harlem and other places. This senator told me that his constituency were concerned with auto theft and graffiti. Some legislators tried to—in exchange for their support—demanded the reopening of some fire companies for their support that had been closed in an effort to save money.[25]

Dinkins' proposal did generate a lot of publicity, but it did little to change his prevailing image. A Marist Institute poll found that 62 percent of the respondents had heard of the proposal, 70.7 percent thought adding ninety-six hundred police officers, new jail spaces, and courts was a good idea, and 24 percent thought it would not make a difference. Only 5.2 percent thought it was a bad idea. The same poll found that 82 percent of the respondents supported the idea of a twenty-five-cent surcharge on lottery tickets, 76.2 percent supported the payroll tax, and 62 percent supported raising the property tax.[26]

Mark Voorhees' essay in the *Manhattan Lawyer* analyzed the proposals and found little linkage between felony rates and proposed staffing levels. He claimed that safer precincts received a disproportionate number of new police officers. Voorhees found that "uniformed strength at the 15 precincts with the highest felony rates would rise an average of 50.8%, while the increase at the 15 lowest-felony rate precincts would average 56.2%."[27] Voorhees questioned the statistics used in Commissioner Brown's report and his overall community policing plans. He interviewed the mayor and the police department spokespersons, none of whom provided an explanation for this discrepancy.

When Governor Mario Cuomo entered the debate, he upped the stakes by arguing that New York City needed "thousands" of new officers. Dinkins responded the next month by raising his original request from 3,416 to 9,603 new police officers. The money for these new officers would come from a payroll tax and a twenty-five-cent surcharge on the lottery. Yet the number of potential new officers was reduced by the city council and state legislature to 3,500.

The entire episode brought about a public relations breakdown for Dinkins and his new police commissioner. The mayor seemed unsure of how to enact his safety compact and was perceived to be merely throwing numbers around and overreacting to criticism. Even the announcement of the first drop in crime in thirty-six years did not help Dinkins recover in his public relations battle. Ironically, the 4.4 percent drop in crime should have been a cause for celebration, but it received little attention. Brown lasted two years and nine months on the job, resigning because of his wife's illness in August of 1992. Dinkins' appointment of Raymond Kelly, a veteran police officer and insider, was hailed in the *Times*.[28]

Dinkins' *Safe Streets, Safe City II: A Future Print for Success* was published in 1993. The report stated that "the total FBI index of crime in our city declined 15% since Fiscal Year 1990;

subway crime has declined 31% since 1990; and crime in public housing has declined by 18% during that same period. Notably index crimes are the lower level since fiscal year 1955."[29] The report also said that 6,000 police officers should be added to the three police forces, and it set goals of 31,063 in 1990, 37,133 in August 1993, and 38,310 in February 1994.[30] Leland Jones stated that "every columnist said it was dead on arrival. It did happen and Giuliani is the beneficiary."[31]

This second volume of *Safe Streets, Safe City* came out during Dinkins' reelection campaign. By this time, the police union was publicly opposed to the mayor's reelection. On CNN's *Inside Politics* Judy Woodruff asked the mayor about the perception of crime in the City. Dinkins responded,

> You put the question not inappropriately; that the perception is that crime is not down. But the fact is that crime is down in seven major FBI index categories for the first time in 36 years and for 2 consecutive years because of our Safe Street/Safe City program, which we call Community Policing. The president has praised it. It's working. And it's working well. And we have plans for how to deal with the future. We intend to merge our three police departments, transit and housing and NYPD in one super department. We have, even now, more cops on the street than we have had in recent years and as we achieve our goal, we'll have in excess of 38,000 cops, more than we have ever had.[32]

Woodruff was not convinced and attempted to rephrase the perception question. Dinkins responded to the question by talking about the introduction of a community court to try petty crimes. Woodruff shifted the question to the mayor's slow reaction to the black boycott of Korean groceries. Dinkins grew testy and said, "Just a second, Judy, even for CNN, I cannot permit that kind of misperception." Dinkins asserted that she was asking him to respond to every allegation that Giuliani had made. She assured him that she did not get information from Giuliani. Dinkins went on to list the achievements of the city and scolded Giuliani for ducking a debate. Although in journalistic circles, Woodruff was doing her job by challenging the mayor, this exchange was not good for Dinkins' image, coming as it did a few days before the election.

Throughout the campaign, Dinkins spoke to white audiences about his crime-fighting record, yet his way of answering questions often baffled his audience. One reporter recalled that if Dinkins were asked a question about crime, he would answer with technocratic jargon. The audience would talk about crime, and Dinkins would say, "I am not unmindful of your concern" when he should have said, "I care." He seemed essentially incapable of conveying his message. He would talk about his *Safe Streets, Safe City* reports as if they knew what he was talking about.[33]

The Revolt of "Hessians"

In September 1993, police officers conducted one of the ugliest demonstrations in the city's history. Dinkins recalled that, "the cops demonstrated against me at city hall and Giuliani was out there egging them on. It was ugly, illegal, and improper. He [Giuliani] got away with it as far as the media is concerned."[34]

When police demonstrators called Mayor Dinkins a "washroom attendant," the reference not only tapped into a black stereotype but also weakened safety compact efforts. The *New York Post* ran a series of headlines about crime, and after a Miami tourist was killed in New York City the headline ran, "Savage City." The Patrolman Benevolence Association (PBA) took out a full-page ad in the *Post* entitled "The Shattered Mosaic," which played up on Dinkins' characterization of the city as a gorgeous mosaic and listed a series of grievances with the mayor. The ad ended with "How about making him Commissioner of Tennis, where the issues would be less challenging?"[35] As the reelection campaign progressed, Dinkins tried to make a case for his record. Bob Liff observed, "Like a mantra, Dinkins recites at virtually every campaign stop that for two years crime has gone down in the seven major FBI categories of serious crime for the first time in decades."[36]

Despite employing a famous commissioner, the *Safe Streets, Safe City* report, and the declining crime rate, race had trumped Dinkins' image as a crime fighter. Klein asserted that the real trouble with the "toughest mayor strategy is that Dinkins doesn't buy the law-and-order, beef-up-the cops solution. In his heart of hearts, he remains a social-work liberal of the sort immortalized (and tweaked) in West-Side Story 30 years ago."[37]

Managing Meaning: Media, Mayors, and Crime

As was suggested earlier, once a police commissioner is in place, the media plays a critical role in providing meaning for crime. Journalists give events, what Hall calls "primary definitions."[38] Shootings are either accidental, domestic in nature, drive-bys, or gang related. Whatever official meaning is assigned to an event, journalists supply the language. Several scholars have suggested that journalists' constructions of events tend to contain an elite bias. Gamson and colleagues argue, "The lens through which we receive these images is not neutral but evinces the power and point of view of the political and economic elites who operate and focus it. And the special genius of this system is to make the whole process seem so normal and natural that the very art of social construction is invisible."[39]

In other words, reporters "frame the event."[40] The world is made meaningful by referencing events to official versions or causal explanations. The media helps elected officials frame the nature of the crime, officers' reactions, and predicted resolutions. Police are expected to react differently to each of the shootings described earlier. Framing the event helps the public understand the police officers' reactions.

The entire framing process often follows the politics. Since mayors have become chief salespersons for their respective cities, they often cite crime statistics in their pitches to developers. A high crime rate tends to diminish the attractiveness of cities as sites for home building, recreation, and business. If a city has a reputation for unsafe streets, drug trafficking, and so on, it may lose residents to its suburbs and less crime-prone cities. Industries cite high crime rates as a primary reason for moving out of the inner city. Placing an industrial plant in high-crime districts results in higher insurance rates and expanded security measures. However, locating plants in such neighborhoods means more employment, better retail sales, and the revitalization of community morale.

Dinkins' promotion of a conservative safety compact was explicit in one of the campaign themes: Strong enough to hold the line. Yet his handling of crime incidents where race was a factor undermined his credibility. He was further compromised by his decision to go forward with the Mollen commission against the advice of Commissioner Brown. The ugly police demonstration at city hall reinforced the damage his public image had taken on this issue. Trying to establish a safety compact in the midst of a fiscal crisis is difficult. Bob Herbert of the *Post* put it well, "Now without New York between the terror of an unprecedented crime wave and the horror of déjà vu fiscal crisis—is the time for Dinkins to light up his gorgeous mosaic."[41] In the end, the police department made fun of Dinkins' mosaic. Although crime had gone down during the latter part of Dinkins' tenure, he was not able to capitalize on it. The reelection campaign was, in part, about a more conservative safety compact. Eli Silverman agrees that the Crown Heights incident hurt Dinkins. "Dinkins' castle door was now assailable by candidate Giuliani's battering ram."[42] The *New Yorker* opined that "by falling back instinctively on identity politics, on the static politics of victimhood—a strange position for someone as powerful as the mayor of New York—Mr. Dinkins forfeits an issue about which the public's thinking is evolving rapidly."[43]

The Incident of Crime in New York City

Is crime in large American cities an epidemic? What is too much crime? It is difficult to answer these questions because there arises a dichotomy between the perception of crime and its actual rate or incidence. The Federal Bureau of Investigation (FBI) publishes an annual Uniform Crime Report (UCR), which it acknowledges to be underreported and therefore inaccurate. Nevertheless, the UCR is the only nationwide survey on the frequency of crimes. The report divides crime into seven categories: murder, forcible rape, robbery, aggravated assault, burglary, larceny, and motor vehicle theft. Table 7.1 shows the incidence of crime during the Dinkins tenure as mayor.

Table 7.1 demonstrates that the decline in crime rates is not uniform because a decline may be followed by an upsurge. Often there is no explanation for either change. Good economic news is usually associated with the decline in the rate of crime,

Table 7.1. Types and Rate of Crimes, 1990–1994

Murder & Non Negligent Manslaughter	% Change	Forcible Rape	% Change	Robbery	% Change	Burglary	% Change
1990 2,245		3,126		100,280		68,891	
1991 2,154	–4.05%	2,892	–7.49%	66,832	–33.35%	112,015	62.60%
1992 1,995	–7.38%	2,815	–2.66%	91,239	36.52%	103,476	–7.62%
1993 1,946	–2.46%	2,818	0.11%	86,001	–5.74%	99,207	–4.13%
1994 1,561	–19.78%	2,666	–5.39%	72,540	–15.65%	88,370	–10.92%

Source: FBI Uniform Crime Reports.

but as table 7.1 illustrates, it depends. Mayors take credit for dips, but over time peaks and valleys have little to do with their crime strategy.

The point is that statistics are not always convincing because the public's perception is more important than the actual rates of incidence. The attack of a young woman in Central Park or Riverside Park carries more meaning for the public than a published table that shows the decline of incidents in the parks. The public watches the 6:00 and 11:00 local television news, which tend to lead with crime stories. The news conveys the message that crime is an ever-present menace. During high-crime periods the police are presented in a positive light. The public support for police expansion breaks down when police are involved in questionable actions, such as when they demonstrate at city hall, pass out fear pamphlets to tourists, or take illegal job actions. The supervision of the police is best exemplified when a mayor rigorously investigates a police scandal.

Policing the Police

The New York Police Department has long been the butt of jokes about corruption. Most mayors have been reluctant to take on the department over this issue, but the 1992 drug scandal provided Dinkins with an opportunity to investigate the department. Over the objection of Police Commissioner Brown, Dinkins decided to appoint a commission to study corruption.

Therefore, in June 1992, Dinkins issued an executive order to create an official commission to investigate alleged police corruption in the New York Police Department. This grew out of the arrest of Officer Michael Dowd for drug trafficking and a series of drug-related crimes. A hearing began in September 1992 and Officer Dowd gave testimony that rivaled that of the infamous Knapp Commission. He gave testimony on a police crime group called the "Losers Club," to drug dealing, to brutality in the precincts. Ironically, the commission became a liability for Dinkins. A *New York Post* reporter concluded that, "tales of the so-called Morgue Boys could translate into the political death of Dinkins." McAlary asked, "Can David Dinkins afford to see rank corruption bared in his police department on the eve of an election? Or will the mayor emerge from the fray as the man Who Cleaned Up the police department? It can go either way."[44]

Dinkins asked his deputy mayor for criminal justice, Judge Milton Mollen, to lead a police corruption panel and urged a civilian police review. The Mollen Commission consisted of five members and was designed to investigate allegations of drug dealing and corruption in several precincts. The Mollen Commission issued an interim report in December 1994, resulting in the arrest of several officers. In June 1995, a final report recommended the creation of a "permanent external Police Commission [that would be] independent of the Department." This independent "watchdog" agency, though widely supported in the media was never adopted.[45]

Crime Icons and Symbolic Reassurance

Most crimes are routine events: a man kills his wife, teenagers are caught with drugs, two men rob a convenience store, a rapist attacks another victim. The 6:00 P.M. local television news is full of such events. In fact, news editors must often decide which crimes to cover on television. Some crimes just do not fit with the flow of the news hour. Reporting routine crimes can be dull and repetitive. Moreover, public officials easily manage routine events because they usually include the "usual suspects," and the police have a relationship with the violators. Arresting petty thieves with criminal records is often not considered newsworthy.

The opposite of routine news events are the "accidents." These are crimes by otherwise law-abiding citizens or incidents between individuals of different races. Public officials scramble to give these types of crime meaning. If the crime involves members of different races, the politicians and the media decide what to do with the race angle. If the crime involves an otherwise upstanding member of the community, the reporter will explain why the individual went berserk. However, some of these "accidents" escape or resist official meaning. They are what Bennett and Lawrence call "nonroutine and sensational crime news icons." Journalists treat such events as indicators or metaphors for deeper community problems. On a Channel 4 news forum, Dinkins attacked media hysteria on crime. He argued that Koch was mayor during the city's worse crime wave (1978–1981), but

> media coverage during that period did not speak of a crime wave. . . .
> On the contrary, the mayor was praised and photographed with his
> thumbs in the air calling for the death penalty. . . . Yet in the same
> program Dinkins was asked if he felt that he was being judged by
> a double standard. He gave his standard answer, "Well, it's is not
> so much whether I'm personally being judged by a different standard. I'm not."[46]

The Washington Heights Incident

In the summer of 1992, a white policeman, Michael O'Keefe, shot a Dominican man, Jose "KiKo" Garcia, but the details of the incident were in dispute. The victim's family claimed that Garcia was unarmed, but the police claimed that Garcia had a gun and resisted arrest. Five days of demonstrations ensued. Again, Dinkins was put in a difficult situation. He offered sympathy to Garcia's family and pledged a city investigation. Although Garcia was alleged to be a drug dealer, and the autopsy of Garcia's body revealed the presence of cocaine, Mayor Dinkins arranged for the city to pay for Garcia's funeral and the cost of flying the body back to the Dominican Republic for burial. He came under fire from the Patrolmen's Benevolent Association for making Garcia a martyr, and his prevailing image as soft on crime was reinforced by the incident. An article in *Newsday* quoted Alice McGillon, a former police department spokesman: "The mayor is perceived as someone who is not a proponent of law enforcement and soft on crime and it could affect him politically. I think his image is mixed right now."[47]

Dinkins defended himself by citing his Safe Streets, Safe City program and saying, "I can't see how those who really care about the police department think it is in their interest to have the police department think the administration doesn't care about them. How in the hell is that useful?"[48] Dinkins apparently had no idea that the Garcia incident would be read as an example of his being soft on crime.

Regina Lawrence has identified three key clusters of variables for managing meaning: event characteristics, oppositional communication strategies, and official communication.[49] Dinkins ignored the context of the Garcia incident in an attempt to be evenhanded. If he had sided with the police, the action would not have been enough to reverse the growing alienation of the street officers. Moreover, bringing the Garcia supporter stories into the light, might have gone a long way toward repairing his reputation among the Latino community. The mayor, in attempting to show respect for the Latino community, suffered the wrath of the PBA, the most visible group in his safety compact.

Summary

This chapter began with a discussion of Dinkins' safety compact. Although closed and open compacts are not mutually exclusive, proper mayoral posturing is essential to both. The Dinkins years were replete with stories about improved police productivity and community policing successes. Dinkins was eager to assert his administration's claim of being strong against crime. Dinkins tried to impose a closed safety compact, but it was not convincing. Phillip Thompson concluded that Dinkins' plan was successful in quieting down the media, but the mayor had no long-term policy agenda. He observed, "By acquiescing to the demands for more police, Dinkins had essentially let the media set public policy."[50] Thompson suggested that the police bureaucracy was bloated and that Dinkins had lost an opportunity to reform it. Thompson's conclusion assumes that the police department supported the mayor or was amenable to mayoral reform. In fact, the police officers protested outside city hall and took out advertisements denouncing Dinkins, as well as opposing his reelection. Perhaps the final blow came with the weak endorsement of the Guardians, the black police officers' organization.

As discussed earlier, the appointment of a new police commissioner is critical to the process of building a safety compact. In this succession, imagined change is perceived to be as important as real change. The media's treatment of leadership secession allowed Commissioner Brown to create the perception of change. And although the commissioner must be skilled at framing events, Brown could not frame the Crown Heights incident as a typical neighborhood dispute, because of his race and his status as an outsider. Therefore, journalists were able to make the story about the racial tension between Jews and blacks. Since race is a factor in framing events in the city, a police commissioner is increasingly expected to be able to reassure citizens about the treatment of black citizens and messages about crime fighting.

In most cities, neighborhood or community policing emerges as a mechanism for additional consultation with community leaders. Working together with citizens redefines the police officer's role as a problem solver. Commissioners are now expected to go to community meetings, appear on talk shows, and reassure residents that the police officers are not an army of occupiers. The public wants a face to identify with the fight against crime.

Crime statistics are often cited and referenced in media stories on crime, but the public seems to be less interested in the numbers than they are in attitudes of the police. However, a police commissioner must maintain the delicate balance between taking credit for success and not overshadowing the mayor. Highly visible and articulate commissioners such as William Bratton can and do upstage their mayors.

Finally, the prevailing image of Dinkins was that of a man who had lost the respect of the police. It is true that his administration was somewhat responsible for a decline in crime, but unlike his successor, Mayor Giuliani, Dinkins was not able to take credit for his achievements. Nor could he rely on law and order rhetoric that would have been regarded by some as a code for cracking down on black criminals. Black elected officials in a majority white city will find it difficult to promote their preferred image as law and order zealots. Even Detroit's Coleman Young, with his confrontational posture toward criminals, could not sell that image to his white suburban audience. Dinkins' carefully constructed mild-mannered personality gave him even less of a chance.

CHAPTER EIGHT

THE TURMOIL OF
SCHOOL POLITICS

Introduction

No crisis in large cities is more frustrating than the plight of public schools. Inner-city schools in New York are beset with a plethora of problems ranging from inadequate facilities, incompetent classroom teachers, and poor reading and math scores, to violence within the schools. The public seems to be most concerned about the low achievement scores of public school students. They are also alarmed by the increasing cost of schools. When Dinkins approached these challenges, he carried a certain prevailing image into the policy arenas. Although mayors are not elected to be de facto school superintendents, they cannot safely ignore school politics. School issues are too important to their broader constituency, and school activists have a way of being constantly in the news. Accordingly, city hall has attempted to engage or appropriate many traditional school issues such as fiscal decisions, school management, and safety. Since school politics is already a crowded field of stakeholders and interest groups, mayors have not always been welcome there. Indeed, hostile receptions are not uncommon. Why would mayors run the risk of degrading a positive prevailing image for a policy for which they have limited statutory responsibility? At the beginning of his administration, Dinkins offers an explanation of why he wanted to be an education mayor.

Education is more important to me than I can express. We know that something like 90% of the new jobs in the service area require at least a high school diploma. If we don't fix the system so our youngsters can get educated and trained for the jobs that are available, not only will they not realize their potential and be a drain on the tax base instead of contributing to it, but we are not going to have a labor pool in 10 or 15 years.[1]

Few would argue with his reasoning but in *Black Mayor and School Politics*, it was suggested that public schools are controlled by a "public school cartel" (PSC). The PSC was defined as "a coalition of professional school administrators, school activists and union leaders who maintain control of school policy to promote the interests of its members."[2] Public school cartels are not true cartels in the pure economic sense, but their behavior is similar. Members are able to monopolize effectively the provision of educational services and veto school reform that is at variance with their interest. Accordingly, the PSC is not likely to support mayoral actions if it perceives them as a threat to its control of the public school system. Within school politics the mayor is either an interloper or a bystander. An interloper injects herself or himself into decisions traditionally the province of the school board and the superintendent. In New York, this encroachment was met with some resistance.

This chapter reviews reactions of the PSC to the encroachment of Dinkins. More specifically, I will discuss how the media interprets school politics and the reactions of the respective PSCs to these interpretations. In addition I will examine how the press frames the politics of public schools.

Although the media will cover a mayor/superintendent conflict, that is not where the majority of the school dynamics takes place. In most cities, the PSC is well organized, and its members do not regard the mayor or the superintendent as members of the cartel. As far as the PSC is concerned, both are outsiders. Nevertheless, the media views mayors and superintendents as having joint responsibility for school policies. In reality, mayors and superintendents lack the power to do much about what happens in a highly bureaucratized and traditionally oriented school system. Having one's own appointees on the board does not insure policy compliance, nor do mandates reach the operational side of the system. Having one appointee on the board and a pliant superintendent can take conflicting school politics off the front page, but these two things do not make a mayor an "education mayor."

What Is an Education Mayor to Do?

In recent times many mayors of large cities have begun to align themselves with the movement to improve school systems. School reform is one of those issues that most people can agree needs to addressed immediately. Some mayoral candidates seek structural changes that allow them direct control over the school board and the superintendent.[3]

The election of a black mayor can unleash pent-up demands for school reform. Many in the black community believe that the public schools are working against black educational mobility. Bad schools are blamed for a variety of social ills that beset the black community. White mayors may promise to improve schools, but they are seldom held to their promise, and often escape criticism for their failure in this area. However, if a black mayor promises school reform, black voters expect to see results. Black mayors are expected to solve the conundrum of poor schools and do something about "those teachers who aren't teaching our kids anything." This was the case for former education-oriented mayors Kurt Schmoke of Baltimore and Michael White of Cleveland.[4]

During the Dinkins campaigns, there were repeated calls for more city hall involvement in the public school system management. Dinkins tried to respond to this challenge. As borough president, Dinkins sought to influence school policy by appointing minorities to the central school board and supporting the efforts of the chancellor. He also spoke out against school policies with which he did not agree.

Mayor Dinkins was aware that further deterioration of the schools would affect the city and his own political image. He was forced to assume a proactive posture toward schools because this issue was salient for the general public, and more importantly, the Latino and black communities. Although problems of inner-city schools have always been a subject of mayoral campaign rhetoric, there is no evidence that Dinkins had any idea how to make school reform work. It is easy to say that we need to improve the schools or that every child should be able to read at his or her grade level, but it is difficult to prescribe solutions. The PSC often welcomes a mayor's general interest in the schools but resists any attempt to impose education content or administrative policy or micromanage the system.

The Sixties Deal

Before 1969 the mayor of New York, with the assistance of a screening committee, appointed the members to the board of education. Since 1971 the mayor appoints two members, and each of the five borough presidents appoints one member. The New York City Board of Education sets the overall education policies and administers the high schools. The central board appoints the chancellor of the New York public school system. The mayor does not have a majority on the board and cannot control the selection of the chancellor. As the chief administrator and advisor to the school board, the chancellorship is a very high-profile job that carries several perks and provides visibility for the appointed individuals. The job has been described as the zenith of an urban school superintendent's career. At best, the chancellor is limited by the decentralized and unionized New York school system. Yet it still attracts applicants who either ignore the history of the New York system or cannot resist a challenge. Joseph Viteritti observed,

> Even though the Board of Education selected the superintendent or chancellor of schools, in all but a relatively few instances the person chosen was a product of the professional bureaucracy. Insofar as the power of the Board of Education was concerned, Livingston Street was a classic case of a situation in which the implementation phase of the policy process carried out through the administration far outweighed the impact of original policy formulations. In effect, the superintendent or chancellor had not only been the candidate of the bureaucracy, but historically also functioned as both its instrument and guardian.[5]

Although the central board controls the high schools, the remaining part of the New York public school system is divided into thirty-two community school boards. Each board hires district superintendents who manage the schools. This is due to a reform implemented in 1969 when the city undertook an extensive devolution of its massive school system. At that time many education and foundation leaders thought the system was too large to serve its students adequately. Opposed by the PSC, decentralization became a part of community and borough politics. A new school politics was born that divided schools into ethnic and racial fiefdoms. Brecher and colleagues concluded,

> The election of community school boards has proved to be a disappointing exercise in representative democracy. An infinitesimal share of the potential electorate turns out to vote, and few significant issues are raised or decided in campaigns. The root of the problem is probably the limited authority of the local boards over educational matters, which remain largely under the authority of the central board or state law. Local boards hire district superintendents and control relatively small sums of "discretionary" funds provided by the board, but these powers are not enough to attract candidates concerned with broad issues of education policy. The result is that teachers' unions, religious organizations, and local political clubs dominate local board elections. The nearly 300 New Yorkers who are elected as school board members every three years are not important municipal policymakers.[6]

Thirty years later the politics of local school boards continues to reflect the communities in which they exist. Ira Katznelson predicted the local board politics would "turn inward" into contests among members of homogeneous communities.[7] For some of these three hundred board members, election is just one of the ways of getting into New York politics. The small turnout does not matter, since there is an opportunity to campaign and achieve name recognition in the community. For minorities, the local school boards serve as good training grounds for elections into the city council and other political offices. Since decentralization, there have been several attempts to curb the power of the community boards, thus allowing the chancellor more control over the selection of district superintendents. This effort failed, primarily because groups have lobbied the State House to retain the present system. As a result, the school board does not have the power to intervene regarding the disruptions or poor management decisions among community boards. Described as a labyrinth of political relationships, the *New York Times* called community boards a "nest of corruption and cronyism." In *Black Mayors and School Politics*, it was suggested that mayors who seek to cleanse this corruption would run the risk of alienating arguably some of the best-organized interest groups in the city.[8] However, Dinkins went on record as supporting the chancellor's efforts to control wayward boards.

Dinkins, School Boards, and Superintendents

With 1,069 schools and an enrollment of 1.7 million students, the New York City public school system is larger than most midsize American cities. With an operating budget of over $7 billion, it employs more than sixty-five thousand teachers and four thousand supervisors and administrators. Hence, the New York City school system is a major employer in the city. What is more important, it attracts many first-generation college graduates, particularly minorities. As a result, the school system is used as a vehicle for social mobility. It is also a system that can successfully resist change and subvert management innovations. Norman Chung and David Roger's *110 Livingston Street* chronicles the rise of central board staff and their ability to resist school reform. Chancellors come and go without making much impact on the standard operating norms of the school system. Viteritti adds that "the discouraging predicament of the New York City school Chancellor is that he must function in a political environment that is basically hostile to the interests of the students he serves."[9]

During the 1989 campaign, Dinkins asked, "Why can't we develop an education SWAT team to take hold of failing schools and turn them around?"[10] These SWAT teams were to be formally known as school improvement action teams. Dinkins told an audience, "We owe the next generation of students a renewed public school system, one where the empty chairs of this day will be filled, where corridors and classrooms will be safer and New York will lead not lag behind."[11] Few voters are impressed by such campaign testimony.

After six months in office Dinkins announced plans to appoint an independent investigator to look into allegations of corruption in the community school boards. The Joint Commission on Integrity in the Public School, or the Gill report, had reported widespread corruption in the system. It described the school bureaucracy as a "sleepy-eyed, lumbering brontosaurus primarily interested in grazing."[12]

The New York mayors who have attempted to tame this stubborn behemoth have experienced little or no success. Dinkins believed that he could make a difference. He supported the incoming chancellor's decision to change the rules about the tenure of principals. He called for a Marshall Plan for education and a drug-free school zone. Nevertheless, in the first campaign, Dinkins said that the mayor's role in education should be changed "not by law, but in attitude. I think the central board should set policy. I would convey my ideas to the central board much as any citizen might, except that the mayor has more clout."[13] It was suggested in *Black Mayors in School Politics* that newly elected black mayors believe that they can make a difference in school politics by appointing progressive whites and minorities to the school board. The mayor of New York appoints two of the seven members of the board; the remaining five seats are divided among the five borough presidents. In effect, every appointment is a patronage slot. This highly politicized appointment method has proven to be a triumph for the public school cartel. This arrangement allowed the PSC the opportunity to pit borough appointees against each other and the chancellor. The community boards were even more political, with minorities fighting for limited resources.[14]

In September 1986, Dinkins as borough president appointed Dr. Gwendolyn C. Baker to the school board and then in September 1990 Baker, a black woman and the executive director of the YWCA, became president of the board. This was the first time in the city's history that minorities represented the majority on the board. The board included Carol Gresser, a teacher and administrator from Queens; Irene H. Impellizzeri, an administrator at CUNY; Westina L. Matthews, a former elementary teacher; Michael Petrides, a professor of electrical engineering technology and administrator; Luis O. Reyes, an educator; and Ninfa Segarra, a lawyer and former city official.

Before Dinkins was elected the board had decided to hire Joseph Fernandez, a former school superintendent of Miami who would be the first Latino to head the system. Born in Puerto Rico, Fernandez was raised in Harlem. As a Miami superintendent, he gained a reputation as a reformer. The appointment of Fernandez as chancellor provided a critical opportunity for change. He appointed Stanley Litow as his chief operating advisor and Amina Abdu-Rahman, a former Dinkins staff member, as his deputy for programs. The latter appointment did not sit well with some of the PSC members, because Abdu-Rahman did not have a college degree. However, at the time, she was vice president for education of New York City Partnership. Before taking office Fernandez promoted the idea of school-based management, abolishing the board of examiners and the power of the chancellor to transfer and remove principals. All of the 1989 candidates for mayor supported Fernandez in his effort to remove ineffective principals. Dinkins said, "If the principal is not doing his job, it is not possible for the school to do well."[15]

The Great Budget Fight

Five months into his term Dinkins asked for massive cuts in the education budget. The first rumor was that public education would have to make a $190 million cut from its $6 billion budget. In May 1990 the mayor recommended that the board of education take over $48 million in spending cuts, which could have meant elimination of school aides and the board of examiners. Eight months into his administration, Dinkins instructed city agencies to cut their budgets for the current fiscal year and the next by a total of $1.1 billion to cover an expected gap of $1.8 billion. For the board this meant a 2 percent cut, or approximately $94 million. Fernandez refused to accept the cuts, stating, "We refuse to agree to cuts that will irrevocably harm the education and the futures of thousands of New York City school children."[16]

What started out as a good working relationship with the chancellor became a contentious one as Fernandez made only a 1 percent cut instead of the 2 percent cut requested. A public fight ensued involving Budget Director Phillip Michael aided by Deputy Mayor Steisel and the chancellor. Fernandez asserted, "We represent twenty-three percent of the (city) budget. We are asking the city to treat us fairly."[17] Fernandez' strategy was to paint a frightening picture of what would happen if they accepted the mayor's mandated 2 percent cut.

On May 10, 1991, Mayor Dinkins proposed another series of budget cuts for the Board of Education. Dinkins wanted to make a 10.4% cut in the school budget for the 1992 fiscal year. The $579 million cut would come just months after the Board was forced to cut $90 million from its current budget. Fernandez stated that the cuts could result in as many as 10,000 teachers being laid off. Dinkins's budget director Phillip Michael asserted, "We think it's more like 3,000." Michael later admitted that his projections "may not be entirely right." Reporter Joe Klein asserted that the "mayor's budget review has reflected two essential Dinkinsian qualities: paralysis and denial. Rather than take charge himself, he kicked responsibility back to his commissioners, who did what commissioners almost always do: They cut the most high profile programs."[18]

A *New York Times* editorial asserted that "the New York school system is at a critical point of transition." It urged the board to support Fernandez and "to act like a corporate board of directors."[19] The school board president, Robert Wagner Jr., the son of former Mayor Wagner and a leader of the progressive wing of the Democratic Party, had been instrumental in persuading Fernandez to become a candidate.

Wagner resigned in June 1990, and Gwendolyn Baker, a Dinkins appointee, became the new president of the board. Baker had a substantial background in education and great credentials. A board member since 1986, she fought for an affirmative action policy and multicultural education. However, once she assumed the presidency, Baker's leadership came under fire. Five board members had never served before. Fernandez felt the new members did not understand the "differences between policy making and administration." He wrote "All the signs were there for a bad marriage: the way members structured meetings; the way they postured in front of the TV cameras at board headquarters; the endless memos and time-consuming demands they made on staff to chase down niggling requests for information (I finally had to step in on that one); and an abysmal lack of control by the president."[20]

Baker's leadership was never accepted by the cartel, and she was forced to resign in June 1991. Fernandez believed her election to the chair was a "mistake."[21] The Baker resignation left only two other black members, Dr. Westina L. Matthews, a vice president at Merrill Lynch, and H. Carl McCall, a local black politician on the Board of Education. Dinkins' choice was H. Carl McCall. McCall was considered a rising political star in New York politics. However, even with three appointees on the board, Dinkins could not recruit another vote to control board affairs. These appointees were frustrated by the fact that Koch appointees still dominated board policy making. In his 1991 *Reform and Renaissance* package, Dinkins asked the state to give him the power to appoint the majority members on the board and was denied that power. Again, in February 1993, Dinkins asked the state legislature for the power to appoint the majority of the seven-member board. He failed in this attempt.

Dinkins and the Multicultural Curriculum

Americans have always disagreed over the content of the basic curriculum. This conflict is probably a plus for public schools because it keeps the public's attention. In 1985 the New York City Board of Education adopted a policy that directed the chancellor to take appropriate steps to eliminate "practices which foster attitudes and/or actions leading to discrimination against students, parents, or school personnel on the basis of race, color, religion, national origin, gender, age, sexual orientation, and/or handicapping condition."[22] We expect schools to foster the American idea of equality and tolerance. In New York, the espousal of such ideas is consistent with its liberal tradition.

In 1989 the board directed the chancellor to submit a comprehensive multicultural education plan. Fernandez presented the Children of the Rainbow curriculum, which ironically cost him his job. The curriculum was designed to teach respect and tolerance of differences, starting at the first-grade level. Agard-Jones concluded,

> Media presentation heightened fear and played on homophobic feelings in the city. Religious leaders who support the multicultural curriculum effort were not given as much visibility as those who oppose it. Many people attempted, and perhaps succeeded, in further polarizing city residents with rhetoric. . . .

... Most of those who objected had not read the relevant curriculum documents. They were reacting to what they heard. In an
era of sound and visual bites of information, people act on very little information, unfortunately trusting the bearer of the message
to bring truth rather than rumor.[23]

Agard-Jones claimed that Children of the Rainbow was not a
gay curriculum, nor did it include a discussion of sexual orientation.[24] However, the curriculum did contain a section on families
that seemed to endorse same sex families. Fernandez agrees
that only 2 out of 443 pages made reference to "tolerance of
"non-traditional" (including homosexual) family structures. My
supporting opinion was that if we're ever going to be in this
country together, we have to deal with such biases early, even in
the first grade. The board didn't buck me on that one."[25] After
the curriculum guides were circulated to the community boards,
parents began to object to the proposed curriculum. Many parents read it as the schools determining moral education for their
children. Since colonial schools began, people have held different views as to what is appropriate to teach in schools and make
available in books. The twentieth-century Scopes trial, which involved teaching of evolution, is the best-known example of this
kind of controversy.

Public school curricula today are no less controversial and no
less emotional. For example, sex education has incited some re-
markable battles in recent years. Fernandez's proposal to give
free condoms to the city's 261,000 high school students met
with criticism from both parents and the Catholic Church. The
free condom program was designed to help in the fight against
AIDS, but it was read as encouraging teenagers to have sex. In
February 1991, Dinkins went on record in support of Fernandez's proposal to distribute condoms with parental consent. Fernandez recalled, "We got Mayor Dinkins to endorse the plan, but
we had to go get him. He didn't volunteer."[26] Dinkins' appointee
and board president Baker also supported the idea, although in
1986 she had stated, "I think if you stood on the doorsteps of the
schools and gave out condoms, I don't think it would make any
difference among youngsters."[27]

The entire discourse about the new proposal revolved around
parental consent. Some parents are vehemently opposed to any

sex information classes, while others prefer only physiological information. Yet others support a comprehensive sex education. In New York, sex education became the third-rail political issue. Ninfa Segarra, a board member, was called a "political prostitute" because she changed her mind on the issue.[28]

The controversies summarized above may appear to be pseudo-issues, but the symbolic significance of such issues is that they allow board members to posture and assess the relative political acumen and agility of the superintendent.

Fernandez and His Critics

After Fernandez was selected he promised to cut 200 of the 5,200 board of education jobs. Accordingly, he took office challenging the core interests of the members of the public school cartel, the continuing influence of the central staff. The teachers' union, United Federation of Teachers (UFT), warned him that he should not try to duplicate the innovations that he had made in Miami. New York City's PSC was very organized and could resist even the most innocuous change. Fernandez did not heed these warnings and proceeded to call for stripping community boards of their hiring power and instituting a scheme for giving teachers and principals more decision-making powers, resulting in endless confrontations.

In May, Carl McCall resigned to become the state comptroller. Westina Matthews followed him. Dinkins' allies on the board were abandoning ship. Carol Gresser of Queens became the first nonmayoral appointee to be elected president of the board. Dinkins responded by appointing Victor Gotbaum, a retired labor leader who had a reputation for being a good negotiator. He also appointed two African Americans—Esmeralda Simmons, a Medgar Evers College administrator, and Dennis Walcott, president of the New York Urban League—to the board.

Despite a record that showed some improvements in dropout rates and math scores, Fernandez's critics began to grow. His stand on condoms,[29] AIDS education, and the Rainbow curriculum made him a controversial figure in the city. In May 1992 Segarra began supporting the abstinence advocates. Fernandez asserted,

Ninfa Segarra, of all people—the woman with relatives who had died of AIDS, the representative whose district included the South Bronx, home of the nation's highest percentage of AIDS infection and the highest teen pregnancy rate in the state. Segarra voted with the previous minority for a 4–3 turnabout to levy an impossible restriction on the curriculum: that every class, every lecture, every written lesson or videotape involving AIDS must henceforth include a greater emphasis on abstinence than on any other preventative measure.[30]

Dinkins' image as a centrist mayor got caught up in the board infighting over the condom controversy. Although the idea had editorial support from newspapers, the mayor was not able to get away from the negative fallout generated by the controversy. A harbinger of things to come, the 4–3 vote against the plan showed that Fernandez was losing the support of the new majority on the board. Discussions about Fernandez's tenure had become a discourse about morality. Board members chose to keep their distance from Fernandez. Board members Irene Impellizzeri and Michael Petrides became the most vocal critics of condoms and advocates for inclusion of abstinence training in the curriculum.

In February 1993, Fernandez was forced out on a 4–3 vote.[31] Gresser was one of the members who voted against Fernandez. Dinkins publicly criticized the board's action. Sandra Feldman, the president of the UFT, joined him. Fernandez admitted that he had made mistakes. He said, "I have fought for children. I will always put their welfare ahead of political or special interest." His advice to the next superintendent was simply, "Don't come." Fernandez' dismissal made national news, prompting the *New York Times* editorial board to call the board of education "a rogue school board."[32]

The board decided in a highly charged and split vote 4–3 to hire Ramon Cortines, a Mexican American and former superintendent from San Francisco, as the new chancellor. Cortines had objected to the condom distribution program implemented in San Francisco. Dinkins had suggested Gerald Tirozzi, a white former Connecticut state education commissioner. A reporter at *Newsday* pointed out that Tirozzi's race "could pose a problem for a board headed by a white president and a white vice president in a system made up of more than 80 percent minority students."[33] Since Dinkins had come out publicly in support of Tirozzi, Cortines' hiring was seen as a rebuff of the mayor. Carol Gresser told *USA Today*, "Ramon Cortines impressed us with his passion for education and his recent hands-on urban experience. He's a consensus-builder."[34]

On July 12, *Newsday* ran an article titled "Ed Board Snubs Mayor," reporting that Dinkins' request for twice-monthly updates from the board after Fernandez's resignation were ignored.[35] By August 1993 Dinkins' prevailing image was one of a weak mayor in jeopardy of losing his job in four months. After failing to convince the state legislature to change the law on board appointments, no board members appointed by the borough presidents had reason to fear Dinkins. A *New York Times* editorial asserted, "That support may have galvanized Mr. Dinkins' opponents and boosted the prospects of Mr. Cortines as an alternative to Mr. Dinkins' choice. It seemed they wanted to embarrass Mr. Dinkins by boxing him into opposing a Hispanic candidate, and also to deny him any gain among whites from supporting Mr. Tirozzi."[36] Here the PSC demonstrated its knowledge of New York politics and Dinkins' situation. Cortines would be a stopgap superintendent at best.

The *Economist* concluded that "the new chancellor is also an outsider, with no previous knowledge of New York. Even the most Machiavellian insider might have problems asserting a sense of new direction. As an outsider, Mr. Cortines will find the structure stacked against him."[37] Dinkins denounced the Cortines appointment and in his speeches began to promote the idea of the local board replacing the central board. Dinkins' 1993 opponent, Giuliani, had also endorsed the idea.

The New York public schools, which were not improving as Dinkins had believed, became a campaign issue in his 1993 reelection bid. Dinkins abandoned his bystander position and became an interloper in school decisions. He unveiled his Parents and Children First Plan in September 1993, which proposed expanding the school board from seven to eleven members and giving the mayor six appointees. The plan would also end the power of thirty-two community boards to hire paraprofessionals, principals, and assistant principals. It would also establish a $200 million Endowment for Public Education to fund new education programs. Dinkins recommended expanding the city's Beacon School Program and extending the public school year. He also wanted to transfer school maintenance from the school board to the School Construction Authority and require custodians to report to principals. (Only in New York would this be considered a controversial proposal.) In addition, Dinkins was to establish a security trust fund to hire over one thousand new police officers for the schools. Dinkins asserted, "Accountability is the only way we get there, and I want this fall's election to be a referendum on school governance."[38] Despite the fact that the proposals received positive initial reviews,[39] Dinkins had lost his credibility with the New York City PSC. Furthermore no one thought the board changes would pass the state house.[40]

The Asbestos Crisis

The big crisis of Cortines' tenure would be asbestos hazards in the city's 1,069 school buildings. Dinkins had ordered the asbestos re-inspection before Cortines arrived but the inspections were incomplete. The School Construction Authority certified only fifty schools, and there were still some questions. As a result of the incomplete inspection, some children could not return to their school buildings, delaying the start of school year by eleven days. This became known as the "asbestos scandal." The *New York Times* editorial reminded the public of the meaning of the delay. "This is a great inconvenience to parents who must now make new and possibly costly arrangements for childcare. It also throws the school year, which requires a minimum number of class days, into further chaos."[41] After blaming all of city hall, the board, and the School Construction Authority, the *New York Post* speculated that many parents were going to keep their "kids away even after the certification has been made."[42]

Giuliani attacked Dinkins for using his deputy, Steisel, instead of getting an outside expert to oversee the asbestos crisis. A *New York Post* article stated, "Mayor Dinkins was protecting himself, not seeking to protect the children, the teachers and parents of the city."[43]

As Dinkins' stock declined, his former supporters abandoned him. Robert Wagner Jr., a former president of the board who had supported some of Dinkins' efforts to reform the board, endorsed Dinkins' opponent, Giuliani, for mayor. The Wagner endorsement of Giuliani was yet another sign that Dinkins had serious problems with some liberal progressive supporters. In October, the United Federation of Teachers, one of Dinkins' supporters in 1989, voted to remain neutral in the 1993 mayoral race. A spokesperson reported that the decision was greeted by a "loud and prolonged applause"[44] from the three thousand delegates. It was a big blow to the Dinkins reelection campaign. Giuliani would use Dinkins' woes with the board as a part of his campaign.

The Politics of Superintendent Turnover

The relationship between the mayor and the school superintendent is a complex one that consists of vexing image challenges. In many cities mayors have aligned themselves with superintendents, while in other cities a traditional institutional distance is carefully maintained. Superintendents are not a part of the school cartel. They might be characterized as itinerant workers who move from one school system to the next.[45]

Vacancies in the superintendency always make for great excitement and anticipation within the PSC. Members of the board get to review countless resumes and receive numerous telephone calls from community leaders. In this instance they interviewed four or five candidates. The media allowed that ethnicity should not be the only criterion for the next superintendent. The subtext was that they had had two failed black superintendents and felt that it was time for a nonminority to try.

In New York great care is given to make the selection of school superintendent appear to be a joint decision. However, none of the committees select individuals without consultation with local politicians. Politicians react to such behavior by refusing to deal with appointed superintendents and, in effect, make them permanent outsiders. Despite all of the claims of citizen control and parental input, the selection of the superintendent remains the most important administrative function of the board. What the public understands about school politics comes from the newspapers. Television news may report a particular superintendent selection but does not discuss the politics of the selection.

The Media and School Politics

The responsibility for reporting on schools lies with the media. If test scores are falling, the media has a responsibility to say so. Occasionally, the media will make an effort to compare test scores among various cities. In New York, reporters were assigned to cover all aspects of school politics. However, many reporters are not familiar enough with the dynamics of school policy to present a useful analysis. Therefore, reporters end up "superintendent watching" and, more problematically, "test score reporting." Only on rare occasions do they delve into substantive issues such as reviewing the qualifying processes for teachers or the climate of the classrooms.

The saliency of the school crisis should force the media to play a critical role in school politics. First, the media has a basic monopoly on citywide communication. Second, the media has access to school leaders, allowing them to report news about the activities of school board members and the superintendent. Third, the media interprets the news about local schools. Fourth, the media can influence local public attitudes about schools. Finally, the media can set the agenda by conducting polls, uncovering corruption, and focusing on inner-city versus suburban school disparities.

In the 1990s big city public schools resegregated and inner-city schools consistently performed below the standards of some third world countries. The media noted these problems but was distracted by claims that a new superintendent would make a difference. Although the coverage of low test scores for reading and math was fairly consistent, the public seemed more interested in the turnover of superintendents, the rising school budgets, and the violence within schools. New York City public schools were in a period of many small crises.

During small crises, some reporters feel obligated to make school news interesting. The media is aware that negative and sensational news draws more readers, so scandals of all types are quickly reported. Public school muckraking is practiced with the same fervor as regular city politics. Although commentaries are often done on the editorial pages, it is not uncommon for a paper to slant or tilt its coverage toward a popular superintendent or mayor. The Wong and Jain research suggests that the media also supports the position of the governing alliance. They found that the media usually supported city halls in school disputes.[46]

Summary

Changing school policy from city hall is not an easy task.[47] The mayor does not appoint all members of the school board, and the board members appointed by the borough president can safely ignore the mayor. Unlike his successor, Michael Bloomberg, Dinkins did not control the majority of the board, and the chancellor did not report to him. Moreover, aside from having multiple veto points, the PSC can stall.

During Dinkins' time mayors intervened in school policy through collective bargaining, board appointments, and the budgetary process. It was not until 2002 that the New York state legislature granted the mayor the power to appoint the majority members of the school board.[48] Dinkins shared that appointment power with independently elected borough presidents.

In this chapter I examined Dinkins' intervention into the superintendent selection process with the hope of finding an individual with whom he could work. When Dinkins announced a major reorganization plan during his reelection bid, it turned out to be a poor strategy. It is also clear that Dinkins' board appointees were never able to impose any of city hall's policy preferences on the board. Dinkins admitted, "I could never get a majority vote on the Board."[49] Mayoral appointees competed with borough appointees, and they lost. The other board members never accepted his appointees as anything except mayoral appointees. This explains, in part, why they resigned so quickly. The New York media never fully explained the internal dynamics of the board to the public. The Fernandez controversy was a classic case of how framing controversial issues can entangle city hall. Fernandez's multicultural curriculum and the condom initiative was a good story, but framing it as a religious issue created the subtext of a struggle between the white, working-class Catholics in the outer boroughs and the so-called Manhattan liberals. It is not clear whether Mayor Dinkins understood that his ruminations on these issues would further alienate those voters.

New York Times reporter Joseph Berger was partially correct when he characterized borough appointees on the board as partisans. He found that borough presidents enjoyed considerable leverage over their appointments. He asserted, "Board members almost never defy the people who appoint them. Some want to make sure they get reappointed. Others need the support of the mayor or a borough president for any higher political ambitions they possess."[50] The borough presidents want their appointees to speak up for their own borough, rather than for the unitary interest of the board.

The PSC was aware of the limits of borough and mayoral coalitions when it supported the 1969 reorganization plan. Once the mayoral appointees were in place, the mayor discovered that either his appointees were socialized into the norms of the public school cartel, or they were isolated from the decision-making process.[51]

The chancellor of New York is the chief school politician. He or she survives to the extent that he or she can stay on good terms with the board and elected officials. Despite all claims to the contrary, school purchasing, construction, and hiring policies still interact with local patronage arrangements. Even with numerous management studies and reform programs to make schools more effective, schools continue to disregard them. Although a chancellor is the city's most visible appointed official in the school system, he or she has little control over the overall school system and is a representative for a bureaucracy with its own culture and ways of doing things.

Finally, a word must be said for the continuing significance of framing. One would think that with the growing information tide, the public would be able to challenge the framing of the school situation. There are several reasons why this is not the case. There is no multiple framing of public school politics. Framings by television, radio, and print media are almost identical. Rarely is there follow-up on most stories. Occasionally, there is a feature article on a special student or a teacher. The coverage is at best inconsistent. When school is out for the summer, the coverage usually ends.

CHAPTER NINE

CONCLUSION

Throughout this book, I have attempted to anatomize the complex theater of everyday politics in New York City. Like an opening of a new Broadway play, a newly elected mayor is always met with anxious anticipation. We sort through the dialogue and encounters to discern the plot and determine the protagonists and antagonists, but before we render our evaluation of the presentation we have witnessed, we wait for the reviews. Reviews offer us clarity, comparisons, summary characterizations, and a reframing of what we saw, heard, and read. And so it is with the media and politics.

Electing David Dinkins, an African American, mayor of New York City, the nation's largest and arguably one of the most important cities in the world, had within it a larger meaning. What had the voters of New York done? Had they just voted for a politician who won the Democratic primary, or was it a message of color blindness? Was it a triumph of the city's inclusive spirit or was it a harbinger of a slow-moving transracial transition? Did the election represent the regime change for which some city activists had hoped? Would it be a theater of embarrassment, sentiment, or racial redemption? The pending drama created an opportunity both for David Dinkins to prove his mettle and for reporters (reviewers) to record this historical event. After all, many of them knew the former borough president and liked him. However, they were obligated to cover him and events in an objective manner. The election of a black man provided an opportunity to revise the ongoing political discourse about whose city it was and to identify changes in ethnic hierarchies implicit in the transition. The public needed to know the meaning of the

Dinkins administration. This is why Dinkins' image was so important. In the early nineties, a black man who touted himself as a deracialized politician attracted doubting journalists.

This book discussed the social, structural, and economic changes that Dinkins inherited. It was a more difficult tenure than Ed Koch's twelve years earlier. The new charter eliminated the Board of Estimate and gave the city council a larger role in the budgetary process and land use policy. Adding more voices to land use policy did not improve the planning process. The city continues to limp along from project to project rather than developing a more comprehensive policy.[1] The budget became Dinkins' nemesis as he sparred publicly with actors ranging from labor leaders to New York City school chancellor. Like his predecessors Dinkins discovered that the school bureaucracy is not amenable to mayoral directions. The recession lingered throughout his tenure, and no one could have predicted that the fusion regime that Dinkins tried to create would face an insurmountable political communication problem.

Political Communication and the Third Era

Although the nascent third era of political communication is continuing to unfold, it is having an effect on city politics. This new era is characterized by multiple sources of the news, intense competition among reporters and outlets, multiple narratives, and a more information-conscious public. The mayor in a postmodern society has to work harder to convince others that city hall matters. Otherwise the metanarrative of any city will lose its grip on the imagination of its residents. The mayor has to govern as well reassure the public that the city's story will remain faithful to its plot.

For the first time in urban history there is a large quantity of information available anytime and all the time. As William Knoke has pointed out, we live in a placeless society—everything is everywhere. The same holds for information. This is not to say that the segmentation of messages has been discontinued. The message for new audiences is more segmented because the mayor has to cater to a more sophisticated public. This is why speaking style is open to more criticism than it used to be in political communication's first era when messages were produced, interpreted, and delivered by political parties and other interest groups.

Mayoral Style and Substance

All politicians are products of their political environment. Detroit's Coleman Young was a product of the rebellious labor movement of the thirties and forties. The movement ideology shaped his sometimes-cantankerous personality. Atlanta's Andrew Young was a product of the civil rights movement and his role as the movement's diplomat. Thomas Bradley was a product of the coalition of Los Angeles's white progressives and its nascent minority politics. Dinkins was a product of Harlem and the eastern version of white liberal/black coalition politics. As a creature of his environment, Dinkins could not be another Coleman Young because he did not have the background or the majority minority constituency, nor for that matter, could he be another Rudy Giuliani or Michael Bloomberg.

It is notable that Dinkins always presented himself as what James McGregor Burns calls a "transactional leader" not a "transformational leader."[2] The former focuses on exchanges between leaders and followers. Such leaders are bargainers and negotiators. They seek inclusion and social equilibrium. Dinkins won the 1989 election by promising to bring the various ethnic and racial communities together. Transformational leaders seek fundamental changes in the status quo and in doing so raise the aspiration of their followers. Dinkins may have raised the hopes of his black and Latino constituencies, but he never promised to change the city economic arrangements. The fusion regime his constituency hoped for never had the resources to be consummated. In the last days of his administration, the nascent fusion regime gave way to a developmental regime.

As we saw in the chapter on staffing, Dinkins tried to respond to the feedback he was getting from the communications system by changing or replacing members of his staff. In the Red Apple and Crown Heights incidents, he experimented with different styles of presentation. Because he was caught between the skills he learned in the second era of political communication and the new, less controlled third era, he found it difficult to cope. This is why Dinkins' responses to the Red Apple and Crown Heights crises appeared so ineffective.

Although Dinkins seemed amenable to coaching and cues from his speechwriters, his speaking style and ways of relating to the press did not change. It was, after all, *his style*. Different mayors use different styles with the press. Koch used wit and intimidation in his relationship with the media. Keeping the media at bay sometimes allowed Koch more space to frame issues and make his case to the public. At the same time, he supported a prodevelopment regime. He was able to keep his act going for twelve years. Dinkins, coming as he did after Koch, wanted to distance himself from his predecessor because he did not like Koch's style and thought it led to Koch's downfall.

The Koch years had built up some antagonism between city hall and the media. Some of the residual effects spilled over into the Dinkins tenure. This explains why Scardino, Dinkins' first press secretary, observed, "I think it was a peculiar moment when somehow journalists thought they were the enemy of politicians and politicians thought some of the journalists were the enemy."[3] As we suggested earlier, some black mayors believed that some white reporters were out to get them. The *Amsterdam News* published an editorial to that effect.[4] The black reporters working for a white paper, Dinkins' city hall staff surmised, were supporting their white colleagues and not calling them out on issues because they were currying favors from their white editors. The mayor under siege can become the mantra of a city hall staff. They, in turn, can see themselves as defenders of mayoral prerogatives. Reporters become even more aggressive as they feel that they are being stonewalled and misled. The result can be a low point in the coproduction of the news and in many ways contribute to an onset of an imperiled mayoralty. Political Scientist Larry Sabato has called this aggressive journalistic behavior "Inquisition, American Style." He asserts,

> It has become a spectacle without equal in modern American politics: the news media, print and broadcast, go after a wounded politician like sharks in a feeding frenzy. The wounds may have been self-inflicted, and the politician may richly deserve his or her fate, but the journalists now take center stage in the process, creating the news as much as reporting it, changing both the shape of election-year politics and the contours of government. Having replaced the political parties as the screening committee for candidates and officeholders, the media propel some politicians toward power and unceremoniously eliminate others. Unavoidably,

this enormously influential role—and the news practices employed in exercising it—has provided rich fodder for a multitude
of press critics.[5]

Throughout his administration, Mayor Dinkins never attacked the media directly because he thought the public would
think he was blaming them for his problems. "I think we [may-
ors] are afraid to complain because to complain is to blame the
media for his failures."[6] A month after taking office Dinkins said,
"I know that reporters feel that they're doing their jobs. . . . [I]t is
impossible, very difficult for anyone, maybe impossible, to be totally objective. . . . And so what [we] have to do is rely on reporters and their consciences to be fair. I think that by and large
they are fair."[7] In a National Press Club speech, Dinkins made a
point of addressing his remarks to the New York City reporters.
Dinkins was just acknowledging what every mayor soon discovers, that reporters are driven by career interest. They sip at the
substance of public policy issues but they do not take long
drinks. They are more likely to write about winners and losers
and political rivalries.

The idea that the media can make or break a mayor led journalists to attempt to frame the issues in city elections. Armed with
the notion that they are taken seriously by city readers, listeners
and viewers, reporters attempted to define the beginning of the
nineties as time to restructure the work force, depict labor leaders
as greedy, expose the dysfunctional city school system, root out
the black nationalist pretenders, and make the city safer.

This discourse offset Dinkins' civility and cooperation rhetoric. Although Mayor Dinkins and his staff fought this effort, they
could not stop it from happening. The media was also busy producing trivial news (personal tidbits about the mayor's tax returns and pseudo-issues about the mayor's dressing and bath-
ing habits). This kept tabloid readers anticipating the next day's
paper, provided talk radio hosts with material, and allowed television stations to use their video libraries to make a point. Print-
ing the fact that a PBA protester called the mayor a "washroom
attendant" certainly got the attention of the readers. The bottom
line for both the New York print and broadcast tabloids was
holding on to their readers and listeners.

News and Entertainment

New Yorkers are mayor watchers. The mayor of New York is a celebrity. Dinkins tried to graft himself onto the glitterati but was less successful than his predecessors and successors. The fact that he was expected to be a celebrity tells us a lot about the uniqueness of the city's politics. Voters want entertainment with their local politics. As William Gamson and associates told us, media-generated images of the world are presented in ways that make them seem natural. Michael Parenti makes the argument in *Invented Reality* that the media distorts reality by concentrating on distractions or political sideshows rather than delving into serious public policy issues. For him journalism never examines the impact of capitalism on society. There is also competition among media outlets and reporters. Television stations are in competition with each other more than with the print media because the nation is less print dependent than formerly. Television stations are in the entertainment business, and local news for them is part of their entertainment fare. When polls find that most people get their political information from television, one wonders if they are referring to local news programming or national news broadcasts.

In fact there is never enough local news. Most television programs began with a crime story—if it bleeds, it leads. When one reads the transcripts of the 6:00 news a few bare sentences are devoted to the local issues. Local news is so concerned about ratings and the appearance of their anchorpersons that important stories are seldom fully developed, and follow-up stories are practically nonexistent. The Sunday morning talk shows are not substitutes for everyday coverage.

The local print media is somewhat better. In the dailies there is the obligatory cover of national news and often the local material is covered in the metro sections. The *New York Times* does a fairly good job of covering local news, but it sees itself in competition with the *Washington Post* for national news. The tabloids offer pictures and bold headlines such as "Dave Do Something." That headline will live in infamy, but the article that follows does not provide information about what the city faced in its attempts to manage crime.

Since the publication of Parenti's book there has been more concentration of media ownership and less differentiation of the news product. Parenti was correct when he predicted that the media would anticipate their readers and viewers interest by concentrating on a politician's alleged eccentricities. In Dinkins case, it was his penchant for tuxedos and tennis playing.

This is not to say that news making in city politics has become the commercial enterprise that Parenti lamented. Yet keeping them laughing and gossiping does work. In modern urban politics, the witty and entertaining leader often succeeds in getting the public to suspend its judgment about critical public policy issues. The media prefers this type of leader, which is why they approved Dinkins' predecessors and successors.

Why Image Matters

This book discusses several types of images, *prepackaged, ecological, preferred self, public,* and *prevailing.* Events can change a mayoral image gradually or overnight. Blumler and Kavanaugh pointed out that in the second era of political communication, image consultants played an increasingly important role in elections and afterward. W. Lance Bennett identified three elements of image making.[8] They include *message composition,* a simple theme for thinking about events; *message salience,* saturating the media so that the image becomes salient and dominant among competing images; and *message credibility,* surrounding the message with trappings of credibility (good packaging). What we saw in the Dinkins case was an inability to fashion a message that induced political acquiescence. Without some degree of acquiescence, governing is extremely difficult.

Dinkins' instincts about New York City politics seemed sensible at first glance, but a closer look revealed that he or his aides lost the packaging contest. The racial healing image could not encompass all the social and economic problems facing the city. The transmogrification of Dinkins' image led to serious problems for his image consultants. They made a gallant effort to rescue his image in the reelection campaign ads but were not successful.

Dinkins, like most black politicians, found it difficult to escape prepackaged racial images of blacks. Robert Entman and Andrew Rojecki claim this is the case because whites, lacking personal contact with a variety of blacks, tend to rely on media to categorize blacks. Claire Kim was right when she flagged the tampering with racial hierarchy as one of unspoken issues in the Red Apple incident. When juxtaposed with other racial groups, the tendency is to rank blacks at the bottom of hierarchy. This may be changing, but it is the reality. Even Dinkins' deracialized image could not insulate him from the ranking.

Obviously, the images of Mayor David Dinkins were critical to his governing style. It was Dinkins' ecological image, that is, his relationship to his political environment, that transformed his public image and became his prevailing image. As we demonstrated, images can be misleading. In this case they were misleading because reporters seized upon stereotypes and eccentricities in an attempt to capture the real person. Unfortunately, this practice distracts the public from understanding how an individual copes with the real issues before the city. Despite Dinkins' penchant for tuxedoes and tennis, he never approached the empty suit status of Jimmy Walker. Yet it was easy for reporters to hint at that analogy when discussing Dinkins. Two generalizations can be made about this approach. Colorful writing does not equal insightful or useful writing. Just because an editor likes the copy does not mean it is meaningful political communication.

In marketing, there is a saying, "Image is everything." In city politics, an image is not everything, but it is close. Politicians strive to create a self-serving political image (preferred self-image) to get elected, such as to sell public policy and leave office gracefully. Perfecting an effective image is extremely difficult and even more laborious to maintain. Therefore, most politicians are prepared to accept the second best image (a good public image). The social and political construction of a mayoral image is a fascinating process that often begins with the socialization of candidates, highlighted during the campaign, and is consolidated while in office. Hired by the candidate or officeholder, the political consultant's job is to make the individual likeable and believable. Candidate personalities matter, but the selling of the candidate to voters is a task increasingly assigned to political consultants and the media. Despite a consultant's efforts, unanticipated events can often derail a carefully constructed public image and transform it into a negative prevailing image.

The public may have been willing to accept the image of Dinkins portrayed by the media because it required a minimum
amount of personal investment and thought. The pace of city living demands that readers, listeners, and viewers take mental
shortcuts. Stereotypes work because they are convenient. This
is why comedian Jackie Mason's remark about Dinkins being a
"fancy shvartze with a mustache" and police protesters calling
Dinkins a "washroom attendant" were so revealing and explo-
sive. In a curious way our society seems to yearn for such statements. Once the media reports such an assertion, it forces the
public to take one side or the other. Such statements also provide the listener and reader with permission to agree. It may not
be politically correct to say so, but one can entertain those beliefs in one's mind.

Political consultants believe that there are idiosyncratic cor-
ners in the mind of the average voter and accordingly seek to
shape their client's public posture and messages. If they believe
that calling attention to a stereotype will help their client, they
will find a way to get it done or play it off if someone else does it.
It is not a matter of hoodwinking the public but a strategy to
frame an event or win an election.

Does Dinkins' caricatured image fit Phillis Kaniss's "ribbon
cutter" media type? By all accounts he seemed to enjoy being the
mayor and the ceremonial aspects of the job. He liked attending
community meetings, as he did as borough president. Dinkins
was a community meeting-going politician, but the New York
media interpreted this behavior as somehow overdone. However,
there is no evidence that Dinkins was oblivious to the other aspects of his job. Part of his problem was his staff. Although he
was warned early about the disarray at city hall, he never made
the critical changes necessary to make his administration work,
nor did he connect the negative publicity of his appointees to his
situation or image. Judging from a subsequent interview, Dinkins was not a man who would deny his staff their share of the
publicity. His successor's, Rudy Giuliani's, firing of Bill Bratton,
the police commissioner, surprised him. According to Dinkins,
Bratton was fired, in part, for receiving so much of the publicity
for reducing crime in New York.[9]

The staff problems were compounded by Dinkins' public presence. The way he answered reporters' questions and his choice of

words in a given situation fed into the caricature reporters were making of him. In an attempt to maintain his preferred image, Dinkins did make some confusing and often ambiguous statements. Ostensibly Dinkins seems to have been searching for a way to assure his detractors that he was even-handed and civil. He was very careful not to blame racism for anything, yet his willingness to discard this mantra did not endear him to voters in Queens and Staten Island. Bennett believes the reason that people cling to an original image (in this case a prepackaged one of Dinkins) is that there is no "easy-to-grasp alternative understanding of a situation"[10] (the racial dilemma the Mayor faced).

Speaking and Leading

A closer look at Dinkins' answering style suggests that he was a man caught in a temporal mismatch. Reading Dinkins' responses, it seems that his answers would have been more appropriate for the 1960s, rather than the 1990s. In the 1960s black speakers who wanted to separate themselves from black militants spoke in terms not to offend white members of the racial coalition. Dinkins also felt he could not be candid for fear of sounding like he was blaming the media for his failings. He was careful not to let reporters force him to use the word *racism*. He often asked reporters rhetorically "What do you think?" which may have caused some confusion and misinterpretation. Lacking the wit and penchant for making colorful quotes of his predecessor, Mayor Koch, Dinkins tried to answer questions in a more philosophical manner. This made for dull copy.

In the beginning of the Dinkins administration, Joe Klein, formerly of *New York* magazine, believed a little dramaturgy could help project the mayor's leadership. Klein offered, "[T]he art of politics, however, is to build public confidence, through the illusion of mastery—to seem on top of things. . . . [O]ver the past few months, Dinkins has given the opposite impression. Indeed, he has isolated himself with a passive, unimaginative administration."[11] Subsequent articles by Klein chronicled Dinkins' missed opportunities and misjudgments. Other reporters also questioned whether or not Dinkins was up for the job of being mayor.[12] After a black boycott of a Korean green grocer in

Brooklyn and a black/Jewish conflict in Crown Heights, several more reporters began to question Dinkins' competency.[13]

Dinkins may have been aware that the media's questioning was deflating his image, but he lacked the rhetorical skills to re-frame the question or engage in a diversionary tactic. The gentle-man image that helped to put Dinkins into Gracie Mansion did not serve him well as crisis manager. Dinkins' political socializa-tion as a clubhouse politician did not prepare him to take control and impose his will on political events. He was left with little choice but to be a partisan caretaker mayor.[14] Such politicians rarely transcend their political backgrounds. As suggested ear-lier, politicians like Dinkins were considered organizational float-ers. These individuals do get to the top, but their personalities prevent them from dominating their environment. Typically, they are very careful not to offend any powerful group leaders or coali-tions, and in trying to accommodate a maximum number of interests, they allow their leadership to be undermined.

As I stated above, Dinkins' personality was attractive to voters in 1989 but worked against him when he failed to mediate the racial challenges of the 1990 Red Apple and the 1991 Crown Heights crises. Perhaps the worst image wounds were suffered when public employee union leaders attacked him. After that at-tack, it appeared that all of his friends had turned against him. Yet these personalized attacks did not fully explain why Dinkins lost his bid for the mayoral reelection.

Why Dinkins Lost

In May 1993 a *New York Times*/WCBS poll found that blacks still supported Dinkins (83 percent to 7 percent over Giuliani). Latinos were evenly divided (45 percent to 44 percent) and whites were opposed (27 percent to 60 percent for Giuliani).[15] Apparently Dinkins was able to make up some of those losses in the campaign because he only lost by five thousand votes. In this study interviewees had several theories of why Dinkins lost the 1993 race. Before the 1993 mayoral election, McNickle sug-gested several scenarios of how Dinkins' electoral coalition could come apart. However, his predictions were somewhat off target. For example, McNickle asserted, "David Dinkins's base among black voters is secure."[16] He declared Dinkins "a senior partner in a new racial coalition that governed the city."[17] Both characterizations proved to be false. In 1993, Dinkins suffered the same problems many first-time black mayors have experienced, that is, a drop of campaign enthusiasm and voter turnout in his reelection bid. Dinkins ran as the incumbent mayor with all the trappings of the office but not as a tribune for minorities and liberals. To be reelected, he needed to remobilize his supporters and reach out to those who had voted against him in the 1989 election. He was unable to do this because many of his previous supporters (blacks, Latinos, and liberal whites) now harbored doubts and grievances. Even one of Dinkins' closest aides claimed the "mayor did not get his voters [minority voters] out in 1993." Dinkins won office by a narrow margin; and he lost by a narrow margin.

McNickle correctly predicted the budget crisis as a potential problem for Dinkins. McNickle wrote his book before the 1993 primary and predicted that if a Latino candidate ran in the primary, it could mean trouble for Dinkins. A Latino candidate did run, but Dinkins prevailed in the democratic primary. The Latino community seems to have been particularly disappointed with Dinkins. The firing of Willie Nieves came back to haunt Mr. Dinkins. He asserted, "Mi conciencia esta clara y se lo que tengo que hacer . . . hay que sacar a David Dinkins de la alcaldia a como de lugar."[18]

McNickle rightly pointed out that the fallout from the Crown Heights incident would undermine Dinkins' support in the Jewish community. Although a Jewish Democrat did not win the Republican primary,[19] Giuliani was able to win a larger percentage of the Jewish vote.

Dinkins managed to keep some of his supporters but still lost in the general election to Giuliani. Dinkins, the Democrat, lost the general election to a Republican challenger in an overwhelmingly Democratic city. The simple explanation for Dinkins' loss was the inability to grow his electoral coalition. Perhaps many first-time minority voters, mobilized to register and vote because of the novelty of a strong minority candidate, were not as enthusiastic the second time around. The issues and expectations had shifted during his mayoral term, and he did not change with them. Nevertheless, the *Amsterdam News* enthusiastically endorsed his reelection, as did others.

David Dinkins will be re-elected for the many improvements he has made to the fabric of this City. Numbered amongst these improvements are building the most diverse government New York City has ever known, attention to the protection of the residents of New York City by providing more police officers and putting more of them on the beat; opening libraries six days per week; opening school buildings for recreation, freezing property, water and sewer taxes; persuading corporations to stay in New York City; saving thousands of jobs; provided the vehicle for increasing the number of minorities and women doing business with the City; initiating avenues for building harmony and understanding between the youth of the City; and negotiating fair contracts with the unions operating the city.[20]

Of course, some voters did not share this sentiment. They were less enthusiastic about Dinkins' reelection. Although the media agreed that Dinkins' 1993 campaign ads were better than those of Giuliani, Dinkins' prevailing image was one of a nice man out of his depth. Indeed, Dinkins seemed locked in the "nice man image" when the public preferred a tough guy who could deal with crime. In a *New York Post* article entitled "The Selling of the Mayor," Dinkins was characterized as "Uncle Dave." The characterization was not meant to be pejorative. It seemed to aim at explaining the caring nature of Dinkins, but "uncle" before a black man's name carried historical baggage and racial connotations, and in this case an erroneous one. Although Dinkins never pandered or deferred to his white constituents, it is not clear he understood them or what they expected him to do.

Dinkins' media experts selected this line for reelection ads: "It takes more than tough talk to run a tough city." This was designed to make the viewer question the tough talk by his opponent, Giuliani. Giuliani's media consultants described their candidate as "Doctor Fusion." Giuliani, who got both the Liberal and Republican nominations, was characterized as a man with broad support in several circles. The theme of his first commercial was "we are going to throw aside politics as usual."[21] But it was Giuliani's image as tough on crime that resonated with the voters.

Fear of crime provides a more complicated explanation for Dinkins' reelection defeat. Although the pull of incumbent and party loyalty was strong, the public was never enthusiastic about his proposal for a new safety compact. Marketing a new safety compact was extremely difficult for a man who had sold himself as a "healer" and had avoided the code words that implied that some minorities were members of a criminal class. Giuliani had no difficulty making the argument that he was the "tough guy" in the race. Any credibility accumulated from Dinkins' *Safe Streets, Safe City* program was lost when he was attacked by the BPA. Michael Cottman of *Newsday* reported that even the Grand Council of Guardians, the black police group, gave him only guarded support.[22] The impression was that Dinkins was losing the support of organized black groups. Black members within white organizations were strangely silent about not supporting Dinkins for election. The *Amsterdam News* reported that some black teachers were planning to retaliate, albeit "inaudibly" against the UFT decision not to back Dinkins for reelection.[23]

In retrospect, we know that Dinkins' staff members were unsuccessful in protecting his reputation and image. This task should have been the prime directive. Instead staff members often pursued their own agendas at the expense of the mayor. Having chosen people that helped him get elected and that would promote his all-inclusive administration, Dinkins was faced with several high-profile resignations beginning with his press secretary, Albert Scardino, within the first year of his administration and ending with Phillip Michael, his budget director, during his reelection campaign. These were in addition to the high-ranking Latino appointees' resignations. *Village Voice* reporter Michael Tomasky concluded that "the rumpled genius" Bill Lynch applied the wrong type of solutions in the Crown Heights situations and affected the reelection campaign.[24] Although Dinkins criticized Giuliani's upstaging of his staff, it kept the media focused on Giuliani and helped his image.

Dinkins' successor in the borough president's office, Ruth Messenger, listed three reasons she felt Dinkins lost the mayoral race. First, many of his strongest supporters had lost some energy and passion because they felt he had not done enough. Second, the Crown Heights incident—the Cuomo administration's report on Crown Heights came out during the 1993 mayoral election. Finally, the turnout of fifty thousand Staten Island residents for the referendum on Staten Island succession.

These included many white voters who presumably voted against Dinkins. Bill Lynch also supported the Staten Island succession theory but admitted that unlike the 1989 campaign, there was not as much enthusiasm. In 1989 "it was like a movement. Everybody was trying to vote."[25] Given the budget problems the Dinkins administration could not live up to the high expectations of his core constituency, African Africans, Latinos, and organized labor. Mollenkopf's analysis of voting returns supports the Lynch-Messenger analysis. He found that disproportionately fewer blacks voted in 1993; Latinos also showed a low turnout, and the white liberal areas of Manhattan and Brooklyn "shifted away" from Dinkins.[26] *Village Voice* reporter Michael Tomasky also subscribed to the coalition stagnation theory. Unlike the black mayors in Los Angeles and Chicago, Dinkins failed to expand his coalition. Tomasky asserted that Dinkins "utterly failed to expand his coalition, in that failure reposes the real tragedy of his defeat, and the true nature of the loss as a setback for progressive politics."[27]

Before the vote, Mike McAlary was quite graphic in his characterization of the Dinkins situation. For McAlary Dinkins was a man wounded by events.

> The cuts are suffered with increasing frequency. The Crown Heights Reports opened a sucking chest wound on the mayor. His lungs are singed with asbestos. The Lockheed Report cut him to the bone. Finally, a hopelessly ambitious fire commissioner moving to his prone mayor's body with the wanton glee of a Los Angeles rioter bashed David Dinkins in the head with a resignation letter wrapped in a brick.[28]

Andrew Hacker, a Queens College political scientist and longtime observer of New York City politics, was quoted as saying that "four years ago, there was a sense of He's a decent guy, let's give him a chance. You could almost hear the sigh of relief: Thank God the black people have come up with such a dignified guy. But he just hasn't been able to solidify his coalition. We liked the idea of his being a gentleman. But [being a] gentleman just wasn't enough."[29] Hacker captures some of the disillusion among city voters. Why were they so disappointed? The explanation may lie in the fact they did not know David Dinkins.

Who Is Dave Dinkins?

The dynamics of race and electoral politics include several misunderstandings, misperceptions and miscalculations. Misunderstandings occur when political actors—voters, politicians and reporters—get political meaning wrong. Misperceptions happen when political actors misread the other actor's behavior and motives. Miscalculations are often the product of incorrect information and flawed interpretations. Voters, politicians, and reporters are particularly vulnerable to any of these possibilities when they are watching and evaluating black elected officials. In other words, there are varieties of meanings and motives attached to electing a black person to an important public office. It follows that there will be a range of reactions to that black elected official's behavior while in office. This is why a review of David Dinkins' tenure is so important. What were voters thinking when they voted for Dinkins? Was there any validity to Rev. Calvin Butts' assertion that Dinkins was "as much a machine, clubhouse politician as he is African American."

In many ways, "Dave" was an imaginary figure in the minds of New Yorkers. Different constituencies wanted different things from him. White liberals wanted him to be a standard bearer for black decency and civility. Blacks and Latinos wanted him to represent them and to tell off the rude and racist white police officers. Essentially, Dinkins owed them. Dinkins tried to please all of them, which was impossible. Casting himself as a black man who would bring the city together worked only for a few weeks. Dinkins could not be the kind of person they wanted him to be or as he had advertised himself to be. Dinkins must have confused his listeners more when he returned briefly to the exhausted "healer theme" in his reelection bid.[30]

Then the questions became, who is he, and what is he trying to do? Was David Dinkins the harbinger of a new black, middle-class ascendancy in New York life? Was he trying to prove that blacks had different personalities? Did he believe that his civility would prevail over the uncivil culture of the city? Whatever the answer to these questions, Dinkins could not deliver on the implied promises of his first campaign and "the energy and passion" that Messinger referred to was not there in the second campaign.

The misunderstanding of Dinkins was not entirely the fault of the media. His image as a race healer, partly promoted by the press, was shaken badly by the Red Apple Boycott and the Crown Heights incident. The way Dinkins handled the so-called black militants in both cases proved to be critical for his image. Black critics, particularly ones presenting themselves as militants, can be a problem for any black mayor. Several black mayors have encountered what may be called the "straw militant black man syndrome." Cleveland's Carl Stokes had Fred "Ahmed" Evans, Michael White had George Forbes, Detroit's Coleman Young had Ken Cockrel, Newark's Ken Gibson had Amiri Baraka, and Dinkins had Sonny Carson and Al Sharpton. White journalists seem attracted to the idea of constructing black mayors and their black critics as a good versus bad "Negro" contest. In soliciting comments from the mayor's black critics, reporters seem to want to spike a story. In the case of a racial incident (Crown Heights), this strategy unintentionally created a *wrap around story* that obscured the facts in the event.

Militant black critics also create a political dilemma for the black mayor. If a black mayor denounces black militants, then the white press is inclined to praise him as a "stand-up guy." However, denouncing a critic, particularly one seeking a reputation as a black militant, can erode a black mayor's credibility among his black constituency. It does not matter if the mayor has taken the right side of the issues. Rather, it is a case of race loyalty. This is particularly true if a black mayor is elected with significant white support, as was Dinkins. The black constituency often finds itself looking for signs of selling out. It is sometimes difficult for this constituency to understand why a black mayor would disapprove of anyone "telling white folks off."

If a black mayor does not respond to his black critics or seek to remain neutral, the press interprets that as encouraging the militants (as with Dinkins and the Red Apple incident). Accordingly, black mayors find themselves being towed in different political directions. They understand that race rhetoric keeps their base contented, but using it can alienate their white supporters. Knocking down straw men is not without its perils. Serving both constituencies can be very difficult as Dinkins' troubles demonstrated.

Although Dinkins was never employed to solve the city's economic problems, the continuing recession reinforced the lingering and underlying perceptions of incompetence. In the waning days of Dinkins' administration, the feeble attempts at promoting new policy initiatives were seen as desperation, not innovation. In the end it did not matter that crime was declining in New York City and that the Girgenti report partially exonerated Dinkins. The prevailing image was reified.[31]

Dinkins became a social construction, a construction of the safe black man protecting whites against the "great undisciplined [black criminal element and black militants]." At first Dinkins embraced this construction—"I am the man who will bring us together." When presidential candidate Richard Nixon said that in the 1968 presidential campaign, most people dismissed it as campaign rhetoric. Such a statement by Dinkins provided a certain reassurance, and his constituency held him to it.

The construction that had given him access to white liberals and moderate political circles also put Dinkins into a bind. The mantle may have fit his first campaign, but it was mangled during the public safety crisis. The Crown Heights incident gave closure to the "incompetent" image that reporters were creating in the public's mind. *Impato,* the Latino newspaper, was even more colorful when it called Crown Heights Dinkins's Waterloo.[32] In 1993 New Yorkers wanted a strong man, not a conciliator. This yearning for a man on a white horse brought a quick end to Dinkins' tenure. Besides, for some a black man riding a white horse does not work well as an image.

White New York politicians generally liked Dinkins, but they were unable to give him the small victories he needed in the Crown Heights case. Without that victory (social accounting success) Dinkins was unable to build the credibility necessary to remain in office. There was no workable stratagem for his reelection campaign. Party loyalty was not enough, and since Dinkins had not been cast as a programmatic individual, he was judged on his handling of the various racial crises.

Political scientists have generally accepted the notion that electoral alliances cannot automatically be converted into governing alliances. Dinkins' coalition never expanded, and members of his own racial group abandoned him. Dinkins never complained that he was hamstrung by white intransigence, but in retrospect maybe he should have. This explanation might have protected his base among blacks and Latinos during the various crises. If Dinkins' first term had been uneventful, then Dinkins might have been able to make a case for reelection. However, events worked against him. As his predecessor, Abraham Beame, discovered, nice guys are voted out of office at the first sign of trouble. In 1959 Sayre and Kaufman commented: "For lesser men the office of Mayor is an office of weakness. Average men as Presidents are more fortunate; the office reinforces the man. But the mayoralty is a vulnerable symbol of all defects in the city and its government. It is within close reach of its critics."[33]

Richard Wade, a noted urban historian and a New York City political activist, made an interesting comment about the early part of Dinkins' tenure. "It's like the fellow who is falling out of the 12-story window—nothing has happened yet." It was only after Crown Heights that Dinkins' staff realized something had happened, and Dinkins would later lament, "Crown Heights will be in my obituary."[34]

As I suggested earlier, Dinkins had a complicated image. He was an enigma within the great puzzle of the city's politics. Reporters reacted to Dinkins by trying to interject some drama into his stories. Among Jeffrey Pressman's lists of the preconditions for effective mayoral leadership was a supportive press.[35] A hostile or even a second-guessing media can make leading constituents more difficult. Mayors cannot lead under conditions of media-contested *social accounting*. For this reason we will further examine the role of the reporter.

Reporters, Messages, and Mayors

The relationship between the mayor and the media is complex. Every city is different. In cities with a strong mayor and a weak media, the advantage goes to city hall. This is particularly true in cities with large dailies with absentee ownership. Strong media cities such as New York put the mayor at disadvantage. When a weak mayor is elected, then he or she has to set boundaries between city hall and the media (for example, Koch) or have the boundaries imposed on him or her (for example, Dinkins). Table 9.1 shows the monitoring of Dinkins. Media questioned his abilities and decisions but were also able to sustain decisions that fit the overall city interest.

Table 9.1. Media Relationship with David Dinkins

	Questioning	Sustaining
Continual	Staffing Decisions Mediation Skills Leadership Skills Management Skills	Economic Development Choices Lowering Constituency Expectations
Episodic	Lifestyle Choices Choice of Words Overall Vision	Legitimacy Dedication Ceremonial Roles

What this matrix shows is that the monitoring of Dinkins took a discernible pattern. In another city, the monitoring might have a different angle. Nevertheless, reporters considered their sustaining support of mayors as evidence of balanced reporting. They considered questioning the mayor's action part of their job and recognized the difference between elite and mass audiences.

There is always a disinclination to take on the larger economic interest in a city. Reporters know that mayors are out-front spokespersons for a governing coalition and that it is acceptable to criticize them. The political messages seek to activate the audience's ability to associate or disassociate with the incumbent mayor. When there is a difference between portions of the audience's race and that of the mayor, messages are often packaged in racial terms. The prevailing image of the former mayor of Washington D.C. Marion Barry was that of a rascal who incessantly embarrassed the city. Yet the *Washington Post* was not able to alienate Barry's core supporters from him because he was able to frame the attack in racial terms. He was able to defend himself against a "white media." The same tactics, but not for the same charges, were used by former Mayors Coleman Young (Detroit) and Harold Washington (Chicago). Psychologist

E. P. Hollander argues that some individuals have what he calls "idiosyncratic credits."[36] In other words, an individual acquires credits and status for accomplishing something that a constituency values, and those credits can be used to offset deviant behavior. Barry accumulated considerable credits in his work in the civil rights movement and directing War on Poverty programs. Young had credits from the struggles of the labor movement. Washington accumulated credits for being an antimachine politician. In attacking these men, the media racialized themselves and failed in their attempt to discredit them. Whereas in the case of a deracialized mayor, who is also disinclined to regard media criticisms in racial terms, standing up to a media onslaught will be difficult, if not impossible. David Dinkins came to office with few idiosyncratic credits and considerable political debt to those who helped his career. A long career in government alone is not sufficient to maximize the amount of credits one needs in the face of a relatively hostile media. Lacking such credits, Dinkins was at disadvantage in office.

Not in position to fend off attacks, Dinkins often lost the framing of the discourse to reporters. In the Crown Heights situation, reporters were able to challenge what he did, what he said, and what he meant. As I suggested some reporters saw themselves as mere scribes just reporting what they saw and heard, while others consciously and unconsciously had higher ambitions. They saw themselves as reporting, interpreting, and prescribing. Some reporters expect their writings to influence the mayor's thinking or actions.

Obviously Todd Purdum and Joe Klein considered themselves performing all three functions. They always wrote for impact—they had a sense of their own agency. For this reason and because of their reputation among their colleagues, their remarks mattered. Klein pursued a relentless critique of Dinkins. Obviously editors approved of what Purdum and Klein were saying. The *Times* editors apparently approved of Purdum's actions in the Scardino matter. The Purdum letter was acting not just reporting. Joe Klein was important because he was a consistent critic of the mayor. Other journalists read his comments and followed his lead rather than make their own evaluation of the mayor. Klein and Purdum were critical to the construction of the prevailing image of Dinkins, because they activated a stereotyped construct, that race affected the way Dinkins did his job. Comments regarding the mayor's clothing and his fondness for tennis further seem trivial, but they fed the idea that Dinkins was more interested in declaring his middle-class status than doing his job as mayor. Writing about Dinkins in this way activated the African American stereotype, which included the traits of inattentiveness, malleability, and ineptness. There were no reporters who consistently refuted these characterizations, giving them more credibility. It goes without saying that not all of Dinkins' troubles were caused by journalists. Their portrayals of him did not by themselves trigger the backlash against Dinkins, but their characterizations served to activate reservations many white voters had developed during the first Giuliani-Dinkins race.

Neuman and colleagues argued that journalists themselves become part of the process of constructing reality. They concluded, "Journalists reconstruct reality for an audience, taking in account their organizational and modality constraints, professional judgments and certain expectations about the audience. Finally, the individual reader or viewer constructs a version of reality built from personal experience, interaction with peers and interpreted selection from the mass media."[37]

The metaphoric "dance" between most white reporters and David Dinkins, the black mayor of New York, involved the irony of liking him as a person and not respecting him as the mayor. They neither feared Dinkins, nor were they in awe of him. Comparably speaking, he was afforded little deference for the office he held. Obviously race played a role in the situation, but Dinkins also contributed to reporters "getting out of their place." As a congenial personality, it may not have occurred to him that he needed to put reporters in their place. Although he resented some of their writings, unlike Ed Koch, Dinkins rarely scolded reporters publicly.

It is likely that the next African American mayor of New York will be very different from David Dinkins, but some reporters will try to compare the two. Comparison is a natural part of reporting, but every mayor is a product of his political environment and his racial times. Dinkins' white successors learned from his efforts and mistakes and found it easier to assert themselves as the mayor for all the people. However, New York City residents, regardless of race, ethnicity, nationality, and place of birth have a right to expect effective leadership from their mayor because it is after all "their city." They equally have the right to good reporting without biased slanting. W. Lance Bennett asserts, "People are ill-equipped to monitor and guide their own destiny when they look through a news window and see a world of scattered happenings, sketched with stereotypes and colored by ideology."[38] For Bennett the news simply reproduces and creates illusions that we hold about ourselves. The reporting on Dinkins certainly did not challenge New Yorkers to think more critically about the problems facing the city, nor did it probe the meaning for those whites that had trouble reconciling their negative images of blacks and the deracialized, competent, and caring image that Dinkins tried to project. Instead the media personalized the tenure of David Dinkins, reminding the public of the emotionally charged racial history of New York while downplaying the economic conditions that led to the city's fiscal crisis.

The politics that created David Dinkins and his challenges still haunts us today. Race is still a part of New York City politics as it is in most American cities. Exorcising it requires rethinking the social purpose it serves. As we look to the future, we can expect the news producers and consumers to help us make this critical transformation. This objective is a worthy cause for those who yearn for high-quality city government.

NOTES

Preface

1. Robert Turner, "What Makes a Mayor?" *The Boston Globe Magazine* (November 13, 1983) p. 13.
2. Ibid., p. 12.
3. Interview with David Dinkins, October 14, 2002.
4. Ibid.

1. Introduction

1. Jay G. Blumer and Dennis Kavanaugh, "The Third Age of Political Communication: Influences and Features," *Political Communication,* Vol. 16 (July–September 1999) pp. 209–30.
2. This reporter worked for one of the leading local TV stations. His point was that local TV stations just report the news; they do not do research. If they have investigative reporters, they usually restrict them to consumer issues.
3. See Ferdinand Mount, *The Theater of Politics* (New York: Schocken Books, 1973).
4. Phyllis Kaniss, *Making Local News* (Chicago: University of Chicago Press, 1991) p. 175–79.
5. Doris Graber, *Mass Media and American Politics* (Washington, D.C.: CQ, 2002) p. 2.
6. Edward Rubin, *Media Politics and Democracy* (New York: Oxford University Press, 1977) p. 8.
7. See my discussion of boosterism in Wilbur C. Rich, "Vincent Cianci and Boosterism in Providence," in James Bowers and Wilbur C. Rich, eds., *Governing Middle-Sized Cities* (Boulder: Rienner, 2002).
8. For the first time in fifteen years the Gallup poll found that more and more Americans believe the news is biased and inaccurate. They believe it is biased toward the Democrats. See Frank Newport, "Number of Americans Who Feel News Coverage Is Inaccurate Increases Sharply," *Gallup News Service* (December 8, 2000).
9. Kaniss, *Making Local News,* pp. 90–91.
10. John Soloski, "News Reporting and Professionalism: Some Constraints on the Reporting of the News," *Media, Culture and Society,* Vol. 11 (1989) p. 215.
11. Interview with Joyce Purnick, January 12, 2001.

12. Interview with Paul Delaney, February 1, 2001.

13. Joe Saltzman, "New Media Owners, Same Old Problems," *USA TODAY: The Magazine of the American Scene,* Vol. 124, No. 2606 (November 1995) p. 31.

14. Other scholars make a similar observation, see Bartholomew H. Sparrow, *Uncertain Guardians* (Baltimore: Johns Hopkins University Press, 1999).

15. P. Watzlawick, J. M. Beavin, and D. D. Jackson, *Pragmatics of Human Communications* (New York: Norton, 1967).

16. Murray Edelman, *Constructing the Political Spectacle* (Chicago: University of Chicago Press, 1988) p. 104.

17. Limor Peer and James S. Ettema, "The Mayor's Race: Campaign Coverage and the Discourse of Race in American's Three Largest Cities," *Critical Studies in Mass Communication,* Vol. 15, No. 3 (September 1998) pp. 255–78.

18. Robert M. Entman, and Andrew Rojecki, *The Black Image in the White Mind* (Chicago: University of Chicago Press, 2000) p. 48.

19. Entman and Rojecki, op. cit., 49.

20. W. Russell Neuman, Marion Just, Ann N. Crigler, *Common Knowledge: News and the Construction of Political Meaning* (Chicago: University of Chicago Press, 1992) p. 120.

21. Jeffrey Pressman, "Preconditions of Mayoral Leadership," *American Political Science Review,* Vol. 65 (June, 1979) pp. 11–24.

22. In a 1999 Gallup poll 57 percent of blacks felt that there were too few black newscasters and reporters on local and network television news programs. Only 31 percent of whites agreed. See Mark Gillespie "Blacks want to see more diversity; whites generally believe media is racially balanced," *The Gallup New Service,* 1999.

23. Black reporters agree that there is a need for more black reporters. It is not clear to me that that this change would make much difference in the overall direction of the coverage, since the print media rewards negative reporting about politicians. For example, James Campbell of the *Houston Chronicle* made that point in an article about the controversial 1991 mayoral candidacy of Sylvester Turner. see "How Should Houston Blacks Look Back on Mayoral Campaigns? Dirty Politics Wasn't Racism" (December 15, 1991) p. 1.

24. Anju Chaudhary, "Press Portrayal of Black Officials," *Journalism Quarterly,* Vol. 37 (Winter 1988) p. 541.

25. See Carl Stokes, *Promise of Power: A Political Autobiography* (New York: Simon and Schuster, 1973).

26. Felicity Barringer, "Disliking Coverage: Cleveland's Mayor Retaliates," *New York Times* (May 28, 2001) p. 2c.

27. See Adam Cohen, "City Boosters," *Time,* Vol. 150 (August 18, 1997) pp. 20–24.

28. For a discussion of antipower bias, see Barbara Fermen, *Governing the Ungovernable City* (Philadelphia: Temple University Press, 1985) pp. 5–6.

29. Bryan Jones, ed., *Leadership and Politics: New Perspectives in Political Science* (Lawrence: University Press of Kansas, 1989) p. 4.
30. Brian Spitzberg, "The Dialectics of (IN) Competence," *Journal of Social and Personal Relationship,* Vol. 11, No. 1 (February, 1993) pp. 137–38.
31. Tali Mendelberg, *Race Card* (Princeton: Princeton University Press, 2001).
32. Ibid., pp. 6–7.
33. For a discussion of political socialization see David O. Sears "Political Socialization" in Fred Greenstein and Nelson Polsby, *Handbook of Political Science* (Reading, Mass: Addison-Wesley, 1975); also see P. Devine, "Stereotypes and Prejudice: Their Automatic and Controlled Components," *Journal of Personality and Social Psychology,* Vol. 56 (January 1989) pp. 5–18. Blacks also believe that whites hold these attitudes. See Lee Sigelman and Steven A. Tuch's "Metastereotypes: Black Perception of White Stereotypes of Blacks," *Public Opinion Quarterly* Vol. 61 (Spring 1997) pp. 87–101.
34. See Anne Schneider, and Helen Ingram, "Social Construction of Target Populations: Implications for Politics and Policy," *American Political Science Review,* Vol. 87 (June 1993) pp 334–48.
35. Boston's Mayor Thomas Menino was known as Mayor "Mumbles" for a long time. It is unlikely that an inarticulate black man could have been elected mayor of New York.
36. Ironically, the stereotypes about black intelligence stay intact even when a reporter suggests that a black mayor is "really smart." Whites who believe that blacks are less intelligent may also believe that there are exceptions.
37. William Gamson, David Croteau, William Hoynes, and Theodore Sasson, "Media Image and the Social Construction of Reality," *Annual Review of Sociology,* Vol. 18 (1992) p. 374.
38. See Todd Gitlin, *The Whole World Is Watching: Mass Media in Making and Unmaking to the New Left* (Los Angeles: University of California Press, 1980); David Paletz and David Entman, *Media Power Politics* (New York: Free Press, 1981); Michael Parenti, *Inventing Reality: The Politics of the Mass Media* (New York: St. Martin's 1986).
39. See Paletz and Entman, *Media Power Politics.*
40. Benjamin I. Page, *Who Deliberates? Mass Media in Modern Democracy* (Chicago: University of Chicago Press, 1996).
41. John Soloski, "News reporting and professionalism: Some constraints on the reporting of the news" *Media, Culture and Society,* Vol. 11 (1989) p. 213.
42. Cited in Soloski, op. cit., pp. 213–14.
43. See Meryl Louis, "Surprises and Sensemaking: What Newcomers Experience in Entering Unfamiliar Organization Settings," *Administrative Science Quarterly,* Vol. 25, No. 2 (June 1980) pp. 226–51.

44. Jim Sleeper, *The Closest of Strangers* (New York: Norton, 1990), p. 307.
45. Interview with Paul Delaney, February 1, 2001.
46. For a discussion of constructionism and journalism, see Neuman et al, op. cit.
47. For a discussion of the merits of qualitative research, see Jennifer Hochschild, *What's Fair? American Beliefs about Distributive Justice* (Cambridge: Harvard University Press, 1981).
48. "Race, Crime, and the Mayoralty" *The New Yorker,* Vol. 69 (November 1, 1993) p. 6.

2. The Making of a New York Black Politician: David Dinkins

1. See William E. Nelson Jr. and Philip J. Meranto, *Electing Black Mayors* (Columbus: Ohio State University Press, 1977).
2. See Wilbur C. Rich, *Coleman Young and Detroit Politics* (Detroit: Wayne State University, 1989).
3. See Zoltan L. Hajnal, "White Voters and Black Candidates: Why Race Matters Less under Black Incumbents" (Unpublished Ph.D diss., University of Chicago, 1998).
4. A remark by an anonymous political pundit.
5. Cited in Kevin Thompson, "Can the Healer Mend New York?" *Black Enterprise* (January, 1990) p. 49.
6. Phil Thompson develops this point in his manuscript "Double Trouble" (Unpublished, 2001).
7. Michael Oreskes, "Blacks in New York: The Anguish of Political Failure," *New York Times* (March 31, 1987) p. 1B.
8. Charles V. Hamilton, "Needed, More Foxes: The Black Experience," in Jewell Bellush and Dick Netzer, ed., *Urban Politics: New York Style* (Armonk: Sharpe, 1990) p. 360.
9. Todd Purdum, op. cit., 44.
10. Interview with David Dinkins, March 16, 1996.
11. Shirley Chisholm and Mayor Owens are exceptions to this generation.
12. Charles V. Hamilton, "The Patron-Recipient Relationship and Minority Politics in New York City," *Political Science Quarterly,* Vol. 95 (Summer 1979) pp. 211–27.
13. Mayor Fiorello LaGuardia's mother was Jewish, so he was considered half Jewish.
14. Telephone interview with Percy Sutton, November 3, 2000.
15. Sam Robert hints at the change in the political climate since 1977. See Sam Roberts "Years of Contrast: From Sutton '77 to Dinkins '89," New *York Times* (February 16, 1989) p. 1B.
16. Interview with Sutton, op. cit.

17. William Sales and Rod Bush claim, "The Black establishment never forgave Democrat Badillo for undercutting Manhattan's Black Borough President Percy Sutton's 1977 mayoral bid." See "The Political Awakening of Blacks and Latinos in New York City: Competition or Cooperation?" *Social Justice*, Vol. 27, No. 1 (March 31, 2000) p. 27.

18. Interview with Sutton, op. cit.

19. Martin Kilson, "The Weakness of Black Politics," *Dissent* (Fall 1978) pp. 523–29.

20. Charles Green and Basil Wilson, *The Struggle for Black Empowerment in New York City* (Westport, Conn.: Praeger, 1989).

21. Phillip J. Thompson, "Double Trouble" (Unpublished manuscript, 2001) chapter 3, p. 13.

22. Jim Sleeper, *The Closest of Strangers* (New York: Norton, 1990) p. 272.

23. Chris McNickle, *To Be Mayor of New York: Ethnic Politics in the City* (New York: Columbia University Press, 1993) p. 319.

24. Sleeper, *The Closest of Strangers*, pp. 277–78.

25. "Dinkins Faults the Tactics," *New York Times* (June 28, 1988) p. 5B.

26. "Mr. Dinkins and the Brawley Fireballs," *New York Times* (June 30, 1988) p. 22A.

27. David Dinkins, "Criminal Justice System Is at Issue in Tawana Brawley Case," *New York Times* (July 19, 1988) p. 30A.

28. Farrell got 13 percent of the Democratic primary vote against Koch. See Frank Lynn, "Koch Takes Primary Easily," *New York Times* (September 11, 1985) p. 1A.

29. Interview with Ruth Messinger, September 27, 2000.

30. Ibid.

31. Joe Klein, "Mr. Softy," *New York*, Vol. 22, No. 3 (January 16, 1989) p. 21.

32. Interview with David Dinkins, October 14, 2002.

33. A comment by a black activist (Elombe Brath) reflected this point. He told the *Guardian,* "New York City is not Chicago. Our first Black mayor is not likely to be a firebrand." Cited in Barbara Day, "New York: David Dinkins Opens the Door," in Mike Davis, Steven Hiatt, Marie Kennedy, Susan Ruddick, and Michael Sprinker, eds., *Fire in Hearth* (New York: Verso, 1990) p. 167.

34. Donald Baer and Scott Minerbrook, "New York's First and Last Hurrahs," *U.S. News and World Report* (September 25, 1989) p. 26.

35. For an excellent account of the fall of the Koch coalition, see John H. Mollenkopf, *A Phoenix in the Ashes* (Princeton: Princeton University Press, 1992).

36. Joe Klein, "Can Dinkins Do It"? *New York*, Vol. 22, no. 39 (July 31, 1989) p. 32.

37. Scott McConnell, "The Making of the Mayor, 1989," *Commentary*, Vol. 89 (February 1990) p. 34.

38. Ed Koch, *Citizen Koch: an Autobiography* (New York: St. Martin Press, 1992).

39. For a discussion of this scandal, see Jack Newfield and Wayne Barrett, *City for Sale: Ed Koch and the Betrayal of New York* (New York: Harper and Row, 1988).

40. Arthur Browne, Dan Collins, and Michael Goodwin, *I Koch: A Decidedly Unauthorized Biography of the Mayor of the Mayor of New York City* (New York: Dodd, Mead, 1985).

41. Hillary MacKenzie "Edward Koch Loses Bid for New Term," *Maclean Magazine* (September 25, 1989) p. 32.

42. Ken Auletta, "What the Podium Performances Add Up to for Dinkins and Giuliani," *New York Daily News* (September 17, 1989) p. 41.

43. McNickle, op. cit., p. 319.

44. Sam Roberts, "The New York Primary: Finding a Way to Win," *New York Times* (September 14, 1989) p. 1A.

45. Frank Lynn, "Dinkins Joins Mayoral Race against Koch," *The New York Times* (February 15, 1989) p. 1B.

46. This is not what many of them told pollsters; see Asher Arian, Arthur S. Goldberg, John H. Mollenkopf, and Edward T. Rogowsky, *Changing New York City Politics* (New York: Routledge, 1990) p. 113.

47. Frank Lombardi, " Dinkins Lead Drop to 4 Points," *New York Daily News* (October 24, 1989) p. 5.

48. See Basil Wilson, *David Dinkins and the Goliaths of New York City: The 1989 Mayoral Campaign* (Albany: New York African Institute, 1991) p. 42.

49. Gary Langer, "Candidates 'Running Backwards' in New York City's Mayoral Race," *St. Petersburg Times* (October 29, 1989) p. 5A.

50. "For Mayor, Dinkins," *The New York Times* (October 29, 1989).

51. Elizabeth Kolbert, "Two Views of Dinkins: Conciliator of Hesitator?" *New York Times* (August 19, 1989) p. 1B.

52. Ibid.

53. Arian et al., op. cit., p. 157.

54. Interview with a former publisher who wishes to remain anonymous.

55. Wilson op. cit., p. 34.

56. Cited in Barbara Day op. cit., p. 172.

57. John Mollenkopf, "The Dinkins Victory," *Urban Politics and Urban Policy Section Newsletter,* Vol. 3, No. 3 (Winter, 1990) pp. 13.

58. Charles Brecher, Raymond D. Horton, with Robert A. Cropf and Dean Michael Mead, *Power Failure* (Oxford University Press, 1993) p. 109.

59. See Raphael J. Sonenshien, *Politics in Black and White* (Princeton University Press, 1993).

60. See Mahar, op. cit.

61. Ken Auletta, op. cit., p. 41.

62. McConnell, op. cit., p. 29.

63. See "Hizzoner's Bed," *Newsday* (October 10, 1990) p. 52; also "Making His Honor's Bed," *Newsday* (October 15, 1990) p. 7.

64. Andrew Kirtzman, "Dave's Bed of Woes," *Daily News* (October 8, 1990) p. 8.

65. Ned Zeman and Lucy Howard, "A Headboard Investigation," *Newsweek* (October 22, 1990) p. 8.

66. Telephone Interview with Albert Scardino.

67. Todd Purdum, "Dinkin's $2000 Lesson: City Officials Fly Coach," *New York Times* (January 17, 1990) p. 31.

68. Todd S. Purdum, "Fire Tests Dinkins as Leader in Crisis," *New York Times* (April 3, 1991) p. 4b.

69. Interview with Leland Jones, August 19, 1998.

70. Joe Klein, "The Great New York Panic," *New York*, Vol. 23 (October 1, 1990) pp. 28–30.

71. "Charm Kills," *The New Yorker*, Vol. 68 (December 21, 1992) p. 48.

72. Jonathan P. Hicks "Where Politics Is Always Local," *New York Times* (October 17, 1999) p. 1.

73. Maggie Mahar, "Mr. Dinkins's Dilemma," *Barron* (March 12, 1990) p. 21.

74. Ibid.

75. Phillip Hamburger, *Mayor Watching and Other Pleasures* (Toronto: Clarke, Irwin, 1958) p. 75.

76. Maggie Mahar, op. cit., p. 21.

77. Jeffrey Schmalz, "Dinkins Gets a Police Guard after Remarks by Farrakhan," *New York Times* (October 10, 1985) 2B.

78. Paul La Rosa and Ruth Landa wrote an article entitled "Dave to Jews: I'm running, not Jesse," *Daily News* (October 24, 1989).

79. Ibid., p. 4.

80. Interview with David Dinkins, op. cit.

81. Interview with Norman Steisel, September 18, 2000.

82. Herminia Ibarra, "Provisional Selves: Experimenting with Image and Identity in Professional Adaptation," *Administrative Science Quarterly*, Vol. 44 (1999) p.7651.

83. Ibid., p. 766.

84. Ken Auletta, "What the Podium Performance Adds up to for Dinkins and Giuliani," *New York Daily News* (September 17, 1989) p. 41.

85. Peer and Ettema, op. cit., 256.

86. Nayda Terkildsen, "When White Votes Evaluate Black Candidates: The Processing Implications of Candidate Skin Color, Prejudice and Self-Monitoring," *American Journal of Political Science*, Vol. 37, No. 4 (November 1993) pp. 1032–53.

87. Ibid.

88. Charles V. Hamilton, "De-Racialization: Examination of Political Strategy," *First World*, Vol. 1 (1977) pp. 3–5.

89. Ibid., p. 4.

90. Charles Bagli and Michael Powell "Bright Lights, Battered City: New York from Koch to Dinkins," *Dollars and Sense,* No. 155 (April 1990) p. 16.
91. Sites asserts that Dinkins' housing policy was not very different from that of Koch; see William Sites, "The Limits of Urban Regime Theory: New York City under Koch, Dinkins, and Giuliani," *Urban Affairs Review,* Vol. 32, No. 4 (March, 1997) pp. 536–57.
92. Jim Sleeper, op. cit., p. 278.
93. Anne Colamosca, "Real Estate Men Favor Dinkins," *Christian Science Monitor* (November 6, 1989) p. 9.
94. Ibid.
95. This is a common risk among black leaders who are solicited for comments about blacks. On the one hand, they want to condemn bad behavior, but on the other hand they do not want their comments to be taken as antiblack. Reporters are often attracted to the possibility of dissent and disagreement among black leaders. Often to the dismay of a black commentator, their words are used to construct them as "reasonable," "thoughtful," or "responsible," whereas other blacks are "irresponsible and thoughtless."
96. See Thomas Morgan, "A Poll Shows Less Pessimism among Blacks," *New York Times* (June 26, 1990) p. 1B.
97. Thompson, op. cit., chapter 4, p. 50.
98. Harold Lasswell, *Power and Personality* (New York: Norton, 1948).
99. Logan, op. cit. 74.
100. F. Trippett, "Broken Mosaic" *Time,* Vol. 135 (May 28, 1990) pp. 20–22; Joe Klein, "Dinkins's Fractured Mosaic," *Newsweek* Vol. 122 (October 11, 1993) p. 35.
101. "The Shattered Mosaic," *New York Post* (September 13, 1993) p. 11.
102. Todd S. Purdum, "The Angry Civility of David Dinkins," *New York Times Magazine* (September 12, 1993) p. 42.

3. David Dinkins and Regime Change

1. See Clarence Stone, "Urban Regimes and the Capacity to Govern: A Political Economy Approach," *Journal of Urban Affairs* Vol. 15 (1993) pp. 1–28.
2. Tom Fredickson, "Economy: It's Bad, But Not for Long," *Crain's New York Business,* Vol. 17, No. 50 (December 10–16, 2001) p. 1.
3. Thompson, op. cit, p. 49.
4. See Fred Ferretti, *The Year the Big Apple Went Bust* (New York: Putnam's Sons, 1976).
5. Francisco Rivera-Batiz, "The Socioeconomic Status of Hispanic New Yorkers: Current Trends and Future Prospects," *A Pew Hispanic Center Study* (January 2002) p. 24. Also see Mitchell Moss, Anthony Townsend, and Emanuel Tobier "Immigration is

Transforming New York City," *Taub Urban Research Center* (December, 1997) pp. 1–9.

6. Sarah Bartlett, "New York Logan 500,000 Jobs Lost since 1989, a Record High," *New York Times* (April 16, 1992) p. 1.

7. Carol O'Cléireacáin, "The Private Economy and the Public Budget of New York City," in Margaret E. Crahan and Alberto Vourvoulias-Bush, eds., *The City and the World* (New York: A Council on Foreign Relations Book, 1997) p. 27.

8. "Climbing Back: New York City First Hurdle: Defeatism," *New York Times* (October 13, 1991) p. 14.

9. See Demetrios Caraley, "Washington Abandons the Cities," *Political Science Quarterly*, Vol. 107, No. 1 (Spring 1992) pp. 1–30.

10. Ibid.

11. Stephen Moore and Dean Stansel, "The Myth of American Unfunded Cities," *Policy Analysis* (February 22, 1993) p. 1.

12. William Knoke, *Bold New World* (New York: Kodansha International, 1996) pp. 20–21.

13. For a discussion of the changes in the budgetary process, see Ester R. Fuchs, *Mayors and Money: Fiscal Policy in New York and Chicago* (Chicago: University of Chicago Press, 1992) pp. 224–25.

14. Todd Purdum, "On Estimate Board's Agenda, Last Item Is Its Demise," *New York Times* (August 16, 1990) p. 1.

15. Michael P. Smith and Joe Feagin., eds., *The Capitalist City: Global Restructuring and Community Politics.* (New York: Blackwell, 1987); also see Saskia Sassen, *The Global City: New York, London, Tokyo* (Princeton, NJ: Princeton University Press, 1991).

16. Nathan Glazer, "Fate of a World City," *City Journal*, Vol. 3, No. 4 (Autumn 1993).

17. Mahar, op. cit., p. 20.

18. Fred Siegel and Joel Kotkin, "Urban Renaissance? Not Yet," *The Wall Street Journal* (November 6, 1997) p. 22.

19. It was estimated that New York City lost 350,000 jobs between 1989 and 1993; see Alan Finder, "Dinkins Outlines Plan for Future Economic Growth," *New York Times* (September 22, 1993), p. 3B.

20. Tom Schachtman, *Skyscraper Dreams: The Great Real Estate Dynasties of New York* (Boston: Little Brown, 1991); see also Eugene Rachlis and John E. Marquesee, *The Land Lords* (New York: Random House, 1963).

21. "Press Conference Urban Summit of Mayors," *Federal News Service* (May 15, 1991) p. 3.

22. See William R. Taylor, *Inventing Times Square: Commerce and Culture at the Crossroads* (New York: Sage, 1992).

23. See Tony Hiss, *The Experience of Place* (New York: Knopf, 1990); also see Savitch and Kantor discussion, op. cit., p. 205–06.

24. Douglas S. Massey and Nancy A. Denton, *American Apartheid: Segregation and the Making of the Underclass* (Cambridge: Harvard University Press, 1993).

25. Ibid., p. 76.
26. Robert Fishman, *Bourgeois Utopias: The Rise and Fall of Suburbia* (New York: Basic Book, 1989).
27. Ibid., pp. 42–43.
28. William J. Wilson, *The Truly Disadvantaged* (Chicago: University of Chicago Press, 1987).
29. Fuchs, op. cit., p. 287.
30. Curtis Skinner, "Measuring Skills Mismatch New York City in the 1980s," *Urban Affairs Review*, Vol. 36, No. 5 (May 2001) p. 689.
31. Ken Auletta, *The Underclass* (New York: Random House, 1982).
32. See Peter Eisinger, "The Politics of Bread and Circuses: Building the City for the Visitor Class," *Urban Affairs Review*, No. 3 (2000) pp. 316–33.
33. See Ingrid Sturgis, "NYC Adopts M/MBE Plan," *Black Enterprise* (May 1992) p. 22.
34. "New York City's New Goals," *Engineering News-Record*, Vol. 228, No. 9 (March 2, 2005) p. 15.
35. See Clarence Stone, *Regime Politics Governing Atlanta 1946–1988* (Lawrence: University Press of Kansas, 1989).
36. Telephone Interview with David Dinkins, op. cit.
37. Ibid.
38. See Economic Policy and Marketing Group, Office of the Deputy Mayor for Finance and Economic Development, "Strong Economy, Strong City: Jobs for New Yorker, Job Creation Strategies for the Global City of Opportunity," September, 1993.
39. Anna Quindlen, "Wanted: A Persona," *New York Times* (June 13, 1991) p. 29A.
40. Personal communication from Clarence Stone, May 9, 2005.
41. Scott McConnell, op. cit., p. 31.
42. Ibid.
43. Anne Colamosca, "Real Estate Men Favor Dinkins," *Christian Science Monitor* (November 6, 1989) p. 8.
44. Calvin Sims, "Former Chase Manhattan Official Named Deputy Mayor by Dinkins," *New York Times* (March 24, 1992) p. 1.
45. H. V. Savitch and Paul Kantor, *Cities in the International Marketplace* (Princeton: Princeton University Press, 2002) p. 203.
46. Kevin Cox and Andrew M. Mair, "Locality and Community in the Politics of Local Economic Development," *Annals of the Association of American Geographers,"* Vol. 78, No. 2. (1988) pp. 307–25.
47. Calvin Sims, "Advisor to Dinkins Again Tops List of City Lobbyists," *New York Times* (April 1992) p. 3B.
48. See Wayne Barrett, "The Power of Property: City Real Estate Board Beat the Budget," *The Village Voice* (July 9, 1991) p. 11.
49. See Josh Barbanel, "Access Is Money for City Hall Lobbyists," *New York Times* (March 28, 1991) p. 1B.

4. The Staffing of Dinkins' City Hall

1. Theodore Lowi, *At the Pleasure of the Mayor* (New York: Free Press of Glencoe, 1964).

2. Ibid., p. 3.

3. Cynthia Bowman, "We Don't Want Anybody Anybody Sent: The Death of Patronage Hiring in Chicago," *Northwestern University Law Review*, Vol. 86 (Fall 1991) pp. 57–95.

4. Frank Lynn, "Dinkins Slow to hire them, Democrats Say" *New York Times* (May 19, 1990), p.25.

5. Cited in Todd Purdum, "Dinkins Wanted an Unusual Group to Run His City and Here It Is," *New York Times* (April, 1 1990) p. 20.

6. Nathan Grundstein, "Future Manpower for Urban Managers," in *Emerging Patterns of Urban Administration*, F. Gerald Brown and Thomas Murphy, eds. (Lexington, MA: Heath Lexington Books, 1970).

7. See Edward Sermier, and Paul Marcone, "The Challenge of Governing: Getting Things Done," *Public Productivity and Management Review*, Vol. 16 (Summer 1993) pp. 409–14.

8. Gail Collins, "We Expected More from Mayor," *Newsday* (October 23, 1992) p. 4.

9. Interview with Norman Steisel, September 18, 2000.

10. Thompson, op. cit. p. 49.

11. Bagli and Powell call that appointment "particularly inauspicious" because she presided over a decline in small business loans while working for Koch; see Bagli and Power, op. cit. p. 17.

12. Fran Prial, "New Administration: Profiles of Dinkins's Eight Appointees," *New York Times* (December 9, 1989) p. 28.

13. Ibid.

14. Telephone interview with William Murphy, May 25, 2001.

15. Sam Roberts, "Same Message, but without the Messenger," *New York Times* (February 18, 1991) p. B1.

16. Telephone interview with Albert Scardino, June 25, 2004.

17. Ibid.

18. Todd Purdum asserted that it was his intention to get Mr. Scardino fired. "I was not speaking on behalf of the *Times* and it was not my intention to get Albert fired, but rather to bring to the mayor's attention an unfair matter involving a scoop at a rival paper (*Daily News*). But I cannot deny that there was widespread dissatisfaction about the conduct of the mayor's press relations." Telephone interview with Todd Purdum, January 7, 2005.

19. "The Case for Dr. Myers," *New York Times* (January 19, 1990) p. 34.

20. Joe Klein, "Is He up to It?" op. cit.

21. Ibid.

22. Robert Jervis, *The Logic of Images in International Relations* (New York: Columbia University Press, 1989) p. 18.

23. Interview with Ruth Messinger, September 27, 2000.

24. Arnold Luchasch, "New Administration: Profile of Dinkins's Eight Appointees," *New York Times* (December 9, 1989) p. 28.
25. Wallace Sayre and Herbert Kaufman, *Governing New York City* (New York: Norton, 1959) p. 222.
26. Ibid., p. 223.
27. Interview with Andrew Hacker, May 23, 2001.
28. Reported by Tony Case, "City Hall Controversy," *Editor and Publisher: the Fourth Estate*, Vol. 123 (December 22, 1990) p. 8.
29. Telephone interview with Scardino, op. cit.
30. Case, op. cit.
31. Interview with Scardino, op. cit.
32. Sayre and Kaufman, op. cit., pp. 223–24.
33. An anonymous member of the city administration.
34. An anonymous member of the city administration.
35. "Best Thing for New York since Sliced Bread," *Amsterdam News* (February 23, 1991) p. 12.
36. Ibid.
37. Jim Sleeper, "Koch Aides Litter Dinkins's City Hall," *Daily News* (October 3, 1990) p. 35.
38. Mark Voorhees, "Schmertz's Return," *Manhattan Lawyer* (March 1991) p. 1.
39. George E. Jordan and Jennifer Preston, "Schmertz Sacked, Dinkins Axes Labor Chief," *Newsday* (March 10, 1991).
40. Evelyn Hernandez, "Don't Kick the Daylights out of Union," *Newsday* (March 18, 1991) p. 43.
41. "How the Mayor Can Help Himself," *New York Times* (March 12, 1991) p. 22.
42. Albert Hirschman, *Exit, Voice and Loyalty: Responses to Decline in Firms, Organizations, and States* (Cambridge, Mass.: Harvard University Press, 1970).
43. Interview with Normal Steisel, op. cit.
44. David Gonzalez, "Dinkins Appoints Adviser for Hispanic Affairs," *New York Times* (February 10, 1991) p. 36.
45. Andrew Kitzman, "Latino Chief Resigns while Being Ousted," *Daily News* (October 10, 1990) p. 4.
46. Interview with Norman Steisel, op. cit.
47. Richard Steier, "Dave: Traitor Fire Boss Is Just Blowing Smoke," *New York Post* (September 1, 1993) p. 4.
48. Rob Gurwitt, "New York Forum about Latino: The Coalition of Color Fades," *Newsday* (September 9, 1993) p. 104.
49. Interview with Norman Steisel, op. cit.
50. Todd Purdum, "In Dinkins Inner Circle, Persistent Disarray," *New York Times* (February 21, 1991) p. B1.
51. Correspondence from a Dinkins appointee, June 25, 2003.
52. See "Sound Leadership for Police," *New York Times* (October 17, 1992) p. 24.
53. Bagli and Powell, op. cit., p. 16.

54. Sites, op. cit., p. 548.
55. Interview with David Dinkins, October 14, 2002.
56. Interview with Hacker, op. cit.

5. Racial Events, Diplomacy, and Dinkins' Image

1. See Arthur Miller et al., "Political Issues and Trust in Government: 1964–1970," *American Political Science Review* (September 1979) pp. 951–72; also see Richard Bendetto, "Confidence in Government at Low in Poll," *USA Today* (March 26, 1993) p. 7A.
2. *The New York Times* (June 26, 1990) p. 2b.
3. William Murphy, "Poll Cites City New Outlook on Dinkins-Disapproval Rating the Mayor," *Newsday* (September 28, 1990) p. 5.
4. F. Glenn Abney and John Hutcheson, "Race, Representation and Trust: Changes in Attitudes after Election," *Public Opinion Quarterly*, Vol. 45 (Spring 1981) p. 100.
5. For a theoretical discussion of political support, see Edward Mullen and Thomas Jukan, "On the Meaning of Political Support," *American Political Science Review*, Vol. 71, No. 4 (December, 1977) pp. 1561–95.
6. Robert Bies, "The Predicament of Injustice: The Management of Moral Outrage," in L.L. Coming and B. M. Shaw, *Research in Organizational Behavior* (Greenwich, Conn: JAI, 1987) p. 294.
7. Jeffrey Pressman, "Preconditions of Mayoral Leadership," *American Political Science Review*, Vol. 65 (June 1979) pp. 11–24.
8. Robert Stallings, "Media Discourse and the Social Construction of Risk," *Social Problems*, Vol. 37, No. 1 (February 1990) p. 80.
9. Andrew Valls, "Presidential Rhetoric: A Social Constructionist Approach," in Mary Stuckey, ed., *Theory and Practice of Political Communication Research* (Albany: State University of New York Press 1996).
10. Sue Newell and Jacky Swan, "Trust and Inter-organizational Networking," *Human Relations*, Vol. 53, No. 10 (2000) p. 1295.
11. See G. Jones and J. George, "The Experience and Evolution of Trust: Implications for Cooperation and Teamwork," *Academy of Management Review*, Vol. 23, No. 3 (1998) pp. 532–46.
12. See M. A. Farber, "Black-Korean Who-Pushed-Whom Festers," *New York Times* (May 7, 1990) p. 1B.
13. See Claire Jean Kim, *Bitter Fruit* (Chicago: University of Chicago Press, 2000).
14. Howard Kurtz, "Bonfire of Inanities: How News Fuel Racial Tension," *The Washington Post* (May 10, 1990) p. 1B.
15. See Don Terry, "Diplomacy Fails to End Store Boycott in Flatbush," *New York Times* (July 16, 1990) p. 1B.
16. M. A. Farber, "Black-Korean Who-Pushed-Whom Festers," *New York Times* (May 7, 1990) p. 1B.

17. See Kim, op. cit., p.2.
18. Russell W. Baker, "New York's Korean Grocery Turmoil Rooted in Cultural and Economic Conditions," *Christian Science Monitor* (May 31, 1990) p. 7.
19. Ibid., p. 11.
20. "All for the Price of a Lime," *Economist*, Vol. 315 (May 19, 1990) p. 31.
21. "Sonny Carson, Koreans and Racism," *The New York Times* (May 8, 1990) p. 28A.
22. Ibid.
23. Cited in David Seifman and Rita Delfiner, "Ed: I'd Personally Bust Boycott of Korean," *New York Post* (May 10, 1990) p. 3.
24. Ibid.
25. Sam Robert, "Metro Matters; Which Mayor Knows Best on the Boycott?" *New York Times* (July 30, 1990) p. 1B.
26. Todd Purdum, "Dinkins Steps Up Criticism of Brooklyn Protesters," *New York Times* (May 10, 1990) p. 3B.
27. Sam Roberts, "From an Unlikely Source, Praise for Koch," *New York Times* (February 2, 1990) p. 161.
28. Todd Purdum, "Judge Critical of Dinkins over Boycott," *New York Times* (May 11, 1990) p. 1B.
29. Ibid.
30. Rita Delfiner, "Dave 'Diplomat' on Korean Boycott," *New York Post* (May 9, 1990) p. 7.
31. Ari L. Goldman, "Racial Unity and Dissent in Brooklyn," *New York Times* (May 28, 1990).
32. Sales and Bush, op. cit., p. 28.
33. Todd Purdum, "Dinkins, The Volume Up in a Speech on Race: The Mayor Responds to Complaint that He Hadn't Said Enough," *New York Times* (May 13, 1990) p. 1.
34. Ibid.
35. Ibid.
36. "Talking Like a Leader," *New York Times* (May 13, 1990) p. 18.
37. Reported in Rita Delifener, David Seifman, and Karen Phillip, "Raves and Raspberries for Dinkins Speech," *New York Post* (May 12, 1990) p. 5.
38. Todd Purdum, "Dinkins Asks for Racial Unity and Offers to Mediate Boycott," *New York Times* (May 12, 1990) p. 1.
39. "This City Is Sick of Violence: Dinkins's Address," *New York Times* (May 12, 1990) p. 27.
40. The comment got coverage in several out of town media. See "Korean Store at Center of Racial Strife," *St. Petersburg Times* (May 17, 1990) p. 1A.
41. Sleeper, op. cit., p. 301.
42. David Gonzalez, "Korean See a Gain from Boycott: Unity," *New York Times* (September 25, 1990) p. 3.
43. Don Terry, "Dinkins to Ask State Inquiry on 2d Boycott," *New York Times* (August 29, 1990) p. 1B.

44. Lee Daniels, "U.S. Report Faults Mayor on Boycott," *New York Times* (February 28, 1992) p. 1B.
45. David Gonzalez, "Koreans See a Gain from Boycott: Unity," *New York Times* (September 25, 1990).
46. Larry Simonberg, "For Mayor Dinkins: A Few Don'ts," *Daily News* (October 7, 1990) p. 47.
47. Miquel Garalazo, Rocco Parascandola, David Seifman, Anne E. Murray, and Don Broderick, "Race Riot in B'lkyn," *New York Post* (August 22, 1991) p. 19.
48. Ibid.
49. Dean Chang, "Fatal Crash Inflamed Old Feelings," *Daily News* (August 21, 1991) p. 6.
50. Mike McAlary, "Hate Lines Both Sides of Eastern Parkway Gantlet," *New York Post* (August 21, 1991) p. 191.
51. Interview with David Dinkins, October 14, 2002.
52. David Seufnab, "Unmarked Cop Care Led Rabbi Convoy," *New York Post* (August 22, 1991) p. 3.
53. Ibid.
54. Miguel Garalazo et al., "Anarchy Grip Crown Heights," *New York Post* (August 22, 1991) p. 2.
55. Ibid.
56. Interview with Dinkins, op. cit.
57. Telephone interview with Bill Lynch, January 21, 2005.
58. Ellen Tumposky, "Dinkins Watches, Wait: No Tour of Areas for Now," *New York Daily News* (August 21, 1991) p. 32.
59. Ibid.
60. Joel Sigel and Ruth Landa, "Insults, Bottles Fly," *New York Daily News* (August 22, 1991) p. 27.
61. Don Singleton, "In the Melting Pot, It's Hot Ethnic Stew," *New York Daily News* (August 21, 1991) p. 6.
62. "Streets of Rage," *New York Daily News* (August 22, 1991) p. 1.
63. Bob Herbert, "Blood Feud in Crown Heights," *New York Daily News* (August 22, 1991) p. 2.
64. Ibid.
65. "Cooling Crown Heights Is a Long Term Job," *New York Daily News* (August 22, 1991) p. 3.
66. Earl Caldwell, "The Fire Next Time Is Alarmingly Near," *New York Daily News* (August 13, 1991) p. 32.
67. Charles Sennott, "Dinkins Mourns Mosaic's Tiles," *New York Daily News* (August 26, 1991) p. 21.
68. Ellen Tumposky, "After Week of Tension, Dinkins Left City Hall to Watch US Open," *New York Daily News* (August 27, 1991) p. 15.
69. "Crown Heights: Crisis Not Over Yet," *New York Daily News* (August 27, 1991) p. 32.
70. Eric Breindel, "Race and Riot in New York," *Wall Street Journal* (November 18, 1992) p. A16.

71. David Remnick, "Waiting for the Apocalypse in Crown Heights," *New Yorker*, Vol. 68, No. 44 (December 21, 1992) pp. 52–57.
72. Joel Siegal, "For Me, It's a Lose-Lose," *New York Daily News* (August 28, 1991) p. 5.
73. Ibid.
74. Wayne Barrett, "Dinkins Dilemma," *Village Voice* (December 1, 1992) p. 1.
75. Ibid.
76. Martin Gottlieb, "Report for Cuomo Cited a Chain of Failures in 1991 Disturbances," *New York Times* (July 21, 1993) p. 1.
77. Interview with Leland Jones, op. cit.
78. Herb Boyd, "Crown Heights Report Exonerates Mayor Dinkins from Any Blame," *Amsterdam News* (July 3, 1993) p. 3.
79. Wilbert Tatum, "Governor's Report on Crown Heights: A Redundancy at Best," *New York Amsterdam News* (July 24, 1993) p. 1.
80. Martin Gottlieb, "The Crown Height Report: The Overview; Crown Heights Study Finds Dinkins and Police at Fault in Letting Unrest Escalate," *New York Times* (July 21, 1993) p. 1A.
81. Bob Herbert, op. cit.
82. David Dinkins, "Reason, Respect and Reconciliation in New York City," *New York Amsterdam News* (November 28, 1992) p. 12.
83. Michael Tomasky, "How Dave Botched Crown Heights," *Village Voice* (November 24, 1992) p. 14.
84. Interview with Sam Roberts, March 15, 2001.
85. Carol Conaway, "Framing Identity: The Press in Crown Heights" (Cambridge: John F. Kennedy School of Government Research paper R-16, December, 1996).
86. *CBS Morning News* (November 26, 1992).
87. Ibid.
88. Telephone interview with Albert Scardino, June 25, 2004.
89. "Race Relations," *MacNeil/Lehrer Newshour*, Transcript 3735 (May 18, 1990).
90. Ibid.
91. David Dinkins maintained this position in our interview. Interview with Dinkins, op. cit.
92. Ibid.
93. Kim, op. cit., p. 189.
94. Ibid.
95. "Simmer in the City: Boiling Point: Korean Grocers Meet with Attorney in Attempt to Crush Boycott," *48 Hours* (July 12, 1990).
96. Todd Purdum, "Maze of Troubles Posing Challenges to Power and Popularity of Dinkins," *New York Times* (January 16, 1991) p. B3.
97. "New York Mayor Dinkins Faulted," *New India-Times* (November 20, 1992) p. 55.
98. James Besser, "Crown Heights and Beyond: Is the Tension between Blacks and Jews in Brooklyn the Harbinger of a National Crisis?" *Baltimore Jewish Times* (December 25, 1992) p. 36.

99. Interview with David Dinkins, op. cit.
100. Ibid.
101. Martin Gottlieb, July 21, op. cit., p. 1.
102. Wayne Barrett, "Girgenti's Ghostwriter: How Cuomo Shaped the Report," *Village Voice* (August 3, 1993) p. 11.
103. Interview with Paul Delaney, February 1, 2001.
104. Interview with David Dinkins, op. cit.
105. Debra Cohen, "Dinkins Asks G.A. Leaders for Help in Healing Rift with Black Community," *Jewish Telegraphic Agency* (November 13, 1992) p. 4.
106. "Mayor Dinkins, Blacks, Jews: A Turning Point?" *New York Amsterdam News* (November 21, 1992) p. 12.
107. David Saperstein, "Op-ed: The Paradox of Crown Heights: Situation Unique, Lessons Universal," *Jewish Telegraphic Agency* (December 18, 1992) p. 12.
108. Herbert Daughtry, *No Monopoly on Suffering: Blacks and Jews in Crown Heights* (Trenton, N.J.: Africa World, 1997) p. 263.
109. Mike McAlary, "Dave Lets City Wound Fester," *New York Post* (August 23, 1991) p. 7.

6. Who Runs the City? Union Bosses or the Mayor?

1. Steven Malanga, "Who Runs New York?" *City Journal*, Vol. 13, No. 4 (Autumn 2003) p. 46.
2. Wilbur Rich, *The Politics of Urban Personnel Policy* (Associated Press, 1982) p. 71.
3. For a classic statement on this point see Robert Dahl, *Who Governs?* (New Haven: Yale University Press, 1961).
4. The literature suggests that it does matter whether it is the mayor or a chief negotiator. See Kevin O'Brien, "Does It Matters Who's Bargaining for the Municipality? Evidence for Police and Firefighter Bargaining Outcomes," *Journal of Economics*, Vol. 21, No. 2 (Fall 1995) pp. 107–14.
5. Raymond D. Horton, *Municipal Labor Relations in New York City: Lessons of the Lindsay-Wagner Years* (New York: Praeger, 1973) p. 15.
6. Alessandra Stanley, "The Labor Man in the Middle," *New York Times* (December 10, 1991) p. 1B.
7. Llewellyn M. Toulmin, "The Treasure Hunt: Budget Search Behavior by Public Employee Unions," *Public Administration Review*, Vol. 48, No. 2 (March/April 1988) pp. 620–30.
8. Voorhees, op. cit. p. 3.
9. Ibid.
10. See Barron, op. cit.
11. "What's Fair for Unions, and the City?" *New York Times* (September 18, 1990) p. 26.
12. Joe Klein, "Root-Canal Work," *New York* (April 8, 1991) pp. 14–20.

13. Joe Klein, "To Dave: Get Real!" *New York,* Vol. 24 (May 27, 1991) p. 12.

14. Bruce Lambert, "Year Later, Dinkins's Friends in the Unions Are Facing Their Contract's End," *New York Times* (September 30, 1990) p. 30.

15. Marcia Kramer, "City, and Unions Start Negotiation," *Daily News* (October 16, 1990) p. 55.

16. Bruce Lambert, "New York Agrees to Raise of 5.5% for City Teachers," *New York Times* (October 2, 1990) p. 1.

17. Todd S. Purdum, "Dinkins's Moves: Costly Plan of Action," *New York Times* (October 2, 1990) p. 1.

18. Paul LaRosa, "Teachers Win 5.5%," *New York Daily News* (October 2, 1990) p. 8.

19. Cited in Marcia Kramer, "$1.8 B Plan Draws Fire," *New York Daily News* (October 3, 1990) p. 3.

20. Joe Klein, "Is He up To It," *New York,* Vol. 23, No. 43 (November 5, 1990) 37–40.

21. Marcia Kramer, "Union Issue Grim Warning," *New York Daily News* (October 2, 1990) p. 4.

22. "Press Stakeout with New York Mayor David Dinkins," *Federal New Service* (May 15, 1991).

23. Joe Klein, "The Real Deficit Leadership," *New York,* Vol. 24, No. 28 (July 22, 1991) p. 2S.

24. Interview with Bill Lynch January 21, 2005.

25. Sam Roberts, "A Stack of Messages: First Said to Lack Leadership, Mayor Is Now Said to Go in Many Directions," *New York Times* (October 5, 1990) p. 4.

26. Bruce Lambert, "Layoff? Dinkins Lied, Irate Union Chief Asserts," *New York Times* (October 5, 1990) p. 4.

27. Ibid.

28. Ibid.

29. Joseph Berger, "Dinkins Was Told of Risks in Teachers Pact," *New York Times* (October 10, 1990) p. 1.

30. Klein, op. cit.

31. "Dinkins Aide Denies Image of 'Confusion,'" *New York Times* (October 14, 1990) p. 30.

32. Martin Dickson, "The Rot Goes Deeper in the Big Apple," *Financial Times* (June 10, 1991) p. 15.

33. Felicia R. Lee, "Dinkins Cutting Pay for Officials and for Himself," *New York Times* (October 23, 1990) p. 1.

34. Todd Purdum, "For Dinkins and Unions, Friendship Has Its Price," *New York Times* (November 4, 1990) p. 4.

35. Ibid.

36. Ibid.

37. Joe Klein, "The Pinochle Club," *New York,* Vol. 23, No. 42 (October 29, 1990) p. 9.

38. Sam Roberts, "Mayor Dinkins: Every Day a Test," *New York Times* (April 7, 1991) p. 28.

39. Joe Klein, "The Pinochle Club: Dinkins and the Dinosaurs" *New York,* Vol. 23, No. 42 (October 29, 1990) p. 19.

40. Kevin Flynn and William Murphy, "City, Unions in Agreement," *Newsday* (January 3, 1991) p. 5.

41. "Not Perfect but Realistic," *Newsday* (January 6, 1991) p. 3.

42. Klein, op. cit.

43. "Still Missing: A City Labor Policy," *New York Times* (October 2, 1991) p. 22.

44. Calvin Sims, "Dinkins Gains Tentative Pact on Sanitation," *New York Times* (February 14, 1992) p. 1B.

45. David Dinkins, "Reform and Renaissance," a televised speech, July 30, 1991.

46. William Murphy, "Unions Will Parade Criticism of Dinkins," *Newsday* (September 6, 1992) p. 27.

47. "A Missed Opportunity on City Labor," *New York Times* (January 13, 1993) p. 20.

48. Todd Purdum, "Giuliani Campaign Theme: Dinkins Isn't Up to the Job," *New York Times* (October 245, 1993) p. 1.

49. Telephone interview with Scardino, op. cit.

50. Paul Light, *The President's Agenda* (Baltimore: John Hopkins, 1982).

51. Joe Klein, "The Red Sea," *New York,* Vol. 24, No. 3 (January 21, 1991) p. 14.

7. Crime Coverage, Mayoral Images, and Signaling

1. Joe Klein, "The Red Sea," *New York,* Vol. 24, No. 3 (January 21, 1991) p. 14.

2. Kandel, Bethany "NYC to 'Flood' Streets with Police" *USA Today* (October 3, 1990) p. 3A.

3. See Harrell Rodger and George Taylor, "The Policeman as an Agent of Regime Legitimation," *Midwest Journal of Political Science,* Vol. 15, No. 1 (February, 1971) pp. 72–86.

4. See Robert M. Fogelson, *Big City Police* (Cambridge: Harvard University Press, 1977).

5. D. Zillman, "Fear of Victimization and the Appeal of Crime Drama," in D. Zillman and J. Byrant eds., *Selective Exposure to Communication* (Hilldale, N.J.: Lawrence Erlbaum) pp. 141–56.

6. Lee P. Brown, "Community Policing: A Partnership with Promise," *The Police Chief* (October 1992) p. 45.

7. See Michael Lipsky, *Street-Level Bureaucrats* (New York: Russell Sage Foundation, 1980).

8. *Jewish Press* (May 23, 1990) p. 1.

9. Joe Klein, "Is He up to It?" op. cit.

10. "Crime-ravaged City Cries out for Help: Dave, Do Something!" *New York Post* (September 7, 1990) p. 1.

11. Jerry Nachman, "Dave Style Is Too Measured for a War," *New York Post* (September 7, 1990) p. 5.

12. Thompson, op. cit., p. 78.

13. Joe Klein, "The Panic of 1900: Dinkins and the Vision Thing," *New York,* Vol. 23, No. 38 (October 21, 1990) p. 30.

14. Ibid.

15. David Seifman, "Dave Fight Back," *New York Post* (September 8, 1990) p. 5.

16. Interview with David Dinkins, op. cit.

17. *Safe Streets, Safe City I: An Omnibus Criminal Justice Program for the City of New York Summary* (October, 1990).

18. Carl Pelleck, "Today, Neighborhood Kids Resort to Guns," *New York Post* (September 7, 1990) p. 4.

19. Interview with David Dinkins, op. cit.

20. Adam Nagovrney, "Anti-Crime and Critics," *Detroit News* (October 3, 1990) p. 27.

21. "The High Price of Safety," *Daily News* (October 3, 1990) p. 26.

22. Ibid.

23. "To Restore New York City—First, Reclaim the Streets; No Time to Give Up on Crime," *New York Times* (January 8, 1991) p. 20.

24. Joe Klein, "Fantasy in Blue: Is Dinkins Crime Plan DOA?" *New York* Vol. 23, No. 40 (October 15, 1990) p. 37.

25. Interview with David Dinkins, October 14, 2002.

26. Marist College Institute for Public Opinion, op. cit., p. 7.

27. Mark Voorhess, "Safe Streets, Safe City" *Manhattan Lawyer* (November 1990) p. 1.

28. "Sound Leadership for the Police," *New York Times* (October 17, 1992) p. 24.

29. *Safe Streets, Safe City II: A Futureprint for Success* (September 1993) p. 2.

30. Ibid., p. 1.

31. In our interview, Dinkins was particularly unhappy that Giuliani got most of the credit for reducing crime.

32. "Mayor David Dinkins Interviews on 'Inside Politics'" (October 22, 1993), Transcript 445–3.

33. Interview with William Murphy, May 25, 2001.

34. Interview with David Dinkins, op. cit.

35. "The Shattered Mosaic," *New York Post* (September 13, 2001) p. 11.

36. Bob Litt, "Dinkins' New York Crime and Punishment More Cops, but Fewer Arrests" *Newsday* (October 4, 1993) p. 7.

37. Joe Klein, "The Panic of 1990," *New York* Vol. 23, No. 38 (October 1, 1990) pp. 28–30.

38. Stuart Hall et al., *Policing the Crisis* (New York: Holmes and Meier, 1978).

39. William Gamson et al., "Media Images and the Social Construction of Reality," *American Review of Sociology*, Vol. 18 (1992) p. 174.
40. Erving Goffman, *Frame Analysis* (New York: Harper and Row, 1974).
41. Bob Herbert, "Time for Mosaic to Get Together," *Daily News* (October 18, 1990) p. 4.
42. Eli Silverman, *NYPD Battles Crime* (Boston: Northeastern University Press, 1999), p. 78.
43. "Race, Crime, and the Mayoralty," op. cit. p. 8.
44. Mike McAlary, "September Won't Be Pretty for Pols," *New York Post* (September 2, 1993) p. 1.
45. See Annette Gordon-Reed, "Watching the Protectors," *New York Law Review*, Vol. 40, Nos. 1/2 (1995) pp. 87–111.
46. Cited in Mark Mooney, "Dave Attack Press' Hysteria on Crime," *New York Post* (October 1, 1990) p. 4.
47. Michael H. Cottman, "Dinkins the Peacekeeper or the Anticop," *Newsday* (August 14, 1992) p. 35.
48. Ibid.
49. See Regina Lawrence, "Managing Meaning: Media, Officials, and Police Brutality" (PhD dissertation, University of Washington, 1996); also see her "Managing Meaning," *Political Communications*, Vol. 13, No. 1 (1996) pp. 140–42.
50. Phillip J. Thompson, "The Election and Governance of David Dinkins as Mayor of New York," in Huey L. Perry ed., *Race, Politics and Governance in the United States* (Gainesville: University Press of Florida, 1996) p. 70.

8. The Turmoil of School Politics

1. Kevin Thompson, op. cit. p. 50.
2. Wilbur C. Rich, *Black Mayors and School Politics* (New York: Garland Publishing, 1996).
3. See Jeff Henig and Wilbur Rich, eds., *Mayors in the Middle* (Princeton: Princeton University Press, 2004).
4. See Jeffrey R. Henig and Wilbur Rich, *Mayors in the Middle: Politics, Race, and Mayoral Control of Urban Schools* (Princeton: Princeton University Press, 2004).
5. Joseph Viteritti, *Across the River: Politics and Education in the City* (New York: Holmes and Meier, 1983) pp. 11–12.
6. Brecher, op. cit., p. 59.
7. Ira Katznelson, *City Trenches* (Chicago: University of Chicago Press, 1981) p. 186.
8. Rich, op. cit.
9. Viteritti, op. cit. p. xv.
10. Celestine Bohlen, "Dinkins Urges Help for Schools in Crisis Areas," *New York Times* (June 24, 1989) p. 27.

11. Larry Bivins, "Dinkins' Schools Plan Unveiled," *Newsday* (June 24, 1989) p. 7.
12. Cited in Sylvia Moreno, "Mayor to Name School Watchdog," *Newsday* (June 1, 1990), p. 19.
13. Bohlen, op. cit. p. 27.
14. See Vergie R. Muhammad, "Black Leader' and Black Administrators' Opinions and Perception about the Decentralization of the New York City Schools, 1969–1988" (Unpublished PhD diss., Columbia University, 1988).
15. Josh Barbanel, "New York Mayor Rivals Support School Innovations," *New York Times* (October 29, 1989) p. 36.
16. Sylvia Moreno, "Fernandez Just Says No to More Cuts," *Newsday* (November 9, 1990) p. 5.
17. Nick Chiles and Joseph Gambardello, "Defiant Fernandez Offers His 'One Percent' Solution," *Newsday* (October 25, 1990) p. 5.
18. Joe Klein, "New York to Dave: Get Real!" *New York* Vol. 24, No. 21 (May 27, 1991) p. 12.
19. "The Right Role for the School Board," *New York Times* (July 14, 1990) p. 20.
20. Joseph Fernandez, "Predicting the Fall," *Executive Educator,* Vol. 15 (April 1993) p. 21.
21. Ibid.
22. Joseph Fernandez, *Tales out of Schools* (New York: Little, Brown, 1993) p. 243.
23. Leslie Agard-Jones, "Going over the 'Rainbow,' Curriculum for Multicultural Education," *Education Digest,* Vol. 59, No. 7 (March 1994) p. 12.
24. Ibid., p. 14.
25. Fernandez, "Predicting the Fall," op. cit. p. 22.
26. Fernandez, *Tales out of Schools,* op. cit., p. 249.
27. Jane Perlez, "Educator Is Critical of Sex Plan in Schools," *New York Times* (October 9, 1986) p. 1B.
28. Fernandez, "Predicting the Fall," op. cit., p.21.
29. The court agreed with Fernandez that distribution of condoms was not a violation of the parents' freedom of speech or a violation of their due process rights to raise their children as they saw fit. See *Alfonso v. Fernandez* 584 NYS.2d 406,413 (Sup. Ct. 1992).
30. Fernandez, *Tales out of School,* op. cit., p. 248.
31. See "School Boss Gets the Boot," *New York Post* (February 11, 1993) p. 1.
32. "The City's Rogue School Board," *New York Times* (March 26, 1993) p. 28.
33. Anthony M. DeStefano, "Tirozzi Is Dinkins' Choice Praises Chancellor Candidate" *Newsday* (August 21, 1993) p. 7.
34. Bruce Frankel, "NYC School Decision Leaves a Political Aftertaste," *USA Today* (August 31, 1993) p. 3A.

35. Liz Willen, "Ed Board Snubs Mayor," *Newsday* (July 24, 1993) p. 12.

36. See "New Chancellor, Old Politics," *New York Times* (August 31, 1993) p. 16.

37. "New York's Schools Begin Again," *The Economist* (September 4, 1993) p. 60.

38. "Dinkins to Wage 'Campaign within a Campaign' to Restructure School System," *New York Amsterdam News* (March 27, 1993) p. 4.

39. Nick Chiles, "They've Got Big Plan, Dinkins Unveils School Program," *Newsday* (September 24, 1993) p. 27.

40. Fernandez thought eleven was "too unwieldy"; see *Tales out of Schools*, op. cit., p. 249.

41. "A Quick Dose of Reality for Mr. Cortines," *New York Times* (September 3, 1993) p. 22A.

42. "Asbestos: The Hype Continues," *New York Post* (September 2, 1993) p. 22.

43. David Seifman, "Rudy Rap Dave on Asbestos," *New York Post* (September 9, 1993) p. 12.

44. Nick Chiles, "Teachers Flunk Dinkins," *Newsday* (October 14, 2001) p. 8.

45. Kenneth Wong and Pushpam Jain, "Newspapers as Policy Actors in Urban School Systems: The Chicago Story," *Urban Affairs Review* vol. 35, no. 2 (November, 1999) pp. 210-245.

46. Ibid.

47. Richelle Stanfield, "Bossing City Schools," *National Journal*, Vol. 28 (February 1997) pp. 272–74.

48. Charles Mahtesian, "Handing the Schools to City Hall," *Governing*, Vol. 10, No. 1 (October, 1996) pp. 36–40.

49. Interview with David Dinkins, op. cit.

50. Joseph Berger, "Dinkins Shores Up Power in Condom Vote," *New York Times* (September 13, 1991) p. 1B.

51. Rich, op. cit.

9. Conclusion

1. Academics had been complaining about the city planning process since 1980. See Norman Fainstein and Susan Fainstein, "Economic Restructing and the Politics of Land Use Planning in New York City," *Journal of the American Planning Association* Vol. 53 (Spring 1987) pp. 237–48.

2. James M. Burns, *Leadership* (New York: Harper and Row, 1978).

3. Interview with Scardino, op. cit.

4. "David Dinkins: His Struggle with the Anti-Black Mayor, White Racist New York City Press Corp," *New York Amsterdam News* (January 19, 1991) p. 14.

5. Larry J. Sabato, *Feeding Frenzy* (New York: Free Press, 1991) p. 1.
6. Interview with Dinkins, op. cit.
7. "National Press Club Luncheon Speaker David Dinkins, Mayor of New York," *Federal News Service* (February 26, 1990) p. 4.
8. W. Lance Bennett, *News: The Politics of Illusion* (New York: Longman, 1988) pp. 73–74.
9. Interview with David Dinkins, October 14, 2002.
10. Bennett, op. cit., p. 97.
11. Joe Klein, "The Panic of 1990," *New York* (October 1, 1990) pp. 28–30.
12. Joe Klein, "Is He up to It?" *New York,* Vol. 23, No. 43 (November 5, 1990) 37–40.
13. See C. Byron, "Wrong-Way Dave," *New York,* Vol. 24, No. 21 (May 20, 1991) pp. 14–15; see also Sam Roberts, "Mayor Dinkins: Every Day a Test," *New York Times* (April 7, 1991) p. 28.
14. See Wilbur Rich, *Coleman Young and Detroit Politics* (Detroit: Wayne State University Press, 1989).
15. Todd Purdum, "New York's Blacks Back Dinkins but Whites Don't, Poll Indicates," *New York Times* (May 19, 1991) p. 1A.
16. McNickle, op. cit. p. 323.
17. Ibid., p. 319.
18. "My conscience is clear. I know what I have to do . . . and that is to take David Dinkins out of the Mayors Office." See Evido de la Cruz, "Willie Nieves justifica su desercion: Abandonan los latinos el barco del alcalde Dinkins," *El Diario La Prensa* (September 21, 1993) p. 2.
19. Ironically, it was Michael Bloomburg who ran as a Republican in 2001 and won.
20. Horace Morancie, "Mayoral Election: The Re-election of David Dinkins Is a Must," *Everybody's Brooklyn,* Vol. 17, No. 8 (October 31, 1993) p. 11.
21. Richard Steier, "The Selling of the Mayor," *New York Post* (September 2, 1993) p. 19.
22. Michael Cottman, "Guarded Support? Black Cops Reluctant to Endorse Dinkins," *Newsday* (July 8, 1993) p. 8.
23. Zambga Brown, "Black Teachers Retaliate against United Federation of Teachers," *Amsterdam News* (October 30, 1993) p. 3.
24. See Michael Tomasky, "The Rumpled Genius Stumbles," *Village Voice* (August 3, 1993) p 15.
25. Telephone interview with Bill Lynch, op. cit.
26. See Mollenkopf, *The Phoenix in the Ashes,* op. cit. pp. 210–11.
27. Michael Tomasky, "The Mayor Lost Because He Couldn't Expand his Coalition," *Village Voice* (November 10, 1993) p. 23.
28. Mike McAlary, "September Won't Be Pretty for Pols," *New York Post* (September 2, 1993) p. 1.
29. Peer and Ettema, op. cit. p. 271.

30. Todd Purdum, "Dinkins Asserts He Is Better Racial Healer," *New York Times* (June 30, 1993) p. B3.

31. See *A Report to the Governor on the Disturbances in Crown Heights, An Assessment of the City's Preparedness and Response to Civil Disorder,* Vol. 1 (Albany: New York State Division of Criminal Justices, 1993).

32. Armando Bermudez, "Crown Heights David Dinkins, Como Napoleon En Waterloo," *Impacto* (August 3, 1993) p. 5.

33. Sayre and Kaufman, op. cit. p. 699.

34. Comments made by David Dinkins, 2001.

35. Jeffrey Pressman, "Preconditions of Mayoral Leadership," *American Political Science Review,* Vol. 65 (June 1979) pp. 11–24.

36. E. P. Hollander, "Conformity, Status, and Idiosyncratic Credit," *Psychological Review,* Vol. 65 (March 1958) pp. 117–27.

37. Neuman et al., op. cit., p. 120.

38. Bennett, op. cit. p. xii.

INDEX